Converging on Culture

THE AMERICAN ACADEMY OF RELIGION
REFLECTION AND THEORY IN THE
STUDY OF RELIGION SERIES

SERIES EDITOR
May McClintock Fulkerson, Duke University

A Publication Series of
The American Academy of Religion and
Oxford University Press

Working Emptiness: Toward a Third Reading of
Emptiness in Buddhism and Postmodern Thought
Newman Robert Glass

Wittgenstein and the Mystical:
Philosophy as an Ascetic Practice
Frederick Sontag

An Essay on the Theological Method, Third Edition
Gordon D. Kaufman

Better Than Wine: Love, Poetry, and Prayer in the
Thought of Franz Rosenzweig
Yudit Kornberg Greenberg

Healing Deconstruction: Postmodern Thought in
Buddhism and Christianity
Edited by David Loy

Roots of Relational Ethics: Responsibility in Origin
and Maturity in H. Richard Niebuhr
Melvin Keiser

Hegel's Speculative Good Friday:
The Death of God in Philosophical Perspective
Deland S. Anderson

Newman and Gadamer: Toward a Hermeneutics
of Religious Knowledge
Thomas K. Carr

God, Philosophy, and Academic Culture:
A Discussion between Scholars in the AAR and APA
Edited by William J. Wainwright

Living Words: Studies in Dialogues about Religion
Terence J. Martin

Like and Unlike God: Religious Imaginations in
Modern and Contemporary Fiction
John Neary

Beyond the Necessary God: Trinitarian Faith and
Philosophy in the Thought of Eberhard
Paul DeHart

AMERICAN ACADEMY OF RELIGION

Converging on Culture

Theologians in Dialogue with
Cultural Analysis and Criticism

EDITED BY
Delwin Brown,
Sheila Greeve Davaney, &
Kathryn Tanner

OXFORD
UNIVERSITY PRESS

2001

OXFORD
UNIVERSITY PRESS

Oxford   New York
Athens   Auckland   Bangkok   Bogotá   Buenos Aires   Cape Town
Chennai   Dar es Salaam   Delhi   Florence   Hong Kong   Istanbul   Karachi
Kolkata   Kuala Lumpur   Madrid   Melbourne   Mexico City   Mumbai   Nairobi
Paris   São Paulo   Shanghai   Singapore   Taipei   Tokyo   Toronto   Warsaw

and associated companies in
Berlin   Ibadan

Copyright © 2001 by The American Academy of Religion

Published by Oxford University Press, Inc.,
198 Madison Avenue, New York, New York 10016

Library of Congress Cataloging-in-Publication Data
Converging on culture : theologians in dialogue with cultural analysis and criticism /
edited by Delwin Brown, Sheila Greeve Davaney, and Kathryn Tanner.
p. cm.—(Reflection and theory in the study of religion series)
Includes bibliographical references and index.
ISBN 0-19-514466-X; ISBN 0-19-514467-8 (pbk.)
1. Christianity and culture—Congresses.   2. Theology, Doctrinal—Methodology—
Congresses.   I. Brown, Delwin, 1935–   II. Davaney, Sheila Greeve.
III. Tanner, Kathryn, 1957–   IV. Reflection and theory in the study of religion.
BR115.C8 C594 2001
261—dc21   00-045647

1   3   5   7   9   8   6   4   2

Printed in the United States of America
on acid-free paper

Preface

Displacing the time-honored importance of the discipline of philosophy, a shift to make cultural analysis and criticism the major dialogue partner of theology is underway in many quarters of academic theology today.[1] This shift bridges most of the methodological differences that have typically divided contemporary theology—for example, differences among postliberal, revisionist, liberationist, pragmatist, and historicist theologies. Cultural analysis and cultural criticism—often borrowed, sometimes initiated by the theologian—are now part and parcel of the constructive efforts of theologies of these sorts, as well as of political theology, public theology, correlation theology in a Tillichian mode, the ethnographic theology of marginalized communities, African American theology and feminist discourse theology. This book, arising out of a 1997 conference at the University of Chicago Divinity School, cosponsored by Iliff School of Theology, is the first of its kind to bring together theologians from a variety of these perspectives to make this bridge-building effort explicit. Sharing the nature of their work until this point, the contributors point the way toward an important new programmatic statement for a theology of the future—one yet to be written, it is true, but one in process of evolving in and through such efforts of mutual information.

Sheila Davaney's essay serves as an introduction to the volume as a whole by making clear the bases upon which we proceed—what brings us together in our thinking about culture and where we differ, most broadly, in approach. On the former point, for example, theology is no isolated intellectual exercise but an integral part of wider forms of social action and comprehensive ways of living, both within and without the churches. It is as power-driven a cultural formation as any of the political, economic, or social arrangements with which it is imbricated. It requires particularistic forms of analysis and construction rather than reflection on perennial questions in their most general forms. It expands beyond the reaches of print culture to the material stuff of culture and the ephemera of everyday lives, and beyond the pronouncements of educated and powerful elites to the beliefs and practices of the ordinary, marginalized, and downtrodden.

On the matter of our differences, a very general one—dividing the book into two—concerns the direction of our interests. As Davaney indicates, before turning to her own consideration of the place of theology in religious studies, some of us (including Davaney herself) are primarily interested in using a cultural stance to reconceptualize the discipline of academic theology for purposes of defense and reform (part I); others of us are trying self-consciously and responsibly to construct theologies that act as forms of cultural analysis and criticism with reference to particular communities of identification and concern (part II).

Both directions of interest help raise the fact of theology's shift to cultural analysis and criticism to the level of sustained theological reflection. Little critical attention to the merits and possible problems of such a move has yet to take place among the many theologians of different stripes now engaged in it; this is one place where the book hopes to make a contribution. What is the impetus behind such a shift and what are its implications? The shift is no doubt propelled by a recognition of the lived concreteness and particularity of religious practice and belief and of religious reflection on them. If religion is not to be examined in general but in its particular cultural contexts, and if theology is reflection on religion so understood, how can theology not draw upon cultural analyses of those religious contexts? But does this recognition also signal a general change in how we understand the nature of theology? How might one theorize such a change? What might it imply about the construction of religious meaning, the character of theological traditions of inquiry, and appropriate procedures for theological education?

The first part of the book takes up some of these issues explicitly, by rethinking the genre of theology as cultural production (Rebecca

Chopp), theology's method (Delwin Brown), its blurred relation to other forms of worldview construction (Linell Cady), its public role as a form of cultural criticism (Victor Anderson), and its contribution to the academic study of cultures (Sheila Davaney).

In keeping with cultural studies' focus on the particular and the situated, and on boundary-violating interconnections among cultural forms, the second part shows concretely what such rethinkings of theology might amount to, in specific rather than in general terms, as they reflect the particularities of commitments and contexts for our work extending beyond the limitations of our academic employment. As these essays in their different ways demonstrate, cultural analysis and criticism help theologians make normative interventions in the communities with which they identify—in and out of church, in and out of the academy (mostly out!)—promoting the ends of community action in the direction of greater effectiveness and self-critical responsibility (Mary Fulkerson, Serene Jones, and Tony Pinn), and furthering processes of liberative social action and reflection (Dwight Hopkins, Mark Taylor, and Ada María Isasi-Díaz.)

We wish to express appreciation to the University of Chicago Divinity School and Iliff School of Theology for their generous support for the founding conference that led to this collection and that launched the Theology and Cultural Analysis and Criticism group. We are also grateful to Maggi Mahan (Iliff) for her work in bringing this publication to fruition and Meredith Underwood for creating the index for the volume.

Note

1. For major statements of this shift, see, for example, Delwin Brown, *Boundaries of Our Habitations: Tradition and Theological Construction* (Albany, N.Y.: SUNY Press, 1994); Sheila Greeve Davaney, *Pragmatic Historicism: A Theology for the Twenty-first Century* (Albany, N.Y.: SUNY Press, 2000); Dwight Hopkins and Sheila Davaney, eds., *Changing Conversations: Religious Reflection and Cultural Analysis* (New York: Routledge, 1996); Ada María Isasi-Díaz, *En La Lucha—In the Struggle: A Hispanic Women's Liberation Theology* (Minneapolis: Fortress, 1993); Mary McClintock Fulkerson, *Changing the Subject: Women's Discourses and Feminist Theology* (Minneapolis: Fortress, 1994); and Kathryn Tanner, *Theories of Culture: A New Agenda for Theology* (Minneapolis: Fortress, 1998).

Contents

Contributors

VICTOR ANDERSON is associate professor of Christian Ethics at Vanderbilt Divinity School. He teaches courses and lectures on religion and cultural criticism, African American religious thought, and theological ethics. He is the author of *Beyond Ontological Blackness: An Essay in African American Religious and Cultural Criticism* (1995) and *Pragmatic Theology: Negotiating the Intersection of an American Philosophy of Religion and Public Theology* (1998). He is currently working on *Divine Grotesqueries: Essays in African American Philosophical Theology*.

DELWIN BROWN is Harvey H. Potthoff Professor of Christian Theology at Iliff School of Theology. His publications include *Boundaries of Our Habitations: Tradition and Theological Construction* (1994) and a number of recent articles on the relationship of theology to religious studies and other academic inquiries in the university. Currently he is working on a book analyzing the theistic pluralism of both historic and modern Christianity.

LINELL E. CADY is professor of religious studies at Arizona State University. Her publications include *Religion, Theology and American Public Life* (1993) and numerous articles on Royce, feminist theology, religion and the public/private boundary, and method and theory in religious studies and theology. She is currently working on *Shifting Paradigms: Theology, Religious Studies and the University*, an edited volume on the relationship of religious studies and theology.

REBECCA S. CHOPP is dean of Yale Divinity School and Titus Street Professor of Theology and Culture. She is the author of *The Praxis of Suffering: An Interpretation of Liberation and Political Theologies* (1986), *The Power to Speak: Feminism, Language, God* (1989), *Reconstructing Christian Theology* (1994), and *Saving Work: Feminist Practices of Theological Education* (1995). Chopp is widely published in the fields of women's studies, Christian theology, and the role of religion in American public life. She is currently president of the American Academy of Religion.

SHEILA GREEVE DAVANEY is professor of theology at Iliff School of Theology. Her most recent book is *Pragmatic Historicism: A Theology for the Twenty-first Century* (2000). She is coeditor with Rebecca Chopp of *Horizons in Feminist Theology* (1997) and with Dwight Hopkins of *Changing Conversations: Religious Reflection and Cultural Analysis* (1996). She has published extensively on historicism, feminist theory and theology, and the relation of theology and the university.

MARY MCCLINTOCK FULKERSON holds a joint appointment in the Divinity School and Women's Studies Program of Duke University. She is the author of *Changing the Subject: Women's Discourses and Feminist Theology* (1994). She is currently at work on a book on theology and culture in the form of an ethnography of an interracial church.

DWIGHT HOPKINS teaches theology at the University of Chicago Divinity School. Along with numerous collaborative works, he is the author of *Black Theology USA and South Africa: Politics, Culture, and Liberation* (1988), *Shoes that Fit our Feet: Sources for a Constructive Black Theology* (1993), *Introducing Black Theology of Liberation* (1999), and *Down, Up, and Over: Slave Religion and Black Theology* (2000). His *Heart and Head: Black Theology Past, Present, and Future* will appear in 2002.

ADA MARÍA ISASI-DÍAZ is associate professor of Christian ethics and theology at Drew University. Born and raised in La Habana, Cuba, she received her Ph.D. from Union Theological Seminary in New York City, where she now lives. Her most recent book is *Mujerista Theology: A Theology for the Twenty-first Century* (1996), and with Fernando Segovia she coedited *Hispanic/Latino Theology: Challenge and Promise* (1996). Currently she is developing a liberating understanding of justice and corporality.

SERENE JONES is associate professor of systematic theology at Yale Divinity School with joint appointments at the Yale Law School and the Department of African-American Studies. She is the author of *Calvin and the Rhetoric of Piety* (1995) and *Feminist Theory and Christian Theology: Cartographies of Grace* (2000). She is currently working on theological aesthetics and the cross.

ANTHONY B. PINN is associate professor of religious studies and coordinator of African American studies at Macalester College. His publications include *Why, Lord? Suffering and Evil in Black Theology* (1995), *Varieties of African American Religious Experience* (1998), *Making the Gospel Plain* (1999), and *Social Protest Thought in the African Methodist Episcopal Church* (2000).

KATHRYN TANNER teaches theology at the University of Chicago Divinity School. She is the author of *God and Creation in Christian Theology: Tyranny or Empowerment?* (1988), *The Politics of God: Christian Theologies and Social Justice* (1992), *Theories of Culture: A New Agenda for Theology* (1998), and *Jesus, Humanity and the Trinity: A Systematic Theology in Brief* (2001).

MARK TAYLOR is professor of theology and culture at Princeton Theological Seminary. His publications include *Remembering Esperanza: A Cultural-Political Theology* (1990), *Paul Tillich: Theologian of the Boundaries* (1987), *Beyond Explanation: Religious Dimensions in Cultural Anthropology* (1985), *The Executed God: The Way of the Cross in Lockdown America* (2001); with Rebecca Chopp, he coedited *Reconstructing Christian Theology* (1994). He is also an activist working to end the death penalty and to build solidarity with Mexico's liberation struggles.

Part One

Theoretical Reflections on Culture and Theology

Theology and the Turn to Cultural Analysis

Sheila Greeve Davaney

As advocates of various intellectual disciplines, methodologies, and institutional locations, scholars often seek to identify and to stress the differences that divide our work or perspective from other orientations. It is by exploiting those differences and arguing that what divides us matters the most that we are able to establish the purported superiority of our own field or position over that of our rivals.

There are indeed differences that, as Richard Bernstein has argued, "make a difference."[1] There are conflicting assumptions and commitments that divide us, and even where we seem to agree on matters, we often interpret their implications in incompatible ways.

However, these differences, both within and across academic disciplines, are attended most often by extensive areas of agreement, similarity, or overlap that allow us to be intelligible to one another, to converse and debate and influence each other. Such arenas of agreement wax and wane in various historical periods. Moreover, what is experienced from within a period as meager overlap against the contrast of vast and deep realms of conflict may, from the vantage point of another historical moment, appear like minor variations on quite similar themes.

The purpose of this essay is to explore some of the trends that are being given wide expression in the academy today and that are finding particularly strong voice in religious studies and especially academic theology. By turning to supposedly common themes with broad credence, I harbor no illusion of false or spurious consensus on these matters. Nonetheless, I think that it is also important to explore the points of convergence, to get a perch on the broader developments that are shaping the enterprise of religious studies and that are affecting how the nature and task of academic theology are being reconceived today. In particular, this chapter focuses on the widespread move to cultural and social theory on the part of religious studies scholars (in the United States perhaps most notably theologians) and to the increasing interpretation in the United States of theology as a form of cultural analysis and criticism.

I want to turn to two tasks.[2] First, I want to rehearse in general what I take to be the central elements that are framing the current developments, that is, I will set forth in the broadest terms the assumptions about culture and about religions as part of culture that are fueling many of the shifts presently underway in the academy. Second, I want to explore what these changes imply for our disciplinary self-understanding and especially for how theology is related to the rest of the study of religion and the academy at large.

The turn to cultural analysis by theologians as well as other scholars of religions has been funded by a variety of different sources that represent quite distinct developments in their own right and that harbor differences that are truly significant. Such sources include critical theory, revisionist Marxism, poststructuralism (especially in its French variations), British cultural studies and their American counterparts, liberationist thought, sociohistorical trajectories (including earlier American ones), and lines of thought developing out of nineteenth-century historicism. Other sources include a variety of postmodernisms and postcolonial perspectives and the disciplinary and theoretical shifts under way in other intellectual fields, especially literary analysis, philosophy, historical studies and historiographical theory, and the social sciences, most notably interpretive sociology, postmodern anthropology, and the new ethnography.

These often disparate sources have contributed to the emergence of claims about three overlapping arenas—claims about culture, claims about religious traditions and communities as located within and as dimensions of culture, and claims about theologians and theologies as producers of culture and as themselves cultural artifacts or expressions. There are competing interpretations of all these, but I will present in an encapsulated form what I take to be influential versions that are shaping theology. As we will see, parallel claims are emerging about each of these areas. Let us turn to culture and how it is being viewed within theology.

Theologians, no less than other intellectuals, have come to view human beings as historical creatures located within the complex matrices of particular cultures and social worlds. Gone, whether forever or for the moment, are the universalisms of both Enlightenment reason and nineteenth- and twentieth-century theological liberalism. Over against notions of rationality and experience as ahistorical, commonly structured, and temporally invariant, there have emerged assumptions of the located, particular, pluralistic, and thoroughly historical nature of human existence, experience, and knowledge.

The cultural domain within which human life is now interpreted as so thoroughly ensconced has also taken on a particular character. Increasingly, culture has come to refer to a multitextured network of relations or total way of life encompassing the myriad relations, institutions, and practices that define a historical period or specific geographical location or formative community or subgroups within larger fields. In contrast to earlier notions of culture as the deposit or accumulation of knowledge or meaning produced by elites, or as a body of beliefs and values shared by all members of a group such as a nation or religious community, culture now is viewed as the dynamic and contentious process by which meaning, and with it power, is produced, circulated, and negotiated by all who reside within a particular cultural milieu. Hence, the notion of culture points simultaneously to the totality of relations and dynamics that constitute human life and to the specificity and concreteness of particular human historical configurations.[3]

There are many dimensions to the notions of culture as processes of historical invention and negotiation. But for our purposes I want to highlight several elements that are having a particular impact on theology's reconceptualization. The first is the already stated assertion that cultures are not static givens but dynamic processes in which all participate and all contribute, albeit with varying degrees of power and influence. Concurring with the claims of the new ethnographers such as James Clifford, Delwin Brown has argued that cultures are not organic unities unfolding naturally but rather "constantly re-negotiated ensembles of diversity."[4] As such they are internally pluralistic, continually in process of being made and remade, conflictual and, importantly, lacking unifying or unchanging cores, essences or centers that provide their inhabitants stable identities, roles, or direction. Culture is the process by which meaning is produced, contended for, and continually re-negotiated and the context in which individual and communal identities are mediated and brought into being.

Accompanying this articulation of notions of culture as dynamic and conflictual processes has been the move away from interpreting culture as exclusively the domain of elites. Of all the shifts that have occurred, the move to popular forms of culture is among the most significant not only for cultural studies but also for modes of theology engaged in cultural criticism. In contrast to those perspectives that have interpreted culture as the province of the powerful that was imposed, either willingly or unwillingly, upon the "masses," many current theories of culture stress the active participation of nonelites in cultural negotiation. "The people" are not just passive consumers of meaning, values, and practices devised by the powerful. They are the producers of culture on multiple levels, including through their resistance to elites, their creative appropriation and reconfiguration of the cultural productions of the powerful, and, not the least, through the creation of cultural meanings, practices, and identities that are their own. In all this, popular culture has emerged no longer as that to be disdained or overcome but as the domain of creative cultural contestation and construction.[5]

Several other shifts concerning the understanding of culture stand out for their relevance in current theology. Significantly, there has been a move away from construing culture as only referring to the theater of ideas and symbolic forms. Increasingly influential now are materialist theories of culture that stress not only the intimate interconnection between ideational forms of culture and nondiscursive social realities but also emphasize that meaning is constructed and produced in nonlinguistic and nondiscursive modes, in social practices and relations, in everything from ritual and the circulation of economic resources, in the valorization of certain bodies and in the absence and invisibility of other bodies, in the construction of public and private spaces, and in the seeming reign of image over idea and surface over substance. Thus not only has there been a move away from great ideas and great men to popular culture, but also there has been an enlargement of the notion of culture itself beyond the scope of ideas, texts, and symbolic productions.

Imbuing all this has been the profound sense that what is at stake in cultural dynamics is the struggle for and the negotiation of power. The languages of otherness, of difference, of struggle, of contestation found in so much theology today all point not to the commonalities that once were thought to hold a society or a tradition or even an intellectual discipline together, but to the fragmentation, inherent plurality, and unrelenting dynamics of domination and resistance that constitute all cultural processes. Moreover, these analyses of power also presuppose in a manner distinct from earlier interpretations of ideology and power politics that power is never located solely in one segment of society—in one class, race, or gender—but is in continual circulation and is constantly being reconfigured. And often accompanying these claims of multiple sites of power is the further Foucaultian contention that power is not just a repressive mechanism that exerts itself through constraint and limitation but that control is also exercised through the construction of new possibilities, roles, identities, and institutions.

This turn to culture has had many effects in relation to the study of religions, but I want especially to highlight one very general effect and two accompanying results. The general change has been that increasingly religion, religious communities, and traditions are now located within the thick matrices of culture. Religious beliefs, practices, identities, values, institutions, and even texts are all now seen as elements within and products of cultural processes.

Certainly there have been trajectories within religious studies that have viewed religions as sociological or cultural phenomena whose emergence, propagation, and function could not be understood apart from other cultural realities. Especially those intellectual traditions that developed along with or as part of the social sciences in the last two centuries have pointed in this direction. But there was also a long tradition that viewed as reductionistic and illegitimate such efforts to naturalize religion as one dimension of culture interpretable by the same means as other cultural elements.[6] Many perspectives within the growing field of the study of religions, including approaches characteristic of the history of religion, for a long time followed the route of viewing religion as a unique phenomenon that demanded its own methodologies and interpretive categories. Even where religions were thought to have cultural expressions that could be studied and analyzed, these were often taken to be rooted in dimensions of reality that would not yield to scientific inquiry.

Theology, for the most part, also assumed the sui generis character of religion. There were some exceptions, most notably the sociohistorical school of the University of Chicago, and certainly from the nineteenth century onward there intensified for theologians among others what Van Harvey identified as the tension between the "ideal of belief" and "a new morality of critical judgment."[7] Most theology, however, both liberal and more traditional, advanced its claims by asserting that religious beliefs and practices were indeed in a class by themselves, or at the very least were grounded in or pointed to realities that escaped the analytical and critical gaze of the ever more powerful natural and social sciences. Whether it was Schleiermacher's appeal in the nineteenth century to nonlinguistically structured religious experience or Karl Barth's assertion in the twentieth century of revelation and faith as realities beyond the scope of ordinary human knowledge, theologians most often assumed the peculiar character of religion—or in Barthian terminology, faith—and its objects.

Today these assumptions are in the process of radical reformulation both for the study of religions in general and for theological reflection in particular. Religions are increasingly viewed as cultural processes and artifacts that are not disconnected from other dimensions of human cultural and social institutions, discourses, and networks of power. They are now taken to be both products of and contributors to the negotiations around cultural resources. As such, religions, like cultures in general, are viewed as always concrete and particular, lacking essences that provide a common character across traditions and a singular identity within traditions. The study of religions thus is making a claim on being an important, if not always recognized, component of the study of cultures. Its focus is increasingly shifting from the search for pristine origins or essences, for transhistorical continuities, transcendent objects, or texts wrenched from their historical context, to the examination of concrete practices and beliefs and their role within the broader cultural domain.

This general shift is further specified by two accompanying innovations in the study of religions and most dramatically in theology. This first is the move, along with many of those disciplines concerned with culture, to ordinary people and their everyday lives and practices—the turn to the realm of the "popular." The second is the concomitant shift from what Lawrence Sullivan has called an "overly literary" approach to religion to a reorientation toward the material practices and dimensions of religions.[8] There has been a long history of the identification and examination of popular religions, most often by those scholars associated with anthropology and sociology who tended to have from the start more naturalized orientations toward religions. Frequently, however, in the study of religions and most certainly in theology, the assumptions referred to above about the peculiar character of religion led to a focus upon either what were taken to be the universal and ahistorical underpinnings of concrete historical religions or what were taken to be the dominant figures and the controlling beliefs, texts, and institutions of a religious tradition. The mass of religious persons and their lives were not interpreted as the location of constructive theological production, nor were their concrete lives and practices the central concern of much of the study of religions. Thus, for example, Christian theology for centuries interpreted itself as commentary on biblical texts and concerned itself with the history of doctrine, the development and transmission of beliefs. Or again, until recently, philology has been the presiding paradigm for Buddhist studies, with the translation of ancient texts and commentary upon them the central focus and with little evidence of interest in everyday life and practice. Glenn Yocum, in a recent article on popular Jainism (something thought not even to exist by many scholars), notes our tendency to study "sophisticated texts, overwhelmingly produced by premodern (male), often ascetic, intellectuals."[9] Yocum further asserts that when these have been the target of religious studies scholars, what we produce are interpretations of religions far removed from what practitioners actually do or say.

Today there are moves afoot across the study of religions and its diverse subfields to broaden the arena of exploration and to reconsider the nature and function of everyday beliefs and practices. And even where texts remain of central concern there is new interest in the social and cultural conditions within which they were produced and in the concrete histories of their transmission and reception. For many scholars, texts and beliefs no longer float free, to be interpreted only in relation to other texts and ideas, but are understandable only within the concrete particularities of historical existence. Thus, the dominance of exegetical, philological, and hermeneutical methods is yielding to social, cultural, and political analysis.

Theologians, especially those whose area of interest is the Christian tradition, have been central participants in these developments. Broadly across the discipline of academic theology, there has been a move away from the study of ideas abstracted from their concrete histories and contexts and a turn to the thick histories and realities of religious communities and individuals. From postliberalism to pragmatic historicism, from liberationist to revisionist theology, there has been sounded the call to attend to the concrete and particular forms of Christian life, practice, and beliefs. Moreover, these locales are now seen not as thin shadows of "real" theology or as unreflective or nonconstructive first-order beliefs that fare poorly when contrasted with the work of professional or academic theologians, but as constructive perspectives that require critical examination and engagement.

Importantly, it is not merely that academic theologians are now turning to the beliefs and practices of particular communities and traditions or that we are less and less treating theological ideas as disembodied abstractions having, in David Kelsey's words, "ghostly lives."[10] Theologians are also increasingly examining our own cultural identity and location as well as the political character not only of the beliefs and practices that we study but of our own claims. It has now become

almost de rigueur for theological works to begin with the detailing of
the theologian's identity and social location, the recitation of which
function both as mechanisms of illumination and explanation and
sometimes as subtle forms of validation. Hence, naive or self-serving
assertions of unconditioned knowledge have been replaced by self-
consciousness concerning the perspectival and value-laden character of
claims to knowledge and of all such claims as forms of advocacy. The
rehabilitation of the concrete has thus been accompanied by the re-
pudiation of the "objective" and the recognition of the political nature
of our enterprise. Both the religious beliefs and practices we study and
our own academic claims are viewed as culturally embedded and socially constructed and hence as politically potent vehicles of meaning
and value.

Each of these moves—to culture, to religion as part of culture, and
to theology as a cultural practice—has not been without problems. A
number of more conservative theologians have used these shifts as justification to retreat to bounded communities and to forgo the difficult
work of justifying their claims in the public realm. Other more liberal
thinkers, especially those associated with liberationist perspectives, have
often engaged in an uncritical romanticizing and valorizing of popular
culture and religiosity that assumes without argument that these are
the site of all liberative and transformative ideas and actions. Moreover,
it seems at times, in our age of sensitivity to our situatedness, that social
location and identity have replaced reason giving as the source of legitimation and delegitimation for our positions.

Despite these problems, all three of these shifts have had salutary
effects upon the discipline of theology. First, these developments have
reconnected academic theology to concrete communities and traditions
of belief and practice in creative, nonapologetic, and noncondescending
ways. Shorn of the illusion that we traffic with ahistorical and universal
truth, theologians have been returned to what Linell Cady has aptly
called the "morass" of lived religion.[11]

Moreover, theologies are not neutral but do their theorizing with a
normative intent. Though there is no consensus within academic theology concerning what cultural purposes theology should serve, there
is growing agreement that academic theology engages cultural realities
not merely as interesting objects of study but as arenas in relation to
which theologians seek to recover an effective voice. Thus, if the theological task is less and less interpreted in terms of the search for ahistorical truth or the unvarying essence of a religious tradition, it is
emerging more and more as a form of cultural analysis and criticism

that seeks a legitimate role both in the academy and in the broader cultural arena.

Second, the rethinking of religion and theology as cultural phenomena offers important new ways of thinking about the study of religions in general and in particular of theology's role in the academy. This issue is of importance today not the least because the current locales of most professional theologians are institutions of higher education, either universities or graduate theological schools. Moreover, these locales especially in the United States are not secure and the professional identity of academic theology is not clear in relation to the rest of higher education, especially to other disciplines broadly and often uneasily residing under the rubric of religious studies or the study of religions.

A number of recent studies and publications have highlighted the issues surrounding the role of religious studies in the academy and the place, if any, of theology in the study of religions. *The Hart Report* on "Religious and Theological Studies in American Higher Education,"[12] the infamous *Lingua Franca* article on the American Academy of Religion,[13] and recent books such as Russell McCutcheon's *Manufacturing Religion*[14] and Talal Asad's *Genealogies of Religion*[15] have all put out for display the lack of clarity and consensus concerning the discipline, its objects of study, and its role in higher education.

The Hart Report and the more polemical *Lingua Franca* article pointed to the even more precarious situation of theologians. According to both, many scholars who define their disciplines as religious studies understand their own work to be modeled on the social sciences or other academic disciplines, to be descriptive and explanatory in nature, and to seek to be neutral and, in Hart's words, as "freed as possible from prejudice."[16] Theology is portrayed, in contrast to religious studies, in the words of various respondents to the Hart study, as inherently "confessional," "dogmatic," "apologetic for a particular faith commitment," and as a mode of activity whose object is "to explore, systematize and study the doctrines . . . of a given faith which are taken for granted or assumed to be true."[17]

From the other side, persons such as McCutcheon have challenged religious studies as covertly theological, as creating a self-perpetuating discipline through the representation of religion as, in his words, "sui generis, autonomous, of its own kind, strictly personal, essential, unique, prior to, and ultimately distinct from, all other facets of human life and interaction."[18] Talal Asad has offered a multilayered assault against religious studies, arguing that the modern construction of the idea of religion is part of the emergence of the modern nation state and its separation of the public and private spheres and is, moreover, an extension of the colonial project that accompanied the West's expansionist moves. Asad adds to this critique the further contention that religious studies remains predicated on medieval Christian theological methods that treat religion as a text to be broken open and decoded through exegetical methods, methods that he finds inappropriate to non-Christian traditions.[19] For McCutcheon and Asad, religious studies is, thus, highly suspect precisely because it is theological while pretending not to be.

I want to suggest that the turn to culture and the interpretation of religion as a cultural phenomenon and of theology as a cultural practice is suggestive for rethinking the category of religion, religious studies, theology, and theology's role in the academy. First, in what may be a supreme irony, theology's rethinking of itself and its subject matter lends strong support to the rejection of interpretations of religions as sui generis and thus of what Wayne Proudfoot has called the "protective strategies" that followed from removing religion from the realm of other historical realities.[20] Religion, in this scenario, takes its place as one dimension of human culture among others, demanding that whatever academic disciplines illuminate religious realities, precisely as forms of historical existence, should be utilized in their study.

Second, these developments in religious studies and in theology's own self-understanding also provide the ground for arguing for the inclusion of theology as an integral part of the study of religion. In important ways, they challenge the unnuanced forms of bifurcation so evident in *The Hart Report* and the *Lingua Franca* article. To many theologians, it seems anachronistic that in our increasingly post-Enlightenment period, when the value-laden character of interpretation and the political dimension of even basic descriptions are broadly acknowledged in almost every other field, many scholars of religions should pursue self-definitions that recapitulate naive notions of autonomy and objectivity. Many North American scholars of religions often appear to commit the twin modern fallacies that we have no convictions (or if we do we can successfully bracket them) and that such convictions, including religious ones, are or should be of little matter to our academic enterprises. Thus, we foster notions of the disengaged scholar studying the artifacts of other people's convictions while keeping our own at bay and steadfastly refusing to enter into serious debate about the value, meaning, truth, and function of anyone's convictions including our own. And this goes on, if McCutcheon and Talal Asad are correct, while many religion scholars continue untenable and unexamined notions of religion, arguing for the discipline on convictions that function but are not acknowledged.

Does this all lead to the view that theology should have a secure place in the academy because in fact everything else is really covertly confessional, that is, theology in disguise? This argument is indeed heard today, but it is one that I want to urge theologians to strongly resist. Instead, I would offer a different kind of argument for the inclusion of theology both as a descriptive-analytical enterprise and a constructive-normative one.

First, just as other aspects of religions, however defined, merit identification and critical analysis, so do beliefs, symbols, and systems of meaning and value that are integral parts of any religious tradition. How could we ever think that we have adequately studied a religious tradition when we have explored texts or rituals or historical events but left out all analysis of beliefs and values, ignored basic convictions about reality, and left unattended exploration of how these flow from and contribute to other cultural and social elements of human existence? The fear of being tainted by association with fideistic theology has resulted in a partial and one-sided treatment of religions that has little justification today. In the view put forth here, theology is precisely that subdiscipline whose major concern is the identification and critical examination of the beliefs and values that are central parts of religious traditions; it is, as Ada María Isasi-Díaz[21] and Delwin Brown[22] have each suggested, an ethnography of belief, or as Kathryn Tanner has recently proposed, the exploration of the meaning dimension of religious traditions.[23]

Even on the level of identifying and critically analyzing beliefs and values, scholars are engaged in normative decisions of which we need to be continually aware. Whose beliefs count? How shall we understand the relation of beliefs and arguments that have been honed over centuries and given authoritative expression in time-honored texts to everyday practices? Should we or our students engage not only in a kind of bland show and tell in which we look from a distance at materials but do not evaluate them, or should we bring to bear upon them critical norms, especially of the university? What theoretical assumptions frame and direct our choices of study? What determines whether we think, to use Glenn Yocum's example again, that Jainism has popular beliefs and practices and that examination of them is very important to understanding that tradition or, to use an example closer to my own interests, that gender is an appropriate analytical tool for understanding beliefs even when women are seemingly absent from the material? All of these

questions press in upon us even on the level of identification and analysis, reminding us that the decisions we make are not neutral or value
free.

Second, I want to argue that theology is not only normative on this
analytical level but that it has constructive dimensions that are legitimate not only in the context of religious communities but also under
the auspices of the academy. Few theologians today would trade all
constructive and normative intent in order to "pass" in the university.
Theologians can and should be able to venture, as their colleagues in
other disciplines do every day, normative proposals about the self, about
human community, about our relation to the natural world, and so on.
The issue should not be, in this age of awareness of the value-laden
character of all intellectual work, the constructive or normative thrust
of a proposal. The issue is whether theologians or any other intellectuals
are willing to venture their proposals without claiming any special privilege for them and with full acknowledgment of their speculative and
interest-laden character and with a willingness that they be publicly
scrutinized and debated. The important point to keep remembering in
all this is that, whether on the level of description and analysis or on
a more constructive level, there is nothing in the subject matter of
religion or in theological analysis or construction that rules out critical
or public analysis and debate.

In arguing that there has been a widespread turn to culture as an
analytical construct in the academy, that religions and religious communities and traditions are increasingly being treated as dimensions of
culture, and that, therefore, the study of cultures is incomplete without
attention to religions, including their beliefs and values, this chapter
has suggested that religious studies is an integral part of culture studies
and theology, like ritology, history, philology, and so on and is an
important part of the study of religions. This discussion assumes a
move to what are termed naturalistic notions of religion, though what
those might be is still clearly a contested issue within the academy
today.

But this chapter also leaves many questions unanswered and many
issues before us. What are the limits of appealing to culture, and what
is left out when human life is so exhaustively portrayed as cultural?
What norms should we invoke for not only deciding what to study but
for critically assessing our subject matter? Is popular always good, and
if not, when is it not and why? What is the relation between the cultural
location of the academic and the traditions and communities he or she
studies? What theoretical construals of religion should at this historical
moment guide our work and how can they contribute to the study of

other dimensions of culture? Surely these are not our questions alone, but they are certainly ones about which scholars of religions should have a good deal to contribute both within the university and within our larger cultural context.

Notes

1. Richard J. Bernstein, "What Is the Difference That Makes a Difference? Gadamer, Habermas, and Rorty," in *Proceedings of the 1982 Biennial Meeting of the Philosophy of Science Association*, ed. P. D. Asquith and T. Nichles (East Lansing, Mich.: Philosophy of Science Association, 1983).

2. I have developed a more extended version of these arguments in *Pragmatic Historicism: A Theology for the Twenty-first Century* (Albany, N.Y.: SUNY Press, 2000). In the essay in this volume I fluctuate between referring to religion and religions. This fluctuation is indicative of the vacillating between more generalizing categories and ones focused on plurality and particularity.

3. See Delwin Brown, *Boundaries of Our Habitations: Tradition and Theological Construction* (Albany, N.Y.: SUNY Press, 1994), and Kathryn Tanner, *Theories of Culture: A New Agenda for Theology* (Minneapolis: Fortress, 1997). Even though culture is appealed to widely, questions are being raised about the usefulness of the term. See Adam Kuper, *Culture: The Anthropologists' Account* (Cambridge: Harvard University Press, 1999).

4. Chapter 3 here, 45.

5. The study of popular culture has become widespread in the academy today. See Celeste Condet, "The Rhetorical Limits of Polysemy," in *Critical Perspectives on Media and Society*, ed. R. Avery and D. Eason (New York: Guilford Press, 1991), 365–86; John Fiske, *Understanding Popular Culture* (London: Routledge, 1989); Stuart Hall, P. Welles, D. Hobson, and A. Lowe, *Culture, Media, Language* (London: Hutchinson, 1980); Raymond Williams, *Marxism and Literature* (Oxford: Oxford University Press, 1977).

6. J. Samuel Preus, *Explaining Religion: Criticism and Theory from Bodein to Freud* (New Haven, Conn.: Yale University Press, 1987), tracks the "naturalization" of religion.

7. Van A. Harvey, *The Historian and the Believer* (Philadelphia: Westminster, 1966; reprinted, Urbana, Ill.: University of Illinois Press, 1996), 38.

8. Lawrence E. Sullivan, "Seeking an End to the Primary Text or 'Putting an End to the Text as Primary,' " in *Beyond the Classics? Essays in Religious Studies and Liberal Education*, ed. Frank E. Reynolds and Sheryl L. Buckhalter (Atlanta: Scholars Press, 1990), 42.

9. Glenn Yocum, " 'On the Ground': Jainism in South India," *Religious Studies News* 12, no. 3 (September 1997): 5.

10. David H. Kelsey, *To Understand God Truly: What's Theological about a Theological School* (Louisville, Ky.: Westminster/John Knox Press, 1992).

11. Linell E. Cady, *Religion, Theology, and American Public Life* (Albany, N.Y.: SUNY Press, 1993), 145.

12. Ray L. Hart, "Religious and Theological Studies in American Higher Education: A Pilot Study," *Journal of the American Academy of Religion* 59 (Winter 1991): 715–827.

13. Charlotte Allen, "Is Nothing Sacred: Casting Out the Gods from Religious Studies," *Lingua Franca*, November 1996, 30–40.

14. Russell T. McCutcheon, *Manufacturing Religion: The Discourse on Sui Generis Religion and the Politics of Nostalgia* (New York: Oxford University Press, 1997).

15. Talal Asad, *Genealogies of Religion: Discipline and Reasons of Power in Christianity and Islam* (Baltimore: John Hopkins University Press, 1993).

16. Hart, "Religious and Theological Studies," 733.

17. Ibid., 731, 737, 738, 742.

18. McCutcheon, *Manufacturing Religion*, 26.

19. Asad, *Genealogies of Religion*.

20. Wayne Proudfoot, *Religious Experiences* (Berkeley: University of California Press, 1985), 16.

21. Ada María Isasi-Díaz, *En La Lucha—In the Struggle: A Hispanic Women's Liberation Theology* (Minneapolis: Fortress, 1993), esp. chap. 3.

22. Chapter 3, here, 51.

23. Tanner, *Theories of Culture*, 70.

2

Loosening the Category That Binds

Modern "Religion" and the Promise of Cultural Studies

Linell E. Cady

As this volume attests, there is a growing interest among theologians in engaging in cultural analysis, including that which falls under the general rubric of cultural studies.[1] It would be easy to greet this development with cynicism, as just the latest example of the search for relevancy, perhaps for a subject, in a discipline that has become increasingly discredited and marginalized in late twentieth-century America. As Van Harvey has noted, "the slightest breezes that have stirred the trees of the groves of academe have been frantically harnessed for the purpose of generating energy for some new theological 'movement'—a 'theology of the death of God,' a theology of play,' a 'theology of hope,' a 'theology of liberation,' a 'theology of polytheism,' a 'theology of deconstruction.' "[2] Perhaps "theology and cultural studies" is simply another episode in this continuing chapter of disciplinary decline.

On the other hand, perhaps not. After all, the burgeoning interest in cultural studies among theologians is not an intradisciplinary phenomenon. Scholars from a wide range of disciplinary locations, including literature, philosophy, anthropology, and history, have embraced the assumptions and methods of this admittedly amorphous interdisciplinary movement—with significant ramifications for the human sciences. There is a widespread sense that the rise of cultural studies signals a paradigm shift within the academy and larger society, a shift most com-

monly depicted as the transition from modernism to postmodernism. It
has fostered new theoretical orientations, often the inverse of those
characteristic of modernism, and has been linked to larger trends, including the globalization of capital, erosion of the nation-state, and
explosion of new technologies.[3] From one angle, this shift is evident in
the intensification of scholarly interest in culture as an analytic category, although from another angle it is more appropriate to speak of a
marked reconceptualization in the notion of culture. Given the broad
transformations that are at play, it would be surprising if theologians
were isolated from their influence.

Although this general depiction of the changing landscape helps to
account for the growing interest in cultural analysis among theologians
(a point to which I will shortly return), the potentially radical implications of this turn for theology only come into focus through the use
of a narrower lens. Rather than limit attention to the revisioning of
"culture" as an analytic category, I am interested in focusing more explicitly on the category of "religion," a cognate term that is variously
understood as a dimension or subset of the former. By tracing the emergence and contours of the modern category of religion, the more particular constraints—intellectual, political, and institutional—that have
curtailed attention to sustained cultural analysis among theologians become clearer. The intellectual and institutional shape of theology in the
past two centuries has been deeply informed by the modern configuration of religion. Until quite recently, the work of this category in
shaping our private and public life has largely been concealed. For a
variety of reasons associated with globalization, the decline of modernism, and the growing reflexivity of postmodernism, its discursive power
has grown more evident, which has challenged, although certainly not
displaced, its continued dominance. Insofar as theological attention to
cultural analysis correlates with problematizing of the category of religion, whether intentionally or not, it harbors a potentially radical shift
within the discipline of theology. To this extent, far from being yet one
more example of theology's penchant for fads, the turn to cultural analysis may carry the seeds of a more sustained transformation, with significant implications for its institutional embodiment and the presumed
expertise of the theologian.

The Historicist Turn

Although a very blunt analytic instrument, the distinction between
modernism and postmodernism does help to clarify many of the major

theoretical shifts that have occurred in the past two decades. The distinction reflects, among other things, the culmination of a historicist turn that has had profound implications for epistemology, ontology, and ethics through broad reconceptualizations of their basic conceptual ingredients: for example, meaning, knowledge, subjectivity, identity, agency, and power. Although it is neither necessary nor possible in this context to explore these reconceptualizations, identifying a few of the more salient themes and their relation to the reconfiguration of culture provides an illuminating backdrop for our more explicit consideration of the category of religion.

First, there has been a clear movement toward more historicist interpretations of "meaning" and "knowledge." Rather than construe the meaning of words or propositions in terms of discrete representations of external reality, meaning has increasingly come to be seen, following Wittgenstein, as a function of its use. Further, the meaning of a word or practice has come to be understood as embedded within a wide web of significations, neither stable nor identifiable in abstraction or isolation. Richard Rorty has suggested that the shift is akin to escaping from a particular picture of the mind, knowledge, and reality that, borrowing Greek ocular metaphors, has captivated modern philosophers since Descartes:

> [T]he picture which holds traditional philosophy captive is that of the mind as a great mirror, containing various representations, some accurate, some not—and capable of being studied by pure, nonempirical methods. Without the notion of the mind as mirror, the notion of knowledge as accuracy of representation would not have suggested itself. Without this latter notion, the strategy common to Descartes and Kant—getting more accurate representations by inspecting, repairing, and polishing the mirror, so to speak—would not have made sense.[4]

Although obscured by the regnant modernist/postmodernist cartography, it is clear that the shift has been gradual, facilitated by a number of nineteenth- and twentieth-century thinkers who variously contributed to the deconstruction of the modernist picture that Rorty paints. The general trend has been an undermining of the ahistorical, individualistic, and referential model for knowledge that has dominated modernity and the fostering of a more social, historical, political, and pragmatic rendering of meaning, knowledge, and truth. As Rorty notes, with the escape from the modernist picture, "our focus shifts from the relation between human beings and the objects of their inquiry to the relation between alternative standards of justification, and from there to the actual changes in those standards which make up intellectual history."[5] It is a move toward an epistemological relativism, which carries with it heightened self-reflexivity as the scholar attends not just to the objects of study but to the discourses by which and through which objects are approached. In other words, rather than presume the possibility of a largely ahistorical, objective knowledge of what is the case—the mind mirroring reality—attention is directed to the highly particular and ever changing factors, material and ideational, that constrain and enable reflection.

This historicizing turn that underscores the constraints in the production of knowledge corresponds with an acute recognition of the intimate connections between knowledge and power, or in Foucault's formulation, to the power/knowledge nexus. The purported neutrality of knowledge as representation gives way to the conviction that knowledge is thoroughly informed by particular interests, that elite interests contribute to the configuration of hegemonic discourses and social practices, and that a hermeneutics of suspicion is an essential component in their interpretation and assessment. Entrusting knowledge to the determination of the "experts," whether medieval clergy or modern professors, is to risk allowing particular interests—vested in, for example, a particular gender, class, ethnicity, or nation—to control what counts for knowledge at any given time. Beyond cultivating a general skepticism toward knowledge, this fundamental change in epistemic framework exposes the limitations of analyzing meaning and texts in isolation from their contexts. It has underscored the importance of interpreting and assessing ideas, texts, and practices within the wider contexts in which they are embedded, attending carefully to the dynamics of power entailed in their production and reception. And it has led to great interest in popular or everyday culture, sometimes on the grounds that the canonical, official, or high culture reflects and furthers the interests of those in power.

These emphases are central to the scholarly work that loosely falls under the umbrella of cultural studies. Although the English roots and American transmutations of this interdisciplinary genre can be traced, it is a designation that resists easy encapsulation.[6] To some extent this reflects the fact that cultural studies is fast becoming "one of the most ambiguous terms in contemporary theory," perhaps a measure of its successful diffusion across the human sciences.[7] Its recurring accents include an emphasis upon the politically engaged character of scholarship and an attention to the everyday, orientations that have been widely embraced. Acknowledging the difficulties of articulating its de-

fining features, the editors of one influential volume on the genre conclude that "cultural studies proclaims a concern to understand life as
it is lived. This propels cultural studies into an examination of social,
political, cultural and historical forces that are brought to bear on the
real complexities of lived experience in particular social formations."[8]
Its protean nature has most recently assumed a form within which
issues of identity of the self and the other predominate. Attention to
gender, sexual orientation, ethnicity, and colonialism—and the correl-
ative issues of power and the politics of representation—have largely
come to define cultural studies in this decade.

The implications of the postmodern shift for the analytic category of
"culture" have been considerable. Generally speaking, there has been a
change from interpreting cultures as bounded wholes, with a large measure of integration and coherence, toward interpreting them as far more
fragmented and contested, with meanings negotiated rather than
shared.[9] In the modernist frame, culture is primarily understood in ideational terms, with a coherence that is analogous to that of a text or
organism. Modernist ethnographic portraits are like photographs that
capture a snapshot of a culture frozen in time; the internal discord that
fuels its continual transformation is thereby obscured. As a result of
the dual privileging of meaning and consensus in the interpretation of
culture, modern ethnographic portraits tend to function as false universals, which legitimate vested interests. Theorizing cultures as coherent wholes, an essentializing move, correlates with the presumption that
clear and distinct borders differentiate one culture from another. It is
an analytic propensity with elective affinities to the global system of
nation-states, wherein each unit is distinguished by the consonance of
geographical region, cultural coherence, and state power. It is not surprising that the erosion of the nation-state in recent decades, under the
impact of the growing movement of capital, information, and people
across national borders, has corresponded to the analytic displacement
of the modernist construal of culture.

"Culture" in a postmodernist framework is largely a historicist reworking of the same ingredients, with a resulting tendency to champion
features that are the inverse of modernist cultural theory. In lieu of
accentuating the essential unity of bounded cultural wholes, postmodernism underscores the fragmentation within and porous border zones
between cultures. The intellectual and aesthetic demand for coherence
is exposed as a strategy for ignoring dissenting voices, and thereby for
legitimating the current configurations of power and privilege. Rather
than interpreting culture as shared meaning, postmodernist theory re-
gards culture as the continual negotiation of meanings in a largely

conflictive discursive field. Hence, there is a fundamental imperative to attend to the continual processes of cultural formation and negotiation as they occur within day-to-day life. Far from presuming that any one interpretation can accurately capture a cultural phenomenon, the post-modern anthropologist disparages the objectivist pretensions of the modern ethnographer, preferring the image of "a cacophony of voices, commenting upon each other."[10] In addition to validating multiple per-spectives and challenging the distinction between high and low culture, this methodological disposition leads to a concerted effort to attend to those voices that have historically been unattended to in the interpre-tation of cultural life. Taken to its extreme, the move is toward viewing the ethnographer as primarily a spokesperson, or medium, for under-represented voices, virtually displacing scholarly aims and virtues in its wake.

The contrast between modern and postmodern theories of culture serves a useful mapping function in sorting out broad trends and their respective orientations and conceptual repertoires. But its analytic power needs to be tempered with a recognition that these alternatives are rarely found in their pure form, existing, rather, as ends of a con-tinuum along which scholarly inquiries can be located.[11] Despite this caveat, the contrast helps to focus our attention on fundamental shifts in the interpretation of culture and the forms of inquiry considered appropriate to its study. As we will see, there are interesting parallels between culture and religion, in terms of their modern incarnation as well as their postmodern problematizing.

The Increasing Visibility of the Modernist
Construction of Religion

Although attention to the erosion of the modernist paradigm—focusing particularly on shifts in the analytic concept of "culture"—does illu-minate broad trends that account for the growing interest in culture among theologians, it does not bring into sharp enough relief the more specific factors that have influenced the discipline of theology. As noted earlier, it is necessary to look more closely at a particular facet of the modernist paradigm, one of its key building blocks—the category of religion. This category has played a central role in the formation of the discursive space within which theology is carried out, a point generally unnoticed or too unproblematic to warrant much attention.[12] Until re-cently it has remained relatively transparent, exerting its powerful role in organizing the intellectual and social landscape without sustained attention to its peculiar assumptions and implications. Its unexamined power is reflected in the widespread western presumption that religion is an empirical category, corresponding to some experience or attitude that is discernible in cultures across time and space. Viewing religion as a generic, universal category appropriate for comparative, cross-cultural study has played a major role in the formation and legitimation of the field of religious studies; of course, the latter's institutional embodiment serves to reenforce the assumption. Why carve up the disciplinary landscape with separate departments devoted to the study of religion unless there is some universal religious experience, attitude, or domain that distinguishes it from other facets of human life, demanding its own investigative methods?

This construal of "religion" continues to exert tremendous power, power that is exercised and sustained not only through separate departments of religion but through numerous other discursive sites wielding far greater influence, ranging from constitutional law to the federal tax code to religion sections of newspapers. Nevertheless, there are increasing signs that the taken-for-granted power of this way of organizing personal and social life is eroding. Seeking to counter the widely shared, largely western assumption that religion has an empirical referent, Jonathan Z. Smith insists that the study of religion invented "religion."[13] As he explains, "There is no data for religion. Religion is solely the creation of the scholar's study. It is created for the scholar's analytic purposes by his imaginative acts of comparison and generalization."[14] Smith hereby challenges any unreflective use of the notion of "religion" by calling attention to the role that scholars have played in its formation and deployment. However, his emphasis upon the role of the scholar, while very much to the point, obscures the influence of the wider sociopolitical world in the formation of this category.

Other scholars have recently begun to fill in this gap. For example, David Chidester's recent account of the emergence of comparative religion in relation to colonial conquest in South Africa underscores the need to locate the imaginings of Enlightenment scholars within a wide social and political field. The heart of Chidester's argument is to demonstrate that "the frontier has been an arena in which definitions of religion have been produced and deployed, tested and contested, in local struggles over power and position in the world. In such power struggles, the term 'religion' has been defined and redefined as a strategic instrument."[15] Far from viewing "religion" as a neutral or innocent label for an empirical referent, Chidester persuasively exposes its ideological complicity in battles that belong not simply to the history of Europe and not simply to the scholar's study, but to the history of colonial conquest and domination. For our purposes, however, the differences between Smith and Chidester are less salient than their common aim: to challenge the deeply entrenched western presumption that "religion" is a universal and natural demarcation of human experience.

Although it is impossible to capture here the complex twists and turns in the historical evolution of the category "religion" that we have inherited, tracing several moments in this process does illuminate the developments that conspired, often unwittingly, to foster this presumption. As we shall see, the general direction in the modern evolution of this category was toward an increasingly universal, reified, and generic model of "religion." This movement facilitated the greater demarcation of religion from other dimensions of human experience and made possible a general comparison of religions on a level playing field. Multiple agendas—intellectual and sociopolitical, theological and secular—converged to produce this interpretation of "religion" as primarily personal not social, private not public.[16] The trajectory was toward the containment of religion as something distinctive, something that was increasingly defined by virtue of what it was not: not politics, not culture, not science, not aesthetics. In establishing a sharp boundary between religion and these other dimensions of human experience, religion increasingly came to inhabit the interior of the self, assimilated variously to conscience, faith, belief, or feeling.

The modern term "religion" can be traced back to the classical Latin word *religio*. Although the etymological roots of the term have been disputed, its most probable derivation, and the one that gained the most currency through Augustine's endorsement, was from *religare*, meaning "to bind."[17] According to historian Ernst Feil, *religio* meant "the careful and even fearful fulfillment of all that man owes to God or to the gods."[18] It was not used as a generic term, but referred rather to concrete ritual obligations, enacted, for example, before political or military events. Hence, it was not a term that lent itself to a comparison of the variety of beliefs and practices of peoples from different times and places.[19] Indeed, *religio* "implied the idea of religio vera," and therefore for Christians referred to their own ritual life and beliefs.[20] During the Middle Ages, "faith" was the more common term. When *religio* was used it primarily designated membership in a monastic order, referring to the careful manner in which obligations to God were fulfilled, a usage that continues in Catholicism to distinguish the clergy from the laity.[21]

A closer look at the development of "religion" as it took shape between the sixteenth and nineteenth centuries reveals the emerging senses of the term that helped to disentangle religion from its social

matrix, laying the groundwork for the sharp analytic distinction between "religion" and "not religion." To get a handle on this labyrinthine
process, several moments that proved particularly salient to this general
trend warrant attention: the Enlightenment contributions to the conceptualization of "religion" and the "religions," and the nineteenth-
century romantic reaction that soon followed. Each of these episodes in
the unfolding narrative of the modern term "religion" has left its distinctive stamp on the conceptual mosaic we have inherited. Each in its
own way, however, has also constituted a strategy of containment,
thereby contributing to the overall trend in the modern period toward
the separation of religion from other dimensions of human life.

The most significant conceptual development in the early modern
period regarding "religion" is the emergence of a generic sense of the
term, primarily a seventeenth-century development that owes much to
the writings of Herbert of Cherbury. The impetus for this conceptual
innovation can be largely traced to the crisis of authority and ensuing
political, social, and religious conflict that followed the fracturing of
Christendom in the sixteenth century. By the dawn of the seventeenth
century, it was clear that the cacophony of multiple authorities, exemplified in the schism between Catholicism and Protestantism and the
latter's splintering into varied sects—each with its own interpretation
of scripture—demanded resolution. Within this context of civil and religious discord, Herbert sought to articulate a theologically convincing
solution that would foster civic peace. Assuming the universality of
divine providence, Herbert attributed to all the multifarious religions
across time and space an essential core composed of five common notions.[22] These notions, according to Herbert, could be discerned through
an innate rational faculty and did not depend upon access to a special
revelation. In this he anticipated the characteristic Enlightenment understanding of a universal reason set in opposition to "history, tradition,
the past—all without rational authority."[23] Herbert's proposal served to
deprivilege the biblical framework through the identification of a universal religious essence, a move that lent theoretical parity to the diverse
religions.

Although, retrospectively, it is obvious that Herbert's five common
notions reflected Christian beliefs rooted in Arminian theology, the theoretical structure and implications of his proposal were momentous for
the emergence of a distinctively modern understanding of religion. By
locating access to true religion in a universal reason, not in particular
faiths, and in attributing to all religions an essential core, Herbert
helped to forge, "a generic concept of religion, a comparative method
initially made possible by the framework of propositional truths, and

the presupposition of some form of equal status among religions."[24] In proclaiming the five core notions "the only Catholic and uniform church," Herbert advanced the trajectory that severed any essential relationship between religion and institution or place. Although he himself recognized the indissoluble connection between the essential core notions and their historical vehicles, his legacy was to foster a sense of religion that could be abstracted from an integrated way of life. Far from being organically rooted in a particular place and time, religion was portable and primarily interior, associated with cognitive assent.

As is evident in Herbert's writings, the development of a generic notion of "religion" in the seventeenth century correlated with, perhaps even was driven by, the conceptualization of diverse religions as comparable systems of belief and worship. This trend was greatly facilitated by the increasing focus on the intellectual component within religion throughout this century, a reflection of the strong taxonomic and systematizing bent of the period. W. C. Smith explains: "In pamphlet after pamphlet, treatise after treatise, decade after decade the notion was driven home that a religion is something that one believes or does not believe, something whose propositions are true or are not true, something whose locus is in the realm of the intelligible."[25] Hundreds of works appeared in the seventeenth century that sought to provide a summary statement of the essential beliefs of "the Protestant religion" or "the true Catholic religion" or just "religion"; one thinker even offered a diagrammatic summary of the Christian religion in a single page.[26] This trajectory corresponded with changes in the mutually elucidating concepts of faith and reason. The earlier sense of faith as trust in a person and reason as reflecting divinely implanted innate ideas eroded and was replaced by an understanding of faith as assent to propositions and reason as a tabula rasa.[27] The objectification of religion during this period not only reflected the fracturing of Christendom, but, as Peter Harrison argues, it correlated with the rise of scientific methods of investigation:

> It would be expected that "religion" and the strategies for its elucidation would develop in tandem. For this reason "religion" was constructed along essentially rationalist lines, for it was created in the image of the prevailing rationalist methods of investigation: "religion" was cut to fit the new and much-vaunted scientific method. In this manner, "religion" entered the realm of the intelligible. It lay open to rational investigation while its specific forms—"the religions"—could be measured against each other, or against some intellectualist criterion of truth.[28]

Interpreting "religion" as a set of coherent propositions facilitated its pluralization into "religions" as clearly distinguishable systems of beliefs that can be compared and assessed, a marked change from the medieval term *religio*, which was only used in the singular.

Despite the enduring Enlightenment influences on the modern category "religion," they must be filtered through the romantic reaction—epitomized in the Schleiermachian turn to religious experience—that soon followed. The Enlightenment disdain for any arguments from authority, whether scriptural or ecclesiastical, combined with the devastating philosophical attack upon metaphysics and religious knowledge in the writings of thinkers such as Hume and Kant, contributed to the turn to experience to locate and ground religious life. First receiving powerful expression in Schleiermacher's writings and sustained through a line of influential thinkers that includes Otto, James, and Eliade, religious experience was understood as a distinctive, autonomous, immediate experience, prior to the concepts and beliefs that expressed it. For Schleiermacher, religion was "an affection, a revelation of the Infinite in the finite" and particular religions the necessary—but very clearly secondary—external manifestations of this religious affection.[29] Addressing the "cultured despisers" of religion, he asked, "Why have you not penetrated deeper to find the kernel of this shell?"[30] The turn to religious experience was an essentializing move that substituted feeling for propositions at the heart of the religious life. It was, however, another strategy of containment, establishing the essence of religion through a series of negations that distinguished it from science, morality, or knowledge.

Much of the recent writing challenging the essentialist model of religion has called attention to the theological roots and interests that it harbors. Consider, for example, the argument that Wayne Proudfoot makes in his influential work *Religious Experience*. His project is to provide a primarily philosophical analysis of the idea of religious experience that originated with Schleiermacher and that continues to exert, he contends, tremendous influence among scholars of religion and the wider culture. The delineation of a separate, autonomous experience has served, Proudfoot argues, as a very powerful protective strategy:

> With this idea of religion as an experiential moment irreducible to either science or morality, belief or conduct, Schleiermacher sought to free religious belief and practice from the requirement that they be justified by reference to nonreligious thought or action and to preclude the possibility of conflict between religious doctrine and any new knowledge that might emerge in the course

of secular inquiry. Religion is grounded in a moment of experience that is intrinsically religious, so it need not be justified by metaphysical argument, by the kind of evidence considered by the proponents of the design argument, or by appeals to its importance for the moral life.[31]

Under the guise of remaining faithful to experience and phenomenological description of this experience, alternate explanations, including reductive explanations, are ruled out. Taking a very different path, Russell McCutcheon reaches much the same conclusion in his recent book, *Manufacturing Religion*. McCutcheon explores, through the general approach and assumptions of discourse analysis, the multiple sites that sustain a view of religion as a discrete, autonomous object, and seeks to expose the problematic assumptions and ramifications of this conceptualization of religion. "The discourse on sui generis religion," he argues, "deemphasizes difference, history, and sociopolitical context in favor of abstract essences and homogeneity. When it comes to taking account of the possibly messy overlap between issues of power and spirituality, it is a powerful 'bracketing device.' "[32] Others have echoed this charge, contending that the implicit ideological agenda in the phenomenology of religion continues in and through the analytical framework that remains operative, regardless of the personal motives or interests of the individual scholar.[33]

The critique of the sui generis view of religion advanced by McCutcheon, Chidester, and J. Z. Smith closely parallels many of the criticisms leveled at the modernist conception of culture, wherein a tendency to provide a coherent, essentialist portrait obviates matters of power, discord, change, materiality, and representation. The analytic limitations of sui generis religion are similar, with problematic consequences that go far beyond the world of scholarship. Wendy Kaminer, a columnist for the *New Republic*, demonstrates as much in her recent tirade against the sacred shroud that is religion, or as she puts it, "the last taboo." Contending that we are living in an age of religious revivalism, she complains that the liberal press bends over backward not to ridicule religion: "In this climate—with belief in guardian angels and creationism becoming common place—making fun of religion is as risky as burning a flag in an American Legion hall."[34] The positive, legitimizing function of religion is all too evident, she suggests, in politicians' invocations to religion that signal their "trustworthiness" and "adherence to traditional moral codes of behavior." Invoking religion is a strategy that, more often than not, successfully sanctions beliefs and behavior and wards off the challenges of a critical reason in relation to that designated as a matter of personal faith and belief.

This critique of "religion" provides a very important perspective on the development and current usage of the term. However, it does not tell the whole story. In suggesting that it has primarily served apologetic interests, other forces that have contributed to its formation and deployment are obscured. As Wilfred Cantwell Smith succinctly puts it, "Religion' in its modern form is a secular idea. Secularism is an ideology, and 'religion' is one of its basic categories."[35] Uncovering the secular roots of the modern concept "religion" complicates our understanding of the emergence and function of this analytic term, revealing the multiple strands with divergent purposes that constitute it. This more complex picture suggests that it makes as much sense to say that "religion"—with its roots in the evolving liberal secular order—has contained theology as to say that theology has controlled "religion." Both observations are true in important respects, and it is only by acknowledging as much that one can account not only for the criticisms of a Wendy Kaminer but for those of a Stephen Carter, who decries the trivialization of religion in contemporary society.[36] Despite the differing agendas of the apologetic and secular strands that are woven together in the concept "religion," they nevertheless conspire to produce a similar effect: the carving out of a particular religious domain, experience, or moment that is segregated from other facets of personal and social life. This demarcation of something intrinsically religious is a containing strategy, protecting that which is inside from threats from without, while simultaneously ensuring that the inside will not contaminate the outside. Both sides—supposedly—win.

The various senses of "religion" and "religions" that emerged in the modern period to facilitate the demarcation of religion from other dimensions of human life reached its apex in the mid-twentieth century. The identification of religion as something separate from other facets of experience converged with the secularization of modern life and its differentiation into autonomous spheres, each governed by its own norms. Although this process of differentiation provided religion with its own space, its protective cocoon came at the cost of its disempowerment and marginalization within modern liberal society. Talal Asad argues that "the constitution of the modern state required the forcible redefinition of religion as belief, and of religious belief, sentiment, and identity as personal matters that belong to the newly emerging space of private (as opposed to public) life."[37] The modern notion of religion, and the public and private landscape that it both reflected and an-

chored, made possible the accommodation within one unified social order not only plural allegiances to the differing Christian churches, but
even more importantly an overriding allegiance to the emerging nation-
state. Asad makes explicit the dynamics that were operative in noting
that "religion was gradually compelled to concede the domain of public
power to the constitutional state, and of public truth to natural science."[38] In this movement, Asad explains,

> we have the construction of religion as a new historical object:
> anchored in personal experience, expressible as belief-statements,
> dependent on private institutions, and practiced in one's spare
> time. The construction of religion ensures that it is part of what
> is inessential to our common politics, economy, science, and mo-
> rality.[39]

According to the conventional liberal take on this historical shift,
this move not only brought freedom of religion, but it fostered social
unity and harmony through the emergence of a shared secular sphere
shorn of divisive religious commitments. In this scenario, the state is
construed as the benevolent keeper of social peace and harmony who
occupies what poses as a neutral secular sphere. This story line fully
endorses the liberal ideology that has functioned to legitimate the secular order of modern societies, leaving hidden the costs and particular
substantive values that it advances. As William Cavanaugh has argued,
liberal ideology contrasts the post-Reformation period of social fragmentation and religious sectarian violence with the achievement of
peace and social order under the watchful eye of the liberal state, con-
veniently obscuring the continued violence carried out to advance the
interests of the secular state. In his succinct formulation, "only killing
in the name of religion is damned; bloodshed on behalf of the State is
subject to no such scorn."[40] Moreover, the fiction of a neutral secular
sphere functions to obscure the substantive values that the nation-state
supports and goes to war to defend, such as "the value of the market,
scientific progress, the importance of choice itself."[41] The liberal ideology obscures the fact that, in John Milbank's words, "the secular as a
domain had to be instituted or imagined, both in theory and in practice."[42]

The western liberal model constituted by the simultaneous construction of the realm of the secular and the realm of privatized, essentialized religion has been exported around the world as the quintessentially
modern form for state and society.[43] Its influence can be discerned, for
example, in the category of "world religions" and the textbooks used to

teach them. These traditions are typically presented in a reified, essentialized fashion, isolated from the political, social, economic, and cultural worlds within which they are embedded and within which they operate. Reflecting upon the problems with the category of "religion" for his studies in India, Timothy Fitzgerald, for example, argues that a scholar fundamentally distorts what is going on by lifting out the religious ideas and activities from the surrounding political, social, and economic context. He only gradually reached this realization, which contravened his theoretical training, as he studied Buddhism in the Indian state of Maharashtra:

> [T]he researcher will notice that on all Buddhist shrines there is a picture of Gotama Buddha and a picture of Dr. Ambedkar. Gotama is dressed in the traditional rags of the renouncer or sitting crossed legged under the bodhi tree. In contrast, Dr. Ambedkar is depicted as wearing a blue suit and heavily-framed spectacles. Frequently in Buddhist iconography Ambedkar is also carrying a large book, which represents either the Republican Constitution of India . . . or else the power of literacy and education in a more general sense. What is being "worshipped" here, and what does liberation mean to these people?[44]

Beyond the distortions that inevitably attend abstracting something that is religious from the context in which it is embedded, scholars have begun to insist—with arguments essentially duplicating those found in postmodern criticisms of the modern "culture" construct—that these "world religion" constructs are abstractions that serve ideological purposes. As Gerald Larson concludes, "each is a singular label disguising what is in reality a pluralist array of cultural traditions."[45] Considering in particular the study of Hinduism, Fitzgerald argues that

> the confusions which abound at the conceptual level in the analysis of 'religion' suggest that, fundamentally, the idea cannot be clearly articulated in its relation to other prevalent analytical categories, and this mistake has been generated in general by cognitive imperialism and specifically by the *de facto* institutional dominance of western theology through the auspices of phenomenology.[46]

That the category of "religion" and one of its exemplifications (Hinduism) fail to illuminate personal and collective life in India provides further evidence of the historically particular formation that lies behind the modern coconstruction of "religion" and the "secular," with its rigid separation between the private sphere and the public sphere. Although the "institutional dominance of western theology" has served to maintain this discursive formation, the mutually elucidating relationship between western theology and religion must itself be located within the economic, political, and social transformations of western Europe as it interfaced with its colonized "others."

The passing of the modern epoch amid the accelerating forces of globalization has brought greater acuity regarding the modern construct "religion" and the ideological purposes—both secular liberal and theological—that it has served. Although it continues to shape personal and social life through a wide range of sites, its exposure as a historically and culturally specific discursive formation suggests its weakening. This is further confirmed, for instance, in the multiplication of historical studies exposing the misleading, anachronistic renditions of early modern Europe that have resulted from an uncritical appropriation of the analytic lens that sustains a sharp categorical distinction between "religion" and "not religion."[47] Jose Casanova's studies of contemporary religious movements that resist the privatization of modern religion in an effort to transform public life provide further evidence of the analytic limitations of this conceptual grid.[48] Roland Robertson, one of the leading theorists of globalization, argues that the "western-led separation of religion and politics began to be reversed in the mid-1970s."[49] For Robertson, "what stands out as unique in historical and comparative perspectives is the strength of the processes of differentiation which yielded relatively separate spheres of politics and religion, as well as the force of the myths that have sustained these processes."[50] The image of an autonomous sphere or enclave for religion that has dominated the modern imagination and become deeply embedded in our legal, political, and social lives no longer appears as self-evident, as universal, or—to many—as appropriate as it once did.

Theology and Religion: A Mutually Defining Relationship

The various strategies of containment that mark the development of the modern category of religion have also contributed to the shape and institutional location of theology. In George Lindbeck's elegant wording, "the habits of thought [the modern category of religion] has fostered are ingrained in the soul of the modern West, perhaps particularly in the souls of theologians."[51] The relative lack of theological attention to a careful analysis of culture is largely explainable in terms of the sequestering of religion from other dimensions of human life. Defining religion through sharp oppositions with what it is not (e.g., not science, not politics, not economics) has fostered an "unfortunate narrowing and specialization" of theology.[52] The growing interest among theologians in studies in culture—an expansive move—harbors an implicit, if not explicit, critique of the categorical distinction between "religion" and "not religion." Furthermore, it holds out the promise of theology's escape from its intellectual and institutional confinement that has contributed to its increasing marginalization and irrelevance. In the remaining pages my aim is simply to identify some of the reasons for welcoming this development.

The deleterious effects of theology's tango with modern religion have been institutionally reflected in the discipline's exclusion from the liberal arts within the university. The rise of the modern secular university, with its roots in the Enlightenment model of an autonomous, universal reason, raised fundamental questions about the intellectual legitimacy of theology. The latter's identification with a particular tradition and its apparent capitulation to ecclesiastical or scriptural authority precluded its status as a field of academic inquiry within the Enlightenment ethos. Kant was as instrumental in resolving the dilemma, with fateful consequences for theology, as he was in creating it by virtue of his epistemology and critique of metaphysics. In *The Conflict of the Faculties*, Kant essentially equated the philosophical faculty with what in contemporary parlance would be the liberal arts faculty, contrasting their methods and mission with the professional agenda of the theological faculty to train ministers. Although this provided a rationale for the continued presence of the theological faculty within the German university, the cost was exceedingly high. Moreover, the rationale was not fully transferable to the American context with its sharp separation of church and state. It led to the exclusion of theology from public and other self-consciously secular colleges and universities and its establishment within seminaries and divinity schools that were understood to have an explicitly religious and professional agenda.

Theology's forced diaspora from the heart of the university eventuated in an increasingly circumscribed curriculum, mirroring the modern containment of "religion" that has isolated it from other dimensions of experience. The narrowing of the subject matter of theology proper was further exacerbated by developments internal to theological studies as it fragmented into the four divisions of biblical studies, church history, systematic theology, and practical theology.[53] This splintering into separate disciplines further contracted the expertise of the theologian, as "the subject matter of theology was, as it were, subcontracted out to New Testament studies, church history, philosophy of religion, and ethics."[54] As a consequence, theological training in recent times has tended to consist of gaining mastery in the theological canon and facility in exegetical and philosophical skills. Theological texts and doctrines are typically approached ahistorically, interpreted and assessed in isolation from their location within a particular place and time. Theologians in the modern era, in other words, have been primarily taught to "polish the mirror," not to approach religious ideas, practices, and texts as strategies whose meaning and value are inseparable from the cultural context in which they are embedded. Reflecting on the developments within the discipline, Harvey observes that "theology is now no longer seen as subject matter that has to do with the clarification of the self-understanding of the ordinary believer and, hence, as having any relevance for the 'life world.' "[55] Because "techniques for reflection on and criticism" of the life world are not a component of the theological curriculum, theological efforts in this direction, as Harvey rightly notes, frequently lack academic sophistication and credibility, indicative of the absence of formal training in the study of economics, politics, and society.[56]

The growing attention to cultural analysis among theologians is an important corrective to the reigning ahistorical, acontextual model of theology. To the extent that it depends upon developing substantive and methodological expertise that has been the province of the human sciences, it also constitutes a fundamental critique of the modern theological curriculum that has been isolated, intellectually and institutionally, from the liberal arts and sciences.

The growing attention to cultural analysis among theologians also contains an implicit critique of the sequestering of religion and theology that has defined their modern incarnation. Developing this trajectory within theology is vital if the discipline is to adapt to the changing religious-cultural landscape.[57] Although the conceptual grid constituted by the modern constructs "religion" and "religions" may never have been a fully adequate map to lived reality, its lack of fit has grown, and grown increasingly apparent. Recent comparative and historical studies in religion and culture have pointed to the limitations of this conceptual grid in ways that are of considerable relevance for theologians. In his recent study of religion and the state in India, for example, Gerald Larson contends that the conventional meaning of "religion," particularly as it is expressed in the "world religions" constructs, has essentially obscured the emergence of new constellations of meaning and value. The "world religions" discourse, reflected in the notion of Hinduism, has facilitated a view of the state as an increasingly secularized entity, thereby deflecting attention from the processes of re-religionization that surround it. Hence, Larson argues, if

> the "notion of religion" or the "religious dimension" is not nec-
> essarily tied to one of the traditional "world religions," then to
> say that a nation-state or an institution has undergone "secular-
> ization" is to say something only about the nation-state's or the
> institution's treatment of its older pre-modern traditional religious
> forms, but it is to say almost nothing about possible new religious
> meanings growing out of the secularization process.[58]

The blind spots produced by the modern "religions" discourse are not limited to nonwestern contexts. Gavin Langmuir argues a strikingly similar point about the conceptual limitations of this discourse in relation to modern European developments in his recent study, *History, Religion, and Antisemitism*. He denies that Europe "passed from a religious to a secular age"; on the contrary, he argues that "what we see instead is that, in response to radically new conditions and a radical change in mentality, old dimensions of religiosity were expressed in new ways and a radically new kind of religiosity developed that engendered a new kind of religion."[59] Despite quite different agendas and areas of expertise, these scholars are making visible the contours of the conventional category of "religion" and helping to expose the costs of remaining captive to its discursive formation. Significantly, their constructive analytic efforts lie in the direction of blurring the sharp boundary between religion and culture and in placing greater emphasis upon what might be called "religiosity" rather than a coherent system of beliefs and practices or "an ancillary province bolted onto the everyday lives of some and not of others."[60] If theology remains ensnared in the conceptual grid of the modern religions discourse, it will be unable to attend to new forms of religiosity emerging in contemporary life.

Consider, for example, the powerful role of films in contemporary American culture. Far from being merely entertainment, films are popular vehicles for narratives and norms that shape individual and collective identity in critical ways. In the words of one newspaper article, "Star Wars is the scripture of our public religion."[61] This analytic perspective has not had much currency among scholars of religion or theologians. Seeking to change this, the editors of one recent collection on religion and film insist that "popular films are powerful vehicles for communicating religious meanings, mythic stories, and bedrock ideological values to millions of people."[62] Taken together, the essays seek to challenge the categorical distinctions that we have inherited, distinctions that suggest religion and entertainment, or religion and secularism, or religion and aesthetics, are easily distinguishable. On the contrary, the volume establishes that "Movies can no longer be viewed as 'just entertainment,' and religion can no longer be viewed as an antiquated or a peripheral institution in a predominantly secular society."[63]

The promise of cultural studies for theology lies in its potential to break down the fairly rigid boundary that has demarcated religion from its surroundings, contributing to the tendency to engage the ideational contents of this sequestered sphere in isolation from their embodiment in the lived world. By tempering the tendency to abstract religion from the larger configuration within which it is located, the gulf that separates professionalized theology and everyday experience can be minimized. Such a move facilitates the consideration of perspectives that have been largely ignored in the theological tradition. Moreover, it more easily allows for the critical engagement of the changing religious/cultural landscape that has spawned new forms of religiosity that oftentimes, although certainly not always, slip through the conventional grid of modern "religion" and the "religions."[64] Struggling with the problem of defining religiosity without privileging its traditional forms, Langmuir suggests that "religiosity is the dominant pattern or structuring of nonrational thinking—and the conduct correlated with it—which the individual trusts to establish, extend, and preserve consciousness of his or her identity."[65] Assuming some such understanding, theology from this view is engaged in the interpretation, critique, and reconstruction of the major religiosities of a culture, which may or may not correlate with its traditional forms. Cultural studies harbors the potential to facilitate this view of theology, not least through the relaxation of the discipline's ties to the modern "religion" construct.

Notes

1. See also Dwight N. Hopkins and Sheila Greeve Davaney, eds., *Changing Conversations: Religious Reflection and Cultural Analysis* (New York: Routledge, 1996) and Kathryn Tanner, *Theories of Culture: A New Agenda for Theology* (Minneapolis: Fortress Press, 1997). I would like to acknowledge the considerable help of Christopher Chesnek, my former research assistant, in revising this essay for publication.

2. Van Harvey, "On the Intellectual Marginality of American Theology," in *Religion and Twentieth-Century American Intellectual Life*, ed. Michael J. Lacey (New York: Cambridge University Press, 1989), 173.

3. For an argument that seeks to locate the emergence of cultural studies in relation to global political and economic developments and to identify their effects on the modern university, see Bill Readings, *The University in Ruins* (Cambridge: Harvard University Press, 1996).

4. Richard Rorty, *Philosophy and the Mirror of Nature* (Princeton, N.J.: Princeton University Press, 1979), 12.

5. Ibid., 389–90.

6. For an excellent overview of the roots and transformations in cultural studies, see Lawrence Grossberg, "The Formations of Cultural Studies: An American in Birmingham," in *Relocating Cultural Studies: Developments in Theory and Research*, ed. Valda Blundell, John Shepherd, and Ian Taylor (London: Routledge, 1993).

7. Ibid., 8.

8. Valda Blundell, John Shepherd, and Ian Taylor, introduction to *Relocating Cultural Studies*, 4.

9. In her recent work *Theories of Culture*, Kathryn Tanner provides a very helpful synopsis, through the use of ideal-types, of the analytical distinctions between the modernist and postmodernist renditions of "culture." My review of these two orientations relies heavily on her analysis. For another helpful articulation of these contrasting approaches to culture, see Robert Brightman, "Forget Culture: Replacement, Transcendence, Relexification," *Cultural Anthropology* 10, no. 4 (1995): 509–46.

10. Adam Kuper, "Culture, Identity and the Project of a Cosmopolitan Anthropology," *Man* 29 (1994): 542.

11. Robert Brightman provides a useful cautionary note about the tendency to juxtapose these theoretical alternatives too sharply in "Forget Culture." He argues that in this strategy, theory essentially trumps history insofar as theoretical interests in the present are allowed to overshadow a decidedly more nuanced past.

12. There are significant exceptions to this point, most notably Karl Barth, whose towering theological edifice was based upon the sharp distinction between revelation and religion. His critique of nineteenth-century liberal theology was rooted in his charge that it had located theology within the human province of religion, cutting it off from God's revelatory Word.

13. Jonathan Z. Smith, "Religion and Religious Studies: No Difference at All," *Soundings* 71 (1988): 234.

14. Jonathan Z. Smith, *Imagining Religion: From Babylon to Jonestown* (Chicago: University of Chicago Press, 1982), page xi; quoted in " 'Religion' and 'Religious Studies,' " 234–35.

15. David Chidester, *Savage Systems* (Charlottesville: University of Virginia Press, 1996), 254.

16. For a variation on this argument, see, for example, Jacob Neusner, "The Theological Enemies of Religious Studies: Theology and Secularism in the Trivialization and Personalization of Religion in the West," *Religion* 18 (1988): 18. Although underscoring the powerful theological and secular forces that conspired to shape the modern interpretation of religion, Neusner writes as if religion is really something else, thereby minimizing the extent to which religion in the modern West came to assume the shape that he deplores.

17. Morris Jastrow, *The Study of Religion* (New York: Charles Scribner's Sons, 1901), 131; Cicero, *The Nature of the Gods*, trans. Horace C. P. McGregor (New York: Penguin, 1972), 153.

18. Ernst Feil, "From the Classical *Religio* to the Modern *Religion*: Ele-

ments of a Transformation between 1550 and 1650," in *Religion in History: The Words, the Idea, the Reality*, ed. Michel Despland and Gerard Vallee, (Waterloo, Ont.: Wilfrid Laurier University Press, 1992), 32.

19. Scholars have noted that the more generic use of "religion" appears to be connected to historical contexts that are marked by religious pluralism and rivalry. See, for example, Wilfred Cantwell Smith, *The Meaning and End of Religion* (New York: Harper & Row, 1962), 24–25.

20. Feil, "From the Classical *Religio*," 34.

21. Ibid., 32; W. C. Smith, *Meaning and End of Religion*, 33.

22. Herbert's five common notions, as Roger A. Johnson lists them, are: (1) there is a Supreme God; (2) this sovereign Deity ought to be worshiped; (3) the connection of virtue with piety is the most important part of religious practice; (4) wickedness, vice, or crime must be expiated by repentance; (5) there is reward or punishment after this life. See "Natural Religion, Common Notions, and the Study of Religions: Lord Herbert of Cherbury (1583–1648)," *Religion* 24 (1994): 217.

23. J. Samuel Preus, *Explaining Religion: Criticism and Theory from Bodin to Freud* (New Haven, Conn.: Yale University Press, 1987), 35.

24. Johnson, "Natural Religion, Common Notions," 213–14, 219.

25. W. C. Smith, *Meaning and End of Religion*, 40.

26. Peter Harrison, *"Religion" and the "Religions" in the English Enlightenment* (Cambridge: Cambridge University Press, 1990), 25.

27. For a discussion of this change, see Peter Harrison, "Religion and the Religions in the Age of William and Mary: A Response to David A. Pailin," *Method and Theory in the Study of Religion* 7, no. 3 (1995): 273–81.

28. Peter Harrison, *"Religion" and the "Religions,"* 2.

29. Friedrich Schleiermacher, *On Religion: Speeches to Its Cultured Despisers*, trans. John Oman (New York: Harper & Row, 1958), 36.

30. Ibid., 15.

31. Wayne Proudfoot, *Religious Experience* (Berkeley: University of California Press, 1985), page xiii.

32. Russell McCutcheon, *Manufacturing Religion* (New York: Oxford University Press, 1997), 4. McCutcheon attributes the term "bracketing device" to Rosalind Shaw, "Feminist Anthropology and the Gendering of Religious Studies," in *Religion and Gender*, ed. Ursula King (Oxford: Blackwell, 1995).

33. Timothy Fitzgerald, "A Critique of 'Religion' as a Cross-Cultural Category," *Method and Theory in the Study of Religion*, 9, no. 2 (1997): 92.

34. Wendy Kaminer, "The Last Taboo," *New Republic*, October 14, 1996, 25.

35. Wilfred Cantwell Smith, "Retrospective Thoughts on 'The Meaning and End of Religion,'" in Despland and Vallee, *Religion in History*, 16. Peter Harrison takes exception to Smith's claim that "religion" was originally a secular term, arguing that it was originally an insider's term that emerged in theological polemics in sixteenth-and seventeenth-century Europe—as is evident in Herbert of Cherbury's writings. Harrison traces a process whereby "religious ideas of religion were secularized." See Peter Harrison, *"Religion" and the "Religions,"* 4.

36. Stephen Carter, *The Culture of Disbelief: How American Law and Politics Trivialize Religious Devotion* (New York: Basic Books, 1993).

37. Talal Asad, *Genealogies of Religion: Discipline and Reasons of Power in Christianity and Islam* (Baltimore: Johns Hopkins University Press, 1993), 205.

38. Ibid., 207.

39. Ibid.

40. William Cavanaugh, "A Fire Strong Enough to Consume the House: The Wars of Religion and the Rise of the State," *Modern Theology* 11, no. 4 (1995): 397.

41. Ibid., 409.

42. John Milbank, *Theology and Social Theory* (Oxford: Blackwell, 1990), 9.

43. For a fascinating portrait of the power of this discursive formation in the shaping of modern Japanese society in the late nineteenth century, see James Ketelaar, *Of Heretics and Martyrs in Meiji Japan* (Princeton, N.J.: Princeton University Press, 1990). He traces the process by which the traditions of Buddhism and Shintoism were essentially disentangled and constructed, and "religion" was placed in opposition to politics, education, science, and cultural enlightenment.

44. Fitzgerald, "Critique of 'Religion,'" 103. See also Timothy Fitzgerald, "Hinduism and the World Religion Fallacy," *Religion* 20 (1990): 101–18, and Jonathan Z. Smith, "A Matter of Class: Taxonomies of Religion," *Harvard Theological Review* 89, no. 4 (1996): 387–403.

45. Gerald James Larson, *India's Agony over Religion* (Albany: SUNY Press, 1995), 31. This book essentially makes the case for this conclusion by a careful examination of "Hinduism" in India.

46. Fitzgerald, "Critique of 'Religion,'" 99.

47. See, for example, John Hedley Brooke, *Science and Religion: Some Historical Perspectives* (Cambridge: Cambridge University Press, 1991); James C. Livingston, "Science and Religion in Culture: Social and Religious Contextualization in Recent British History of Science," *Religious Studies Review* 23 (1997); David C. Lindberg and Ronald L. Numbers, eds., *God and Nature: Historical Essays on the Encounter between Christianity and Science* (Berkeley: University of California Press, 1986).

48. Jose Casanova, *Public Religions in the Modern World* (Chicago: University of Chicago Press, 1994).

49. Quoted in James Beckford and Thomas Luckmann, introduction to *The Changing Face of Religion*, ed. James Beckford and Thomas Luckmann (London: Sage Publications, 1989), 3.

50. Roland Robertson, "Globalization, Politics and Religion," in Beckford and Luckmann, *The Changing Face of Religion*, 12.

51. George A. Lindbeck, *The Nature of Doctrine: Religion and Theology in a Postliberal Age* (Philadelphia: Westminster, 1984), 21. Lindbeck provides a very illuminating analysis of the forms of theology that correlate with several different models of religion that he labels the "propositional," the "experiential-expressive," and the "cultural-linguistic."

52. Edward Farley, *Theologia: The Fragmentation and Unity of Theological Education* (Philadelphia: Fortress, 1983), 17.

53. In *Theologia*, Farley traces the fragmentation of theological studies into separate disciplinary specialties, resulting in the progressive narrowing of theology proper.

54. Harvey, "On the Intellectual Marginality," 188.

55. Ibid., 184.

56. Ibid., 192.

57. It does not necessarily follow that theology should be limited to the development of this trajectory.

58. Larson, *India's Agony over Religion*, 281.

59. Gavin Langmuir, *History, Religion, and Antisemitism* (Berkeley: University of California Press, 1990), 230.

60. John Daniels, "Religions, Religious Studies, and the Life-World," *Scottish Journal of Religious Studies* 18, no.1 (1997): 39.

61. Orson Scott Card, " 'Star Wars' Our Public Religion," *USA Today*, March 17, 1997.

62. Joel W. Martin, preface to *Screening the Sacred: Religion, Myth, and Ideology in Popular American Film*, ed. Joel W. Martin and Conrad E. Ostwalt Jr. (Boulder, Colo.: Westview Press, 1995), page vii.

63. Ibid.

64. Although my primary interest has been in identifying the promise of cultural studies for theology, I want to include a cautionary note. A correction can all too easily be taken as a substitution, in this instance suggesting that theology should—without remainder—be transformed into a variant of cultural studies. Such an overcorrection risks a "hypertrophied" concern for context and too quickly allows respect for multiplicity to eclipse the imaginal moves toward unity. To defend social context over ahistorical structure, as Wendy Doniger notes, "is to choose empiricism over imagination." The challenge for theology, at this juncture, is to move toward a chastened universalism, the accommodation of universalist impulses within a historicist age. The theological turn to cultural studies may help facilitate this transition. See Doniger, *The Implied Spider: Politics and Theology in Myth* (New York: Columbia University Press, 1998), 52. For Doniger's discussion of the dangers of a "hypertrophied" preoccupation with context, see 43–47.

65. Langmuir, *History, Religion, and Antisemitism*, 162.

3

Refashioning Self and Other

Theology, Academy, and the New Ethnography

Delwin Brown

With freedom of choice and with honor, as though the maker and molder of thyself, thou mayest fashion thyself in whatever shape thou shalt prefer.

Pico della Mirandola,
Oration on the Dignity of Man

The ethnographic subjectivity I am concerned with may be seen as [a] late variant [of Renaissance] . . . "self-consciousness about the fashioning of human identity as a manipulable, artful process."

James Clifford,
The Predicament of Culture

On the Academy

The academic study of religion shares the self-doubt of all humanistic disciplines, but for religious studies this doubt is especially intense. The trauma of the humanities generally stems, first, from the loss of the illusion of objectivity within its inquiries. That illusion has been eroded, on the one hand, by the realization that there are no self-evident generalities from which to begin these scholarly inquiries and hence from which equally sure conclusions might be deduced. In religious studies, this means that there are no unproblematic definitions of religion or religiousness, of humans or humanness, of the sacred, of culture, of ritual, of pilgrimage, of theology, of center or periphery, of structure or antistructure, or, for that matter, of the study of religion with which to begin in confidence that we are starting with something firm and clear from which we might deduce conclusions that enjoy a similar certitude. Our inquiries have no sure points of departure.

The illusion of objectivity has also been eroded by the realization that there can be no certainty about the scholar's destination—the specific, concrete subject matter the scholar wishes to identify, focus on, analyze, and thus to understand. To be sure (taking again the example of religious studies), the scholar can identify, focus on, and analyze this particular thing or that, which she or he might call a ritual, a myth, a dance, a doctrine, a tribe, or a Presbyterian, and the result might be quite, as we like to say, "interesting," but how does the scholar come to any sure conclusion that what he or she says and finds interesting in fact fits with or is appropriate to the particularity at hand? Indeed, it is even hard for us to devise a language for what it is we want our conclusions to be, other than interesting; it is difficult to say what we mean by "fits with" or "is appropriate to." But even if we could settle on a language about what we want by way of solid conclusions—other than something distressingly formal—we can never be certain that we have got it, for that would require us to take our conclusions in one hand, so to speak, and the subject matter in the other, and compare them from some third standpoint, which we manifestly cannot do.

In sum, neither the abstract categories with which we begin nor the specific data to which we apply them are sure groundings for our inquiries. Even in the most empirical of humanistic studies, the conditions of objectivity vanish, and thus objectivity itself.

This loss of objectivity is not our only problem, however, for although we lack a desirable certainty about a number of things, we do think we know some things well enough to be obligated to take them seriously. Among the things we now think we know in this middle epistemic register is that the objects of our study do not, in themselves, display the unity we had once thought. They have lost their essences. This is especially evident when we speak of religion and religious traditions. Except for the perennialists, whether of religion or of particular religions, who posit an essence they know not what, most of us are most impressed by the swirling diversity we see when we look at religion in general and religious traditions and phenomena in particular. Precision defies us. It is not just that we cannot know for sure, which comes from the disappearance of objectivity; it is that we can know enough, albeit tentatively, to say that what is actually there before us does not fit terribly well the categories we have imposed upon them. When we try to compare something in Hinduism and Buddhism or Christianity and Islam, for example, what Hinduism and Buddhism or Christianity and Islam mean become very murky, and so, too, does the "something" we were trying to compare in them.

What follows is not that there are not approximate things like Hinduism and Buddhism or prayer and pilgrimage, but that they apparently do not have the structural unity, the neatness of being, we had thought. They lack essences, defining characteristics that once grasped in our analyses will always lead us like a divining rod straight to their authentic manifestations. And lacking essences, religious traditions seem to be rather like galaxies, as I have suggested elsewhere, adapting a metaphor taken from Sam D. Gill.[1] Traditions are not, on the one hand, quite as arbitrary as constellations, which are patterns in the sky invented by human observers. But neither are they, on the other hand, as solidly given as a planet, which is undeniably there whatever else might be debated about it. Viewed from a distance, religious traditions seem to possess rough identities, but the closer we move in on them the more obvious their swirling internal diversity and, equally important, the raggedness of their edges.

What follows from this is not only that analytical comparisons between traditions are complex and problematic but that the problems of such analyses apply just as stubbornly to comparisons within traditions. Whether we are comparing Judaism and Christianity on a particular issue, or subtraditions within Judaism and Christianity, or different traditions within Judaism or Christianity, we are not given a graspable essence with which to capture the one thing and see its similarities to and differences from the essence of another. These data, too, are something there that we can identify and approach, but as we do we are increasingly aware of them as dynamic miscellanies, without clear and abiding centers, that splinter at their boundaries into something quite different.

Given this, how shall we think of the academic study of religion? We cannot begin with self-evidently valid general categories. We cannot clearly confirm our concluding analyses of particulars. But we think we know enough about the particulars, and are sure enough about the generalities with which we approach them, that we can draw some conclusions, one of which is that the things we look at lack the clear defining characteristics we once assumed they had. Essences and objectivity are now denied us. Without these hallmarks of "scientific" scholarship, religious studies and the humanities generally are now in the process of reexamining the status of their investigations, their nature, how they are conducted, and the standards by which these investigations and their outcomes are to be tested.

If the situation in religious studies is a version of the larger reappraisal within the humanities, we might begin by noting that in the humanities a general constructive response to the loss of essences, insofar as there is such a response, is the emergence of what might be called "historicism," and a general response to the loss of objectivity is a rebirth, at least in the United States, of varieties of pragmatism. Hence, to the degree that there is now developing a constructive alternative, it is, I think, what my colleague Sheila Davaney calls "pragmatic historicism."[2] Negatively, this is the judgment that scholarly inquiry is never objectively conducted, never guided by clear categories, and never subject to proof. Positively, pragmatic historicism is the view that (a) with respect to status, our inquiries always begin "in the middle," so to speak, with an inheritance of fallible values and ambiguous categories, that (b) with respect to their nature, they are always conducted via a continuing negotiation among competing views, and that (c) as to standards, they are to be collectively tested along the way in relation to their actual and probable consequences.

Rather than providing a systematic account of historicism, in this essay I want to discuss the new ethnography because I understand it to be an example of what might be termed "practical historicism" or historicism in practice. For the new ethnography is an attempt to "understand the other" without depending on the illusions of sure categories (essentialism) and certain grounds (objectivity), and, equally important, to be self-conscious about the ways the new ethnography therefore differs from older scholarly self-understandings. But I also discuss the new ethnography here because I assume it to be an element of, or a plausible model for, much that properly goes on in religious studies. If this new ethnographic approach could not be the whole of religious studies, it nonetheless could and should be a legitimate component within it. And if that is true, the revised self-understanding fostered, even compelled, by the new ethnography has implications, it seems to me, for how religious studies ought to rethink the status, nature, and standards of its own undertakings, and thus, what does and does not belong within its domain. In particular, the new ethnography ought to cause us to reexamine the relationship of religious studies to a certain kind of theology. Indeed, advancing this reexamination is one of the main goals of this chapter.

On the New Ethnography

The two epigraphs at the beginning of this essay are from the works of James Clifford and Pico della Mirandola, one of the Renaissance sources to whom Clifford refers. Both, however, indicate what I find suggestive in Clifford's work for trying to think through an important dimension of the comparative study in religion.

James Clifford, of course, is the principal theorist of the "new ethnography."[3] The new ethnography might be characterized as a postmodern ethnographic epistemology in which the value-laden, intensely normed character of all scholarly inquiry is kept in the foreground. Its aim is to understand how these "interested" ethnographies are constructed and represented and, more particularly, "how [they] achieve their effect as knowledge of 'others.' "[4] Thus, the new ethnography might also be seen as the incorporation of postmodern philosophical hermeneutics into the empirical study of human cultures.

One of the most significant consequences of this postmodern approach to culture is the radical questioning of the concepts of "culture" and "tradition." Clifford himself is equivocal on this issue. Sometimes he speaks as if we should dispense with all reference to "cultural and social totalities."[5] When he is in this "deconstructive" mood Clifford usually is reflecting on one of two things, either on the contemporary realization that what we have called cultures are at best "differentiating ensembles"[6] rather than the organic, naturally developing unities we had imagined them to be,[7] or on the global "unification" now occurring that seems unique in the history of this planet.[8] But even on these points Clifford is undogmatic about what these developments imply. He notes, for example, that the so-called unification now covering the globe is producing "connections" but not any evident homogenization of customs and values. He reckons further that those who anticipate the disappearance of ancient and exotic peoples are likely to be surprised.[9] Thus, whether or not the ideas of distinct cultures and traditions are rendered passe by developments in the twentieth century seems finally unclear to Clifford.

Clifford's conclusion on the other point—that cultures and traditions never have been the natural, coherent wholes we had thought them to be—is surely firm and convincing. But his claim here is precisely that cultures and traditions have *always* been constantly renegotiated ensembles of diversity, and if they have *always* been that, the fact that they are that *now* does not automatically imply their imminent demise! Thus, at one point Clifford rightly wonders whether his own tendency to "de-

construct" Mashpee tradition might not be a projection of the pecu-
liarly alienated experience of his own class and time.[10] Hence, in my
view, Clifford's more careful conclusion is that it still remains useful to
speak of cultures and traditions as long as we are clear that these pluralistic ensembles are not simply *given* but also *made* through a process
of collective, conflictive, value-laden negotiation.[11] If so, Clifford's view
of the pluralism and dynamism of cultures and traditions simply underscores one of the problems described at the outset of this chapter.
But, as we shall see, his view of culture as the collective negotiation
of values in conflict also reflects his understanding of the new ethnography. The study of cultures, in Clifford's view, mirrors the nature
of cultures.

In rethinking the academic study of religion, therefore, the distinctively promising aspect of Clifford's thought is his portrayal of ethnography as the refashioning of the self and the other. This characterization
emerges out of Clifford's ruminations on what he calls ethnographic
authority, by which he means simply that which warrants the results
of ethnographic investigation.[12] The underlying premise of this discussion is Clifford's postmodern judgment that reality (i.e., what is the case)
is always highly questionable, better captured by surrealist depictions
than by any of the myriad forms of realism that used to dominate
Western intellectual life.[13]

Back when realism reigned, it made sense to think of the ethnographer as a disciplined fieldworker who entered an alien environment
armed with proven methods and human empathy, and who thus managed in due time to experience the heart of what was to be found there.
Ethnographic authority, then, was that of the fieldworker's experience.
Or in a later, more sophisticated form, the trained fieldworker was also
the educated theorist, who, as participant/observer, did not simply experience the heart of the matter, but uncovered it via a theoretically
informed interpretation of his or her experience. In this case, the authority of ethnography was the ethnographer's expertise in interpretation, itself a product of good theory and skilled technique plus a reasonable capacity for rapport with the other.

Eventually, however, the arbitrary, selective, and parochial nature of
this kind of inquiry became undeniable, which led, according to Clifford,
to two additional images of ethnography—ethnography as dialogue and
ethnography as polyphony. In the dialogical setting, the professional
researcher and the informant are really coinformants, each equally authoritative, each proposing interpretations of the subject under scrutiny,
and each challenging and testing the claims of the other until some
reasonably unified portrayal of things comes out of the process as their

common creation. The weaknesses of the dialogical approach are that the governing agenda is still the agenda imposed by the professional researcher, and that the perspective of the informant or indigenous researcher is always, necessarily, but one possible slant on the native situation.[14] Hence, an alternative ethnographic approach is what Clifford calls polyphony or, following Bakhtin, "heteroglossia."[15] This admittedly utopian strategy Clifford characterizes as a "plural authorship that accords to collaborators not merely the status of independent enunciators but that of writers."[16]

In the end, however, Clifford refuses to rule out any of these modes of ethnography. There is a place, he says, for the creative utilization and combination of each—the experiential, interpretive, dialogical, and polyphonic.[17] They do not represent distinct, progressive moments in the history of ethnography so much as necessary elements, to some degree, in every ethnographic investigation.

For Clifford, then, it is the problematic status of ethnographic reality and the ambiguous status of ethnographic authority that leads him to characterize what happens in this ethnographic process as the refashioning of self and other. He writes: "It becomes necessary to conceive of ethnography not as the experience and interpretation of a circumscribed "other" reality, but rather as a constructive negotiation involving . . . politically significant subjects."[18] In ethnography, the "interlocutors actively negotiate a shared vision of reality . . . [as a] mutual construction." The research experience, he says, "tear[s] open the textualized fabric of the other, and thus also of the interpreting self."[19] "Both researchers and natives are active creators or . . . authors of cultural representations."[20] And, indeed, culture itself, Clifford says, is a kind of "generalized ethnography" in which "people interpret others, and themselves."[21] In sum, for Clifford the ethnographic process tears open, negotiates, and cocreates, reconstructs or (to adapt one of his chapter titles) refashions both the self and the other.

I shall return shortly to this notion of refashioning. I want first to discuss the norms or values that I find to be operative in the various levels of the ethnographic process as it is described by Clifford. What Clifford calls the experiential element is simply the act of being there with the data in a manner sufficiently educated and open that it can receive what is there. The values inherent in this level, I should think, are the mastery of technique, as developed within and governed by the norms of the scholarly community, and a receptivity and flexibility that allows the ethnographer to be open to whatever appears, including the unexpected. I shall call these values professional discipline and sensitivity.

The interpretive level of the ethnographic process brings to consciousness the judgment that all receptivity has a preunderstanding or, in its reflective form, a theoretical background for which the investigator is responsible, and that the investigator must therefore be self-critical in the employment of that theoretical framework, being clear about it, being vigorous in assessing it, and being willing to revise it as needed. I shall call these two values theoretical self-awareness and self-criticism.

The values of the experiential and interpretive phases are not individualistic. The ethnographer is a member of a scholarly subculture in relation to which his or her values—discipline and sensitivity, self-awareness and self-criticism—are grounded and constantly scrutinized in a systematic manner. The components of each professional discipline are in some respects the most important of these values but, because they are themselves always open to critique and revision, these norms of acceptable scholarship cannot be stated for every academic field, nor for any field can they be stated for all time. Abstractly, however, these norms can be identified as whatever is taken to be defensible, or at least worthy of continued assessment, within a given field at a given time. In any case, because of these norms the locus of ethnographic control is the ethnographer's professional community and, more broadly, the academy itself within which ethnography must justify itself in order to retain its credibility. That control is not abrogated, but it is relativized when the ethnographic process opens onto a broader social field in what Clifford identifies as the third and fourth elements of the investigation of the other.

The dialogical dimension introduces an additional professional society in a sense, namely, the empowered other being studied. At least once the agenda has been set, the ethnographer and the informant in dialogue become equal partners in criticism and construction. Here the values are the giving and receiving of criticism and the giving and receiving of constructive support. I shall call them mutual support and critique. And here the values of the profession itself are in principle opened to question since the informant is not a member of the scholarly guild, even though the vulnerability of these professional values is still quite limited because the professional investigator is the one who sets the research agenda and selects or dismisses the informant in accord with that agenda.

It is in the polyphonic facet of ethnography, Clifford's fourth dimension, that professional ethnographic values are most vulnerable. That is because polyphony in the nature of the case is open to anyone who can raise a voice, to any view of the data that can manage to get a hearing. In polyphony, the ethnographer's preferences are no more determinative than anyone else's. Here the values assumed and practiced are the democratization of context and the democratization of criticism.

Clifford readily admits that the polyphonic ideal is utopian; it can never fully be realized. But the same can and must be said of the other elements and their values in ethnography: professional discipline and sensitivity at the experiential level, theoretical self-awareness and self-criticism at the interpretive level, and mutual critique and support at the dialogical level. None of these is ever fully realized; each is to some degree utopian. So if real polyphony is harder to come by, as it surely is, the degree to which it is unrealizable by no means excuses the ethnographer from pursuing its values to the extent possible. Thus, at least in principle, and always to some degree, in polyphony the ethnographer's professional context as well as the ethnographer's professional values are radically called into question.

This helps us understand the radical nature of Clifford's concept of refashioning. Professional ethnographers are disciplined, sensitive, self-conscious, self-critical, itinerant critics and colleagues among the local groups, including possibly their own, to whom they apply their skills, opening in the process both their academic perspective and their academic values to the radical critique of the "other" with whom they work. They jointly refashion the other and the other's self-understanding and, in the process, themselves and their own. Ethnographers are not simply observers and recorders. They are colleagues and critics of the other, supporting and challenging native participants as they articulate their structures and values. But, as I say, ethnographers are also challenged, and the self thus called into question is not simply a carefully protected professional facade with its assorted techniques and theories, but a person. What else could be the case? Are the norms, values, and practices of the professional and his or her profession not tied to those of the personal self? At least in Clifford's analysis, what is subject to being torn, negotiated, cocreated, reconstructed, and refashioned is the fabric of the whole self, personal as well as professional.

This kind of refashioning, as far as I can tell, is Clifford's characterization of comparative inquiry. Knowing the other is not discovering some given within the other. It is not finding the other's foundational logic. It is not knowing the other better than, or even as well as, the other knows himself or herself. Knowing the other is constructing the other in critical collaboration with the other, and in the same joint venture being reconstructed oneself.

In the context of this discussion I want to talk next about theology, or at least one kind of theology that is, I contend, methodologically analogous to, if not actually a subset of, the new ethnography.

On Theology

I have argued elsewhere that there are at least three types of theology.[22] By theology in general I mean, quite conventionally, the critical examination and reconstruction of religious ideas. What distinguishes these different forms of theological investigation is not their subject matter so much as the purposes for which, and thus the norms by which, they are conducted.

There are, first, religious theologies, which are conducted for the purpose of clarifying, extending, and defending the conceptual practices of particular religions or religious communities. Religious theologies are thus governed by the values and norms of the religious communities in question. Naturally, there are variations in this genre of theology. In some instances, as in premodern Christianity, the norms of the religious tradition were also thought to be universal norms or at least the norms of the culture generally. In other instances, for example, Barthian theology, the operative norms are said to be at odds with the general norms of the culture. But what is decisive for my understanding of a religious theology is that its examination of ideas is governed by religious purposes and thus by religious norms.

Second, there are personal theologies. In the West, the possibility of personal theologies emerged from the Renaissance through the Enlightenment, precisely the period in which personal autonomy was identified and asserted in independence of the governance and values of religious communities. The purpose of a personal theology is to create an adequate religious worldview for the autonomous individual and is thus regulated by the norms of the autonomous individual. Again, those norms are sometimes thought to be identical to universal values, as was certainly the case with modernist religious thought including, especially, liberal Protestant thought. In other cases there are, so to speak, countercultural personal theologies, such as the religious thought of Tolstoy or Thoreau. Moreover, personal theologies may or may not fit into schools of thought, such as Transcendentalism or Romanticism. But even if they do, they are elaborated not in loyalty to the school but as acts of personal integrity that happen to fit more or less with a mood of the times. Personal theologies are governed by the needs and values of the autonomous individual, not of some cultural school and not in loyalty to some religious tradition.

In the past half-century, along with the rise of self-conscious post-modernism, there has emerged explicitly a third way of critically examining and reconstructing religious ideas. It purports to be rooted in the values and norms defensible and defended in a community, namely, the academic community, even as what it seeks to analyze critically and reconstruct are the ideas of another kind of community, namely, religious communities. As I have said, I believe James Clifford's quite expanded notion of ethnography is a useful model for understanding this third—what I would call "academic"—kind of theology. In Clifford's normatively loaded sense of the term "ethnography," one might say that academic theology is "theography" or, more conventionally, the ethnography of religious belief, just as, for example, a certain form of political science might be thought of an ethnography of a particular political community's beliefs.

To clarify what I mean, compare a theologian of this sort who examines the ideas of a living religious community, such as a group of Christian women, with a political scientist who is examining the claims of the Black Panthers in the 1960s. In the first case, the topic might be gender and its relation, functional and historical, to images of deity in Christian tradition. In the second, the topic might be the role of violence and nonviolence in altering the distribution of power. Let us suppose that both the theologian and the political scientist have read James Clifford. Both will have gained the requisite academic training in the understanding and interpretation of ideas in their social contexts, and thus both will, or at least should, decline to say anything to their "clients" they would not say, or defend having said, to their colleagues in the academy. Further, both will be dedicated, hopefully with skill, to giving the community under study a sensitive hearing. In sum, they will both exhibit professional discipline and sensitivity at the experiential level of their ethnographic inquiry.

The theologian and political scientist, moreover, will have acquired the complex theoretical apparatus necessary for their inquiry. For example, they will have taken on, as operating frameworks, certain theories acquired in the academy about how ideas of deity and gender or violence and power are to be understood, the relationship of such ideas to social reality, how ideas function in various structured social contexts, the relationship of ideas to norms, how these norms are warranted and when in conflict how they are adjudicated, and so forth. And if they are competent scholars, they will be reflective about the adequacy of these theories as they are confronted by the data at hand.

Which is to say, both the academic theologian and the political scientist will be theoretically self-conscious and self-critical.

If, indeed, they have read James Clifford, they will also descend from their privileged perches as participant observers to inquire together with their informants, encouraging the representative of the "other" they are studying to proffer construals of the relevant data and to challenge their own even as they, the academics, elaborate interpretations and criticize those of their dialogical partners. They will even convey critiques of the others' self-understandings and associated ways of life from external standpoints, pointing out the presuppositions of these critiques and the differences they might make were they integrated into the clients' worldviews. Put succinctly, our scholars will embody the values of mutual support and mutual criticism.

And if they have read Clifford carefully, they will attempt to open, in the most radical way, their own scholarly perspectives and criticisms to the scrutiny of an egalitarian polyphony. If they do that, they will have exposed to radical questioning not only their critical analyses of their data, the theories that ground those critical analyses, and the scholarly traditions that generate those theories, they also will have exposed themselves as persons, with all that such potential change— what Clifford calls the tearing of the fabric of selfhood—might entail. This is so because they have valued the democratization of context and criticism.

Two partial illustrations of this type of inquiry in contemporary religious scholarship come to mind. One is *En La Lucha* by Ada María Isasi-Díaz, which is a report of the author's critical exploration into the worldview of a group of Hispanic women.[23] Isasi-Díaz reports quite frankly on her role as midwife of these women's beliefs, as their critic who challenged them within their own framework, and as a cocreator who helped them think through the adequacy of their views in search of better formulations. However, she departed from a Cliffordian model of ethnography in her avoidance of egalitarian inquiry, for she declined to introduce her own critical perspective as one participant among many into the conversation, and thus she insulated these women from external criticism. She helped them reconstruct their worldviews, being self-conscious about their premises and their implications, apparently without, however, exposing them to a fuller range of relevant critical considerations.

That was not a failing of my other partial illustration, *Ritual Criticism* by Ronald Grimes.[24] Grimes is a "ritologist" or ritual theorist, not a "belief-ologist" or academic theologian, but that makes the explicitly constructive, avowedly normed character of his work all the more significant for my purposes. In this remarkable book, Grimes recounts, for review and criticism by his scholarly peers, his role as a critical consultant on specific ritual performances for different religious groups. It is particularly significant that Grimes offers these groups criticisms of their ritual practices not only in light of their own values and norms, but also in light of his, and that he self-consciously engages with them in rethinking their ritual practice as well as their ritual understanding. He calls this "ritual criticism." In a similar sense, I believe academic theology or a Cliffordian ethnography of belief could be called "belief criticism."

I have described the task of the academic theologian in relation to that of the so-called new ethnographer, and I have attempted to clarify further my understanding of academic theology by comparing it to the work of an imaginary political scientist and two actual scholars of religion. To further illustrate the continuities I see between these inquiries, let me conclude with five observations that I think apply to the academic theologian, the political scientist of the sort I alluded to earlier, to the constructive ritologist, and, of course, to the new ethnographer generally:

1. The *techniques and norms* they employ are those judged to be responsible within the community of scholarly inquiry. About everything they say—regarding liturgical action or professed belief, the relationship of ideas of deity and gender roles or the exercise of violence and power—it is appropriate to ask whether they are entitled to make that conceptual move within the canons of academic inquiry.

2. Their *conceptual strategies and performances* are generated out of relevant theoretical frameworks about which they are self-conscious and self-critical, particularly in light of the standing these theories have within the academic community. About what they say it can always be asked, what hypothetical, comprehensive framework can you offer to show how your interpretations of these data fit with other credible claims in the field?

3. The *agenda* of each is collegial analysis, critique and—one should especially note—reconstruction, not only in relation to the academy but also to their clients. This constructive agenda requires a bit of clarification.

If our scholars—whether ritologists, political scientists, or academic theologians—are to remain academics, their constructive efforts will need to be permissible within the framework of norms sustainable in the academic community. Were they to abrogate those norms—acceding, for example, to different and incompatible norms of the client community—they would be religious theologians, Black Panther political analysts, or Roman Catholic ritologists, but not theologians, political analysts, or ritologists in the academy.

Whether a construction is appropriate within the academy depends finally on the logic of the construction and its permissibility in terms of academic criteria. Look briefly at the logic of one of Grimes's constructive proposals regarding Roman Catholic ritual. It amounts to this: If in this ritual you want to preserve the sense of the mystery of your deity, then the ritual, given your context, might better have the following characteristics, and the reason is this, and here is how such a change can be incorporated into your larger theological system. More formally, the logic of his proposal is: If A (which is some specified value), then constructive proposal B is to be preferred, for reasons C, and with supporting connections D. A constructive proposal of this sort might also have been given by the ethnographer James Clifford to the Mashpee regarding their construal of tribal identity and the law, by a nineteenth-century anthropologist to the Indians regarding the deification of the earth and the threat of European encroachment, or by a political scientist to the Black Panthers regarding the use of violence and effective social change. Constructive proposals reflecting the same logic may be made by the academic theologian, regarding, for example, gender equality and ideas of God, or the relation of Torah and community in light of the Holocaust, or on ecological responsibility and ideas of divine creativity.

The issue, to repeat, is the logic of the proposed construction, whether in academic theology or in some other academic inquiry. The issue is not whether a proposal is also consistent with the values of the client community, or contains religious language, or is expansive rather than limited, or changes much rather than little, or has great or small existential import. Collegial analysis, critique and reconstruction—the agenda of the scholars under discussion—are academic if they accord with norms defensible in the academy.

4. In each case, the *vulnerability* of these scholars is their realization that the academy which they represent is a fallible institution that might in the process of inquiry be delegitimated, even in their own eyes. Put differently, they realize that polyphony might conquer academy. In any case, it is their expectation that the roar of heteroglossic negotiation will produce criticisms of the academy that cause the academy to alter itself in ways it could not have foreseen or accomplished left to its own resources.

5. Finally, as to *self-understanding*, these scholars all acknowledge that their inquiries, the negotiations they conduct, and the changes thereby effected cannot be separated from their scholarly values, and

that their values as scholars are tied to their personal values. It is this change in the interpretation of self and other that constitutes understanding, personal and scholarly, between traditions and within them. In other words, they all understand—the ritologist, the political scientist, and the academic theologian—that understanding is the refashioning of the self and the other.

Notes

In writing this essay I have benefited greatly from the research and criticism of Meredith Underwood, a student in the joint Ph.D. program at Iliff School of Theology and the University of Denver.

1. See Delwin Brown, *Boundaries of Our Habitations: Tradition and Theological Construction* (Albany, N.Y.: SUNY Press, 1994), 75–77, and Sam D. Gill, *Native American Religious Action: A Performance Approach to Religion* (Columbia: University of South Carolina Press, 1987), 147–72.

2. Sheila Greeve Davaney, *Pragmatic Historicism: A Theology for the Twenty-first Century* (Albany, N.Y.: SUNY Press, 2000).

3. See especially James Clifford, *The Predicament of Culture: Twentieth-Century Ethnography, Literature, and Art* (Cambridge: Harvard University Press, 1988).

4. George E. Marcus and Dick Cushman, "Ethnographies as Texts," *Annual Review* 11 (1982): 28.

5. Clifford, *Predicament of Culture*, 14, 95, 147, 231.

6. Ibid., 263.

7. Ibid., 46, 95, 117–18f, 233–36, 263, 273.

8. Ibid., 14, 95, 147, 231.

9. Ibid., 16–17f.

10. Ibid., 289–90f.

11. Ibid., 274, cf. 10.

12. Ibid., 21–54.

13. Ibid., 117–51.

14. Ibid., 43–44f.

15. Ibid., 23, 46, 50ff.

16. Ibid., 51.

17. Ibid., 53–54f.

18. Ibid., 41.

19. Ibid., 43.

20. Ibid., 84.

21. Ibid., 22.

22. Delwin Brown, "Believing Traditions and the Task of the Academic Theologian," *Journal of the American Academy of Religion*, 62 (1986): 1167–79.

23. Ada María Isasi-Díaz, *En La Lucha—In the Struggle: A Hispanic Women's Liberation Theology* (Minneapolis: Fortress, 1992).

24. Ronald Grimes, *Ritual Criticism: Case Studies in Its Practice, Essays on Its Theory* (Columbia: University of South Carolina Press, 1990).

Theology and the Poetics of Testimony

Rebecca S. Chopp

In the literature of cultural criticism, a genre has developed that I will call the "poetics of testimony." This genre includes poetry, theology, novels, and other forms of literature that express unique events or experiences outside the representation of modern, rational discourse. Many of us are acquainted with Elie Wiesel's observation, "If the Greeks invented tragedy, the Romans the epistle, and the Renaissance the sonnet, our generation invented a new literature, that of testimony."[1] Wiesel's "invention" has become a common reality of our time. The writers of contemporary literature—African Americans, incest and rape survivors, postcolonial theorists, gays, lesbians, bisexuals—all turn to the term "testimony" to describe their discourse, to tell truth as they see it, as they experience it, and what truth means to their communities.

The poetics of testimony is my way of naming the discursive practices and various voices that seek to describe or name that which rational discourse will not or cannot reveal. Take, for instance, the poetry of Anna Akhmatova, a well-known Soviet poet who helped develop the literary movement away from symbolism to "a poetry of tangible experience," even though her work was banned in the USSR for most of her life. In her poem "Requiem," she chronicles her experience outside the prison in which her son is held. In a section entitled, "instead of a preface," Akhmatova writes:

In the terrible years of the Yezhov terror I spent seventeen
months waiting in line outside the prison in Leningrad. One day
somebody in the crowd identified me. Standing behind me was a
woman, with lips blue from cold, who had, of course, never
heard me called by name before. Now she stated out of the tor-
por common to us all and asked me in a whisper (everyone whis-
pered there):
   "Can you describe this?"
   And I said, "I can."
   Then something like a smile passed fleetingly over what had
once been her face.[2]

Shoshona Felman's definition of testimony helps us to begin describing "this," this practice of the poetics of testimony: "Testimony is, in
other words, a discursive *practice*, as opposed to a pure theory. To testify—to *vow to tell* to *promise* and *produce* one's speech act, rather than
to simply formulate a statement."[3] This genre that I am naming provides
a strong critique of dominant cultural practices and provokes refigur-
ations of the social imaginary, that is, the basic presuppositions, metaphors, and rules that frame cultural operations. The poetics of testimony challenges how the real is both represented and created in culture
by summoning us to question the role of modern theory as the court
of the real.

   In the last thirty years, Christian theologians have increasingly attended to the poetics of testimony. The works of feminist, liberationist,
queer, and post-Holocaust theologies belong to this greater genre of the
poetics of testimony. Many of us who work with this type of literature
do so in order to represent deliberately our communities or movements
within the public arena. But we also do so, I think, because we are
summoned by a moral and theological imperative. The poetics of testimony, expressed in a variety of particular and distinct forms, is fundamentally concerned with human and earthly survival and transformation, and thus renders a moral claim on human existence. This
imperative is also theological, at least for those of us who live Christianity as practices of emancipatory transformation or, in the words of
Albert Schweitzer, as a reverence for life. But there is another dimension
to these testimonies, and that is how they question the shape and definition of theory and help us to reconsider the modern division of theology and witness through the court and judgment of theory itself. In
this essay, I examine the relationship of testimony, theory, and theology
in modern theology from the perspective of current theologies of testimony. My goal is not to denounce the contributions of modern theology but to question what happens to testimony in modern theology

in order to clear new spaces for the power and spirit of testimony in contemporary theology.

As is so common in our theoretical world today, I interrogate (a courtroom term) modern theology's distinction between testimony and theology. I do not offer an analysis of one particular theory of culture and how that theory might travel to transform theology. Indeed, what may be implicit in this essay is a discomfort with, to use the language of Edward Said, how theory travels. I believe with Said that when theory travels it does so successfully only as "intransigent practice."[4] But far more important, as I will demonstrate, I put on trial the notion of theory as determinative of theology, though I will not suggest a displacement of theory from theology, but rather a reshaping of theory within theology as a response to the moral summons of the poetics of testimony. I am interested in interrogating the assumptions of modern theology in order to discover how the nature of theology is confined through particular definitions of theory and witness. In so doing, I will suggest that once testimony itself is refigured and theory is both refigured and redefined, the nature of theology itself is changed. In closing, I identify the implications, as I understand them, of this turn to the poetics of testimony both in and of theology. But let me begin my interrogation with a description of what is at stake in modern theology in the relation of theory and witness.

Interrogating Testimony

We begin by asking if witness is not, in some sense, an innocent bystander in the modern court of reason and the trial of classical conceptions of revelation. The accounts are, perhaps, too familiar. Modern thinkers such as Locke and Lessing, Hume and Kant, Bradley and Troeltsch defined revelation by ordering it as the other of reason. And while these thinkers, perhaps because of political circumstances, did not deny revelation, they did overrule any objection by revelation to reason's first principles and proofs.

Rather than recount this story in full, let us consider one author whose precise language demonstrates what the gap between reason and revelation does to witness, which, after all, must be on one side or the other. Lessing's famous sentence "accidental truths of history can never become the proof of necessary truths of reason," in some sense represents the modern ordering of reason and revelation. Read as a code, the statement already implies two well-developed assumptions in modern thought: Human reason is the chief arbitrator of reality, and rev-

elation does not yield empirical truth as judged by reason. Lessing logically deduces the third law of modern rational reality: Reason will
judge and order even history itself, and historical testimonies will be
subject to empirical investigation and rational ordering.

Lessing arrives at his judgment after observing the power and spirit
of revelation in apostolic times. He comments how Origen was "quite
right in saying that in this proof of the spirit and power the Christian
religion was able to provide a proof of its own more divine than all
Greek dialect."[5] After all, miracles still occurred in Origen's time, and
in this way reason could judge the empirical events. Then Lessing gives,
in a sense, his own testimony: "But I am no longer in Origen's position;
I live in the eighteenth century, in which miracles no longer happen. If
I even now hesitate to believe anything on the proof of the spirit and
of power, which I can believe on other arguments more appropriate to
my age; what is the problem?"[6] The problem is that this proof of the
spirit and power no longer has any spirit or power, but has sunk to the
level of human testimonies of spirit and power.

The problem, so Lessing asserts, is that reports of prophecies and
miracles have to work through a medium—testimonies or reports—that
takes away their power. In this trial by reason, testimonies become powerless, emptied of spirit, not convincing for proof. If testimonies cannot
give immediate power and truth, what use shall be made of testimony,
which is, after all, not only the medium for revelation, but also—and
of increasing importance for modernity—the medium of history itself?
The question is: How do we judge these testimonies?

Perhaps no one poses the question as pointedly as F. H. Bradley, who
was enmeshed in justifying the work of Baur and Strauss on New Testament testimony:

> We ask for history, and that means that we ask for the simple
> record of unadulterated facts; we look, and nowhere do we find
> the object of our search, but in its stead we see the divergent
> account of a host of jarring witnesses, a chaos of disjoined and
> discrepant narrations, and yet, while all of these can by no pos-
> sibility be received as true, at the same time not one of them can
> be rejected as false.[7]

The way to judge these "jarring witnesses" is through an identification of consciousness; so, to say it simply, we reject testimonies that
do not conform to our own experience. The rulings of rationality by
Lessing and Bradley are later upheld by Troeltsch, who articulates the
principles of the ruling: criticism, analogy, and correlation. The theorist,

the protector of reason, must use what is sensible and reasonable to construct a coherent story. The theorist—historian, philosopher, sociologist, theologian—is to judge the evidence and, thus, to give order to history by forming a coherent narrative.

Witnesses and testimonies are the stuff to be judged, and the modern theorist is the judge, prosecutor, and jury. If the testimony matches the consciousness of human experience, it is ruled to be credible and appropriate. If not, it is excluded: ruled as irrational or pagan or simply silenced. In theology, the treatment of testimony is a bit more difficult, given that testimony appears so central to the practice and reception of Christian faith. Yet modern theologians accept the modern mantle of judgment and, robed in various styles, become theorists who decide which witnesses are credible and true.

No theologian has argued this modern mandate that nearly all have voiced as clearly as Schubert Ogden. In a recent work, written during this liminal time of postmodernity, Ogden offers an example of the ordering of modern theology. In this essay, "Doing Theology Today," Ogden articulates a position that has been developing since his earliest work: Christianity is about the existential significance of Jesus. Theology judges if the Christian testimony is appropriate to Jesus as Christians experience him and if such testimony is credible to human existence. Theology asks if this witness is properly Christian (or should be excluded from this court) and if it is in principle worthy of belief—in Ogden's language—"by any woman or man simply as a human being."[8] Ogden is quite clear that theology is distinguished from faith and puts on the mantel of theory itself: "Whereas witness addresses the question on the primary level of self-understanding and life-praxis, theology addresses it on the secondary level of critical reflection and proper theory, which is the only place where the claims to validity that are expressed or implied on the primary level can be critically validated."[9] This essay, written with Ogden's full awareness of pluralism and ideology in the culture and of the impact of these realities on theory itself, indicates the flexibility of this position and suggests that, though it may be tied to one understanding of human existence, understanding itself changes according to changed historical understanding. But the essay also shows that what is at stake in the division of witness and theology is the role of theology as theory: passing judgment, deciding credibility, in short, deciding which of the jarring witnesses will be included and which will be excluded into silence, into powerlessness, as irrational.

Testimony, that to which, in Lessing's phrase, Christianity seemingly "sunk," is divided from theology. Bearing witness is the realm of blooming confusing, the jarring messiness of history itself. Theory, on the other hand, is the clear-headed judge who decides the truth by ordering coherent narratives of history.

Testimony as Interrogation

In what Wiesel says has been invented in this century, and what I call the poetics of testimony, the courtroom seems set up in reverse: The judge, so to speak, is on trial, or perhaps the whole courtroom itself, its procedures and power, and its own ability to speak credibly, are on trial.

The literature to which I refer—some classified as theory, some as poetry and novels, some as theology and philosophy—attempts to speak of the real that is ruled out of court, the real of which language ordinarily does not even know how to speak. Czeslaw Milosz speaks of poetry as naming the real, as "the passionate pursuit of the real." Milosz titled his book, *The Witness of Poetry*, "not because we witness it, but because it witnesses us."[10] Rene Char says it this way: "Born from the summons of becoming and from the anguish of retention, the poem, rising from its well of mud and of stars, will bear witness, almost silently, that it contained nothing which did not truly exist elsewhere, in this rebellious and solitary world of contradictions."[11]

Though I introduce this trope as the "poetics" of testimony, I do not limit it to poetry proper. I prefer to speak of the poetics of testimony for those discourses—poetry, novels, theory, theology—that speak of the unspeakable and tell of the suffering and hope of particular communities who have not been authorized to speak. My use of "poetics" points toward a kind of writing that exists outside much of modern theory. Such discourse is an invention, for it must create language, forms, images to speak of what, in some way, has been ruled unspeakable or at least not valid or credible to modern reason. Compared to rhetoric, poetics seeks not so much to argue as to refigure, to reimagine and refashion the world.[12] Poetics is discourse that reshapes, fashions in new ways, enlarges, and calls into question the ordering of discourse within what Julia Kristeva and Homi Bhabha call the "social imaginary." Thus, poetics uses theory but is not ruled by it; said differently, the imaginative figuration of poetics utilizes even theory as a way to rename and refigure the real against the representations of dominant discourses.

By "testimony" I mean discourse that refers to a reality outside the ordinary order of things, to use Foucault's language. Many of the discourses I consider—the testimonies of Latin America, the bearing witness discourses so common in African-American art, poetry, and novels, and the theologies of spiritual/political expression from around the globe—explicitly use the language of bearing witness and testimony. It is important to observe the peculiarity of these testimonies. Traditionally, testimony is sealed by death, so the martyr seals his testimony by his willingness to die. Emil Fackenheim has pointed out that testimonies of the Holocaust are not about martyrdom (*kiddush ha-Shem*), but about the sanctification of life (*kiddush ha-hayyim*): "In extremity—when the Nazi logic of destruction had become the Final Solution—kiddush ha-hayyim revealed itself as a unique form of resistance no longer indistinguishable from life itself—whether life meant survival for an hour, a day, a week, or even by good fortune until after the evil Unwelt was destroyed."[13]

The telling of these stories is for life, for the mending of life, the healing of life, the ability of life to live and survive and thus conquer this extremity. If, traditionally, we may have made testimony say "this is the truth, I tell it even if I have to die," testimony now becomes "I will live to tell this story, I will survive for an hour, a day, however long I can." If one is not authorized to live, then surviving is both resistance and hope. These testimonies are discourses of survival for hope and of hope for survival.

The language of testimonies asks us to hear this other as the first and most indisputable claim of existence. It is this radical otherness to which we are summoned by testimony. Testimonies enact a moral consciousness and communal, even at times, global, responsibility. Testimonies are neither expressions of a prelinguistic experience nor even of a religious code. Testimonies are neither subjective nor objective; they are collective and social. What appears most common and most identifiable is that testimony is both private and public. One testifies in and to the public space about what one has seen, what one has experienced, what one knows to have really happened. Thus, the categories of public and personal do not hold; the usual split between the subject and object has not been followed. As Muriel Rukeyser has observed, witness "includes the act of seeing or knowing by personal experience, as well as the act of giving evidence."[14] The most basic rules, the public/private and subject/object, are called into question when testimony challenges reason as judge. Although in modernity the construct of "testimony" had to do with miracles and prophecies revealing events that reason could not recognize, in the contemporary period testimonies reveal what reason and its court will not acknowledge. Testimonies call us to an otherness, a reality greater than even the basic rules of individual and public life.

Writing of the will to bear witness by the survivors of the Holocaust, Terrence Des Pres explains:

This response, this response-ability, is what I wish to call "conscience"—conscience in its social form; not the internalized voice of authority, not the introspective self-loathing of the framed "Puritan" or "New England" conscience. And not remorse. If bearing witness were an isolated private act, a purely subjective event, then perhaps the theory of guilt would serve. But as we have seen the survivor's behavior is typical, and more, it is integral to conditions which reach beyond personal involvement. Horrible events take place, that is the (objective) beginning. The survivor feels compelled to bear witness, that is the (subjective) middle. His testimony enters public consciousness, thereby modifying the moral code to which it appeals, and that is the (objective) end. Conscience, in other words, is a social achievement.[15]

Testimony invokes a moral claim—it is from someone to someone about something. Decision is called for, a change in reality is required. This responsibility is, as Carolyn Forché says, a social reality. The moral responsibility is to change the rules, not simply this particular verdict. At a certain level I simply echo the claim made by liberation theologians: It is not enough to add women and stir, not enough to include African Americans and expect them to speak like Anglos, not the point to make the rich the poor, or to "allow" lesbians and gays the privileges of straights.

The poetics of testimony places all theories, even contemporary theories of culture, on trial for their moral responsibility to engage this "reverence for life." Within such testimonies lies something like the claim of Levinas that we are constituted through responsibility to and for the other, a responsibility that is not reciprocal. Testimonies, I suggest, summon even theory to serve those who suffer and hope, those whose voices testify to survival, those who imagine transformation. Theory is neither objective judge nor subjective experience; rather, it is now summoned to help, to aid, to serve.

Such testimonies summon us to attend to the practice of language. The line or difference between literary theory and cultural theory is increasingly fluid as language, representation, and discourse are analyzed as forms of culture. But, as I have already indicated, the language of testimonies is, in some sense, peculiar. The language used in testimonies has a referent that the testifier finds unnameable and yet absolutely necessary to name.[16] Dori Laub, a psychiatrist who is himself a Holocaust survivor, works with Holocaust survivors and writes on testimony. He observes that as testimonies come closer to the event themselves, the language becomes more and more fragmented. Susan Shapiro, from whom I have learned a great deal about the language of testimony, argues that testimonies after the Holocaust have to be written against words—language so fails to express or represent the Holocaust that a hermeneutical antinomy is created: "writing about the Holocaust becomes at once both impossible and necessary."[17] Poetics both refers to unspeakable horror and requests hearing, remembering, reshaping. Witness becomes, in the words of Shoshona Felman and Dori Laub,

> conceptual prisms through which we attempt to apprehend—and to make tangible to our imagination—the ways in which our cultural frames of reference and our preexisting categories which delimit and determine our perception of reality have failed, essentially, both to contain, and to account for, the scale of what has happened in contemporary history.[18]

Indeed, as African American scholars such as Dwight Hopkins, Emilie M. Townes, and Will Coleman suggest, the testimonies are poetic performances that combine elements of diverse experiences and traditions to enact survival.

I want to underscore the importance of respecting and protecting this gap between the named and the unnameable (a gap Christian theologians should know something about). We must resist sublating the gap, assuming that language either captures the event (the modern dilemma) or is itself the event (certain postmodern theorists). In the first mistake, theory assumes full power of judgment because the theorist really sees what takes place, perhaps better than those who see the event themselves. In the second type of error, suffering and hope are occluded and historical events are reduced to a problem of language. Testimonies question the discursive practices of theory both in terms of what it frames or stages (whose voice gets counted) and how it is to be represented. Testimonies describe the real in ways that require people to see these events that reason and theory do not count, do not authorize, do not signify. Testimonies challenge us to reimagine theory as the language that serves the fragments, the uneasy nature, the words against words in order to describe the real.

The poetic quality of testimony not only summons us to attend to the practice of language, but refigures theory: Theory should give voice to particularity and difference, instead of ordering jarring witnesses into pluralistic expressions of one experience, or ruling them as irrational exceptions to true human consciousness. Testimonies offer particular narratives and express particular ways that suffering and exclusion, survival and hope, have been experienced by a group of people. It is necessary to understand that the poetics of testimony resists being one representation of a general category.[19] A testimony requires being heard in its own voice, style, and content, neither as a variation of a common experience nor a representation of that which stands on the margins, opposed by the dominant discourse.[20]

I suggest, therefore, that the poetics of testimony invokes a moral summons to theory. Theory, thus summoned to sanctify life, is refigured and thus redefined. Theory is no longer the objective rule that judges the real by shaping it into a coherent narrative. Rather, through its own poetical character, theory serves as a practical frame for new expressions (critique and constructions) of the real. Theory no longer rules against particularity and difference, the "jarring witnesses," but, as pragmatists and Marxists have claimed, provides orderings of knowledge that propose new relations of norms, rules, and criteria.

Instead of a Conclusion

I have used the poetics of testimony, a genre of diverse discourses that I have drawn together discursively, to interrogate theory and the nature of theology as figured through theory. I have attempted to shake loose the tight relation of theology and theory, both in the sense that theology models itself as judge and court over witnesses and in the sense that theory becomes the arbitrator of witness within theology. Theory is itself now summoned by the moral imperative of testimony, and obligated to protect the brokenness of the language of testimony as well as to respect the particularity and difference of testimonies. Furthermore, my interrogation questions whether theory can be revisioned as a kind of practical and poetical ordering that helps us frame events, listen, make connections of meaning and politics, and explore new possibilities. Remaining to be interrogated are how language works, models of pragmatic reasoning, and how tools of cultural theory operate in theology. Many contemporary theologians are addressing such problems and possibilities.

I close, not in conclusive fashion, but with three observations about the current status and nature of theology, or at least those theologies that respond to a moral summons in and through testimony as I have described it. These summary observations point toward the need to continue the reshaping and refashioning that occupy much contemporary theology.

My first observation is that theology has to be responsive to the moral summons of testimony. To many contemporary theologians the goal, nature, purpose, and point of theology is to address the moral summons revealed through the testimonies of communities and groups outside the court of modern reason and colonial politics. These testimonies do not ground theology, in the way reason provided some sense of absolute explanation for much of modern theology. As I have demonstrated, the moral summons of testimony ruptures the modern identification of theology and theory (or antitheory) within the modern limits of reason. Theology does not become nonrational or irrational, since theology's question and quest are no longer determined by reason. The category for defining or ordering theology has changed from discourse in relation to reason to discourse in response to the moral summons in testimonies.

My second observation about contemporary theology is that in response to the moral summons of testimony, theology gets fashioned through what I call "poetics." I earlier identified poetics as a way of refiguring and reshaping the world; poetics as a discourse works to change what Kristeva and Bhabha call the "social imaginary." Theology now explores domains of imaginative discourse, understanding its ordering discourse as reworking language, symbols, codes, images. In this work, theology is not simply adding or subtracting metaphors but reshaping the moral imaginary.

Perhaps even more so than the pragmatists, poststructuralists, and rhetoricians by whom I am influenced and with whom I identify, I want theological discourse to blur the lines of theory and poetics so as to imagine and create new ways of envisioning human life. Deeply influenced by this side of Paul Ricoeur's thought, I believe poetics is essential to theology. The poetics of theological discourse is about the conversion of the imaginary, which works not only by stirring up "the sedimented universe of conventional ideas," but by shaking up "the order of persuasion" and thus generating convictions as much as settling or ruling over controversies.[21] I have suggested that, in order to respond to the moral summons of testimony, theology must refigure and reimagine the social imaginary.

My final observation is that theology, shaped through poetics as a form of responsiveness to the moral summons of testimony, traces or discerns transcendence as the power and spirit of transfiguration. This "tracking Spirit," to use Mark Taylor's phrase, may sound a bit surprising, given that contemporary theologians have not always spoken positively about transcendence.[22] Feminist theologians criticize the term for suggesting a wholly other God disconnected from social and personal existence. But in the theologies formed as a poetics of testimony, transcendence is a matter of the power and spirit of transfiguration. To say it in traditional terms, transcendence expresses the hope that the memories of suffering will be told and not go unredeemed, the hope that personal and social existence can and will be transformed. God as the term of transcendence functions as hope, the promise of liberation, or in the terms of David Tracy, the mystical-prophetic God.[23] God as the term of transcendence allows for the remembering of the dead and of those who survive, the critique of the present, the creative naming of possibilities for the future. Transcendence is not a conceptual problem but a moral summons to imagine hope.

I introduce this third characteristic of transcendence to open another level of understanding of contemporary theology. First, since it speaks of transcendence through tracing the Spirit, theology may well be more a theology of the Holy Spirit than that of the Father or even of the Son, to use traditional Christian terms. To use the felicitous language of Catherine Keller, "the spirit does the work of the trinity but without the prestige."[24] The poetics of testimony provides a particular account of the real—that which has been ruled out of court—and to morally summon a response. Like the Hebrew prophets, it is more a questioning of what is required of the hearer in this time and place than the Greek inquiry into the limits of being itself.[25] Testimony demands that we see the particular in the absolute, or as Paul Ricoeur would say, that we see the absolute in the testimony of the particular.[26] Second, theologians will provide hermeneutical and pragmatic warrants for transfiguration as the mode of the Spirit and for the task of theology's own discernment. Tracing the Spirit will require theologians to use traditional sources even as they revise tradition to name God in different ways. The variety of testimonies as ways of naming God is not, as in Bradley's time, understood as jarring witnesses, but rather the polyphonic expression of the Spirit working in different ways across the face of the earth. As Francis Fiorenza suggests, "one explicates the content and object of faith neither logically nor deductively, but in relation to history, experience, and practice. History, experience, and practice receive their gestalt and focus from the vision of faith, just as each of these in turn leads to a revisioning of the vision of faith."[27]

Finally, theology traces or discerns the Spirit in order to develop discourses of transcendence, not by uncovering a depth of God's presence or revealing a substance or essence of God, but through negotiating spaces of solidarity, connection, and new creation. Theology continually engages in creating spaces, building bridges, and forming new discourses as practices of emancipatory transformation. One implication, a metaphorical one, is that instead of figuring theology as a courtroom, we will have to imagine theology as practices of negotiating between what is and what can be.[28] Used increasingly in place of litigation in this country, negotiation involves listening, creating safe spaces, and reinventing relationships while remaining attentive to the self-determination of witnesses. (Negotiations do not work if one party cannot feel safe or find terms to express itself adequately).

Understanding theology as engaged in continual negotiation to sanctify life may enable us to keep theology more fluid and more multidimensional—more spiritual—and may allow us a way to combine poetics, rhetoric, and hermeneutics in theology. Imagining theology as engaged in negotiating practices to sanctify life by means of tracing the Spirit allows us to appreciate theology as a type of cultural intervention. Like one meaning of negotiation, theology may help us traverse deep waters in our swirling culture of diversity. Like another common meaning, theology as negotiation may help settle disputes in just fashion. And, like a third, theology may help us imagine new possibilities for our life together before the price of our cultural wars rises too high for us to pay. In all these ways of traversing, settling, and building bridges, theology does its work by speaking the truth about its own moral summons as it discerns the Spirit at work in a particular time and place.

Notes

My deepest thanks to fellow theologian and friend Elaine Robinson, who not only held long and rich conversations with me on the topics of this chapter but also edited my prose time and time again.

1. Elie Wiesel, "The Holocaust as a Literary Inspiration," in *Dimensions of the Holocaust* (Evanston, Ill.: Northwestern University Press, 1977), 9.

2. Anna Akhmatova, "Requiem," in *Against Forgetting: Twentieth-Century Poetry of Witness*, ed. Carolyn Forché (New York: Norton, 1993), 102.

3. Shoshona Felman, "Education and Crisis," in *Testimony: Crises of Witnessing in Literature, Psychoanalysis, and History*, ed. Shoshona Felman and Dori Laub (New York: Routledge, 1992), 5.

4. Edward Said, "Travelling Theory Reconsidered," in *Critical Reconstructions: The Relationship of Fiction and Life*, ed. Robert M. Polhemus and Roger B. Henkle (Stanford, Calif.: Stanford University Press, 1994), 265. I am indebted to Ivan Karp, who suggested to me that Said's own position on how theory "travels" to other locations, changed over time.

5. Gotthold Lessing, *Lessing's Theological Writings*, ed. and trans. Henry Chadwick (Stanford, Calif.: Stanford University Press, 1956, 1967), 53.

6. Ibid., 52.

7. F. H. Bradley, *The Presuppositions of Critical History* (Chicago: Quadrangle Books [1874] 1968), 85.

8. Schubert M. Ogden, *Doing Theology Today* (Valley Forge, Pa.: Trinity Press International, 1996), 9.

9. Ibid., 10.

10. Czeslaw Milosz, *The Witness of Poetry* (Cambridge: Harvard University Press, 1983), 4. Milosz contends that poetry does have a referent—at least

contemporary poetry does as compared to classic poetry, in which language celebrates itself. Milosz suggests that each poet has elements of classism (celebrating structure of poetry) and realism (naming the real): "I affirm that, when writing, every poet is making a choice between the dictates of the poetic language and his fidelity to the real" (71).

11. Rene Char, "Argument," in *Against Forgetting*, ed. Carolyn Forché (New York: Norton, 1993), 253–54.

12. I am guided by the work of Paul Ricoeur on the relation of rhetoric, poetics, and hermeneutics. See, for instance, "Rhetoric-Poetics-Hermeneutics," in *From Metaphysics to Rhetoric*, ed. Michael Meyer (Dordrect: Kluwer Academic Publishers, 1989), 137–49. Ricoeur indicates in this essay that poetics does refer to reality (thus disagreeing with Aristotle).

13. Emil L. Fackenheim, *To Mend the World: Foundations of Post-Holocaust Jewish Thought* (Bloomington: Indiana University Press, 1982), 223–24. I am indebted to Susan Shapiro for this reference.

14. Muriel Rukeyser, *The Life of Poetry* (Masfield, Mass.: Paris Press, 1996), 175.

15. Terrence Des Pres, *The Survivor: An Anatomy of Life in the Death Camps* (Oxford: Oxford University Press, 1976), 46–47.

16. See Susan Shapiro, "Failing Speech: Post-Holocaust Writing and the Discourse of Postmodernism," *Semeia* 40 (1987): 65–92.

17. Ibid., 66. See also Wiesel, "Holocaust as a Literary Inspiration," 7.

18. Shoshona Felman and Dori Laub, foreword to *Testimony: Crises of Witnessing in Literature, Psychoanalysis, and History*, ed. Shoshona Felman and Dori Laub (New York: Routledge, 1992), page xv.

19. Speaking of Fanon and Kristeva's attempt to destabilize symbolic structures, Bhabha observes that "these are not simply attempts to invert the balance of power within an unchanged order or discourse. Fanon and Kristeva seek to redefine the symbolic process through which the social imaginary—nation, culture or community—becomes the subject of discourse, and the object of psychic identification. These feminist and postcolonial temporalities force us to rethink the sign of history *within* those languages, political or literary, which designate the people 'as one' " (Homi K. Bhabha, *The Location of Culture* [London: Routledge, 1994], 153).

20. Indeed, we might even say that these contemporary testimonies of extremity allow us to imagine different ways in which the ordering of the particular and universal or the specific and general might occur. Janet Jakobsen contends that we must reimagine in new ways the relation of particular bodies to the body politic, and thus the relation of general norms to specifics. See Janet Jakobsen, "The Body Politics vs. Lesbian Bodies," in *Horizons in Feminist Theology*, ed. Rebecca S. Chopp and Sheila Davaney (Minneapolis: Fortress, 1997), 116–36.

21. Ricoeur, "Rhetoric-Poetics-Hermeneutics," 143.

22. Mark McClain Taylor, "Tracking Spirit: Theology as Cultural Critique in America," in *Changing Conversations: Religious Reflection and Cultural Analysis*, ed. Dwight N. Hopkins and Sheila Greeve Davaney (New York: Routledge, 1996), 123–44.

23. David Tracy, *On Naming the Present: Reflections on God, Hermeneutics, and Church* (Maryknoll, N.Y.: Orbis, 1994), 22.

24. Catherine Keller, *Apocalypse Now and Then: A Feminist Guide to the End of the World* (Boston: Beacon, 1996), 283.

25. Calvin O. Schrag, *The Self after Postmodernity* (New Haven: Yale University Press, 1997), 137.

26. Paul Ricoeur, "The Hermeneutics of Testimony," in *Essays on Biblical Interpretation*, ed. Lewis S. Mudge (Philadelphia: Fortress, 1980), 119–20.

27. Francis Schüssler Fiorenza, "Fundamental Theology and Its Principal Concerns Today: Towards a Non-Foundational Foundational Theology," *Irish Theological Quarterly* 62 (1996–97): 118–39.

28. Theologians have introduced this practice of negotiation, though sometimes without using the term, to describe how we might think of the nature of theology. Nicholas Lash, for instance, argues against any grand synthesis and pseudouniversalism. He describes theology as mediating interpreters and suggests that such theologies, "seek accurately to reflect cultural particularities depicted in narrative and poetry" (Nicholas Lash, *Theology on the Way to Emmaus* [London: SCM Press, 1986], 32).

Secularization and the
Worldliness of Theology

Victor Anderson

Cultural analysis is an intellectual practice. It is deeply rooted in and dependent on sociological unit ideas derived from the tradition of social theory. Unit ideas such as community and society, authority and legitimacy, status and class, power and domination, alienation and marginalization, and the sacred and secular continue to influence contemporary analysis of cultural practices. In cultural analysis, these categories are used as lenses through which to describe features of social life. The categories of cultural analysis may also disclose problems with and distortions to a particular social subject, whether the individual, groups, or classes. They may also guide one's critique of particular institutions such as government, markets, labor, the academy, or a particular intellectual discipline such as academic theology. This essay is consistent with this third orientation of cultural analysis. That is, I use the categories of marginalization and secularization as a dual lens through which to discuss and understand critiques of academic theology entailed in much of the content of contemporary social criticism.

For social critics such as Richard Rorty, Jeffrey Stout, and Cornel West, cultural analysis is not only fixated on the social and material conditions on which western cultural practices depend, but it also analyzes forms of rationalization that supply culture with meaning and values. Cultural analysis may therefore be oriented toward rational structures of social and moral legitimacy. Through the categories of social theory, cultural analysis criticizes ideas, norms, ideals, learning, and the social systems through which knowledge is brokered. Over the last ten years, academic theology has become a common site of social critique by both contemporary American philosophers and theologians.

My purpose in this essay is to criticize a major thesis among a number of secular critics of academic theology. The thesis is often referred to as "the marginalization of theology in American intellectual and public life." The argument is this: as American intellectual and public cultures have become more secular and worldly, academic theology has grown more marginal in its intellectual and public influence. In the absence of a viable American public theology, secular criticism rises to fill the void. I will argue that the secularization theory that informs this argument is inadequate. Driven by negative dialectical thinking, advocates of the marginalization thesis fail to account for the secularization of theology insofar as the discipline is itself entailed in the secularization of the American academy. From my point of view, what emerges is an increasingly secular and, hence, worldly theology.

The Marginalization of Academic Theology

Elsewhere I have argued that the academic discipline called theology is experiencing a crisis of legitimization.[1] Thinkers such as Richard Rorty, Jeffrey L. Stout, Van A. Harvey, and Cornel West have made the critique of academic theology a significant aspect of their own philosophical and religious projects. Although I have discussed some of their arguments elsewhere, it seems appropriate to rehearse them here only because they have not been widely circulated. In *Contingency, Irony and Solidarity*,[2] Rorty's critique of theology is coincident with his critique of pre-Heideggarian and Wittgensteinian western metaphysical philosophy. Rorty sees theology and metaphysics as discourses that delivered modern western society over to pretensions of moral, cultural, and social perfection, each realm being justified by grand metanarratives of progress, rational ascent, and the substitution of a universal religion of humanity for particularity.[3]

In a revealing passage, Rorty says that these discourses "ask us to believe that what is most important to each of us is what we have in common with others—that the springs of private fulfillment and human solidarity are the same."[4] To be sure, Rorty's criticisms of theology are targeted at the centrality of altruism in Christian theology, which he thinks morally legitimates theology within the schema of social, contractarian liberal political theory. Theology makes social sympathy a natural balance to another basic human disposition shared by all, namely, the feeling of self-interested preservation. The cognitive standing of theology remained intact as long as its legitimacy was found to be in agreement with the grand metanarratives of Newtonian physics, British natural theology and philosophy, and stoic logic. However, with the rise of evolutionary science and philosophy, pragmatism and logical positivism, the internal justifications of theological discourse exploded as these new sciences uncoupled science and philosophy from theology. Radical contingency, private irony, and linguistic solidarity usurped both absolute metaphysics and metaphysical theology.

A discipline whose internal languages are centered on a ultimate reality "beyond time and chance which both determines the point of human existence and establishes a hierarchy of responsibilities,"[5] according to Rorty, is a discourse that is necessarily marginal in our present intellectual culture. Rorty describes our present intellectual culture as one that takes "[our] languages and our culture as much a contingency, as much a result of thousands of small mutations finding niches [with millions of others finding no niches] as are the orchids and the anthropoids."[6] I think that Rorty's point is clear. Just as academic theology ascended in intellectual prominence as a matter of chance and favorable conditions, it has also become marginal in the late twentieth century under these same social and historical conditions. The story that Rorty tells of theology's marginalization is based on a conception of secularization by usurpation. That is, the marginalization of theology is the result of historical movements of thought in philosophy and science which have usurped the epistemic position that theology once held among western intellectuals.

Stout's critique of theology is now well known. According to Stout, academic theologians are in a dilemma of irrelevance.[7] On the one hand, they intervene in public matters in ways that repeat "the bromide of secular intellectuals in transparently figurative speech." On the other, those theologians who propose saying something distinctively theological are "apt to be talking to themselves—or at best, to a few other theologians of similar breeding."[8] The dilemma is this: When theologians speak in a secular tone of voice, they render themselves irrelevant to a secular public that already has good working languages internal to themselves by which they get about relatively easily in public life, without burdening themselves with the weight of theology. Of course, those theologians who insist on speaking in distinctively theological languages are likely to find agreement only among persons like themselves who are familiar with and committed to their particular theological

speech. In either case, academic theology is caught in a dilemma of
public irrelevance.

On Stout's reading of theology, academic theology is not likely to be
helped by theologians making philosophical arguments from phenomenology, hermeneutics, social theory, or deconstruction that will add a
measure of nonparochial legitimacy to their utterances.[9] Moreover, academic theologians are certainly not likely to ascend in public significance by attaching themselves to every new fad in literary, social, and
cultural criticism. The academic theologian's search for new extrath-
eological methods and foundations in the atmosphere of antifounda-
tionalism is not likely to give academic theology more public relevance.
Rather, Stout suggests that the discipline would do as well as it can to
content itself with ministerial education and church dogmatics, that is,
if academic theologians want a hearing at all in the increasingly secular
or worldly culture of American colleges and universities. Stout's account of the marginalization of theology is based on a theory of secularization by displacement. On this view, theology becomes publicly
irrelevant as the secular public increasingly makes use of political and
economic rhetoric to negotiate its needs and establish value, while theological languages recede into the background of the private sphere.

Rorty and Stout exhibit a kind of "secular" piety of pessimism, if not
downright cynicism, about the nature of academic theological discourse
and its public significance. What conditions their attitudes about theology is not altogether clear to me. However, I suppose that a great deal
of their sentiments can be explained as dispositional and misguided
categorical judgments about the practice of theology. For instance, their
talk of theology as a dogmatic, parochial, and quasi-imperialistic discourse appears to me to reflect merely prejudicial assumptions of these
philosophical critics. That is, the legitimacy of their own discourses
requires the opposition of secularism and theology in order for each
thinker to establish a clear line of demarcation between his secular
philosophy and academic theology. In contrast to their evolutionary,
historical, tragic, yet utopian humanism, theology, as a discipline, is the
tyrannical monarch who restricts free thinking, learning, and democracy. Theology becomes the hegemonic discourse against which secular,
historicist, radical democratic philosophers contend for legitimacy.

The problem with these negative criticisms is that they ignore the
critical impact that the modernist impulses of the seventeenth and eighteenth centuries and the evolutionary impulses of the nineteenth century had on academic theology. Much of the successes of modernism,
which secular critics prize, are consequences of the skeptical reactions
of theologians themselves to the inherited traditions of western scho-

lastic theology. Negative critics, therefore, too often ignore the ways that academic theology is part of the secularization processes that made possible much of the secular tenets that they themselves favor. I am not suggesting that the negative critiques of theology are to be dismissed as merely prejudicial. To be sure, Rorty and Stout evoke select, historical memories of the discipline and its functions in higher learning in the West. Notwithstanding their accounts of the secularization of theology, what I find objectionable is their attempts to render theological and secular discourses rationally incommensurable.

One of the more unsettling critiques of theology comes not so much from outside the discipline of theology as from within. In an important essay, Van A. Harvey argues that theology has become irrelevant to most intellectuals.[10] It has become intellectually irrelevant not only because recognizable theological themes, categories, assumptions, and arguments appear foreign to many contemporary intellectuals, but, more importantly, theological argumentation has, in our times, "become virtually a forgotten and lost mode of discourse."[11] Many secularists are not likely to be impressed by theological arguments because they see such languages as historically primitive, antiquarian, and simply obscure.[12] Others find theological rhetoric divisive and not particularly public in character.

Harvey thinks that theologians themselves have been the greatest contributors to the marginalization of American academic theology in American public life. Preoccupied with taking into itself every new wave of critical philosophical and social discourse, academic theology proliferates toward absurdity, producing "theologies of the death of god," "theologies of play," "theologies of hope," "theologies of liberation," "theologies of polytheism," "theologies of deconstruction," and "theologies of God."[13] I find Harvey's trivialization strategy rhetorically persuasive. However, I think that it misses the internal and public motives that drive academic theologies toward contemporary philosophical and social themes and categories.

Harvey is right on target when he claims that major variables in the intellectual marginalization of theology in American public life are internal factors such as the professionalization of academic theology along specialized disciplinary and methodological boundaries. According to Harvey, such a specialization of theological discourse has created a guild mentality among theologians themselves that fragments the discipline into so many instances of atomic and autonomous departments of study. This dispersion of theological labor makes it difficult for either students or theological voyeurs to see any unity of goals and cognitive intentions among the faculties. The lack of consensus among theologians themselves about the nature and scope of theological inquiry also makes it difficult to identify the public significance of theology to contemporary public discourse, says Harvey. Lamentably, Harvey suggests, "it can safely be said that Reinhold Niebuhr and Paul Tillich were the last two public theologians in this country, that is, theologians whose names were recognized because they contributed to those types of discourse that seriously engaged American intellectuals."[14] Harvey also judges American public life intellectually impoverished by their loss; "Not only have we lost the language of moral and communal discourse, . . . but we have lost the sense of what Niebuhr called a 'high religion' and what it might contribute to public life. One does not have to be a Christian to regret this loss."[15]

Cornel West adds his own voice to the company of theological and religious critics. In an essay entitled "The Crisis in Theological Education," West suggests that "our seminaries and divinity schools are not simply in intellectual disarray and existential disorientation; our very conceptions of what they should be doing are in shambles."[16] Like Rorty and Stout, West also ties the marginalization of academic theology in our present intellectual culture to "the demystifying of European cultural hegemony, the deconstruction of European philosophical edifices, and the decolonization of the third world [which] has left theology with hardly an autonomous subject matter (hence a temptation to be excessively frivolous and meretricious in its enactments) and with little intellectually respectable resources upon which to build."[17] West agrees with Harvey that the age in which theologians such as Karl Barth, Paul Tillich, and Reinhold and H. Richard Niebuhr could be counted as "public theologians" has all but come to an end. It has come to an end because "the world, culture, and society that produced and sustained" these kinds of public theologians no longer exist.[18] Academic theologians have consequently tried to assure their discipline by whoring after other disciplines from which they can attach themselves and garner legitimacy. In the end, both their intellectual justifications and public legitimacy stand or fall with the loggias, justifications, and legitimacy of the new disciplines with which they couple themselves.

I do not want to give the impression that for these critics the crisis of marginalization among American academic theologians is peculiar to mainstream theologies of the revisionist, process, empirical, neoorthodox, liberal, deconstructive, or narrative trajectories. As I read them, so-called theologies of the margins (black, Latino/Latina, feminist, minjung, African, mujerista, gay, lesbian, queer, alienated white male North American, womanist, ecofeminist, neopagan reconstructivist liberation theologies) fare no better in overcoming the public marginalization of theology than the mainstream schools against which they assert their differences. Even among the theologies of the margins, driven toward a snowballing proliferation of difference, their public significance remains relatively localized, if not ghettoized, to specialized academies, societies, and particular divinity schools and seminaries where their special interests are nurtured and disseminated.

Thus far, I have primarily operated on the marginalization thesis as if its truth value were self-evident. However, I am not altogether persuaded that marginalization is the best language for describing the present status of academic theology. Three concerns give rise to my doubts about buying this marginalization of theology thesis wholesale. First, a large number of those who propose the thesis are themselves so negatively prejudiced about the very idea of theology (academic or popular) that their descriptions of what they believe academic theologians to be doing appear more like caricatures than "descriptions" (to borrow Rorty's term). For instance, when critics categorically define theology by classic stoic ontology, a priori metaphysics, epistemological foundationalism, absolutism, dogmatism, parochialism, and antidemocratic tendencies, such descriptions simply are inadequate, a historical accounts of the discipline. Most of the contemporary constructive theologies that I read are based on criteria that critics themselves value, namely, history, tradition, and difference. Therefore, I have to judge the critics' negative judgments to be based on outmoded pictures of academic theology and negative prejudices.

My second doubt about the marginalization thesis follows from the first. I call it the fallacy of identification. Having defined theology negatively in relation to a certain discourse that many critics call "secularism," negative critics confuse the processes of secularization with particular principles of their own critical philosophies. That is, they identify the processes of secularization with the tenets of a secularist orientation that favors evolutionary naturalism, conventionalist theories of language and meaning, and radical democracy. However, if these are supposed to be the defining, substantive demarcations of secular philosophy, it can safely be said that what passes today as constructive theology in many theological circles might legitimately be called secular theology.

For academic theology to have entailed itself in such a secularism, one might also presuppose that the same processes of secularization that made possible the secular philosophies of theology's critics also entail the secularization of theology itself. Therefore, like other faculties of arts and sciences in American schools, academic theologians are also involved in a history of secularization. However, for Rorty and Stout, I take it that secularism must also substantively commit its properly initiated adherents to atheism if secular philosophy is to distinguish itself from secular theology, which, according to their descriptions, is categorically theistic. I have argued elsewhere that the opposition of atheism to theism is axiomatic, formal, and categorical.[19] The question of marginalization, which for its critics is an inference from secularization, is historical. Hence, the marginalization thesis requires historical understanding, not caricatures.

The third basis of my doubt for accepting the marginalization of theology thesis wholesale is that many of its advocates infer it from a perceived loss of public of theology or theology's public significance in American public life. They evoke figures such as Paul Tillich and Reinhold and H. Richard Niebuhr to provide evidence that not since their times have any theologians made any significant influences on public discourse. Few, if any, have made the *New York Times* or have been the counsel of presidents. I find this a curious set of criteria for basing a critique of academic theology. To be sure, these figures had significant influence on the public discourses of primarily East Coast intellectuals by virtue of their left-wing democratic political affiliations, the special journalistic organs such as the *Christian Century* and *Christianity and Crisis*, and their impact on university lecture markets. However, it is a long way toward establishing the declining public significance of academic theology by so few examples. It is equally a long way toward defining the normative activity of academic theology by the public engagements of these major figures among an elite, intellectual bourgeois community of scholars, artists (as in Tillich's case), left-wing activists, and New York intellectuals of the 1940s and 1950s.

Mapping public significance might go far toward establishing any strong merit for the critique of academic theology based on the marginalization thesis. For instance, measuring any widespread influence of American public theology would be easy enough simply by developing a quantifiable model based on a questionnaire. One might ask: (1) Have you or anyone in your immediate family ever heard of Paul Tillich or the Niebuhrs? (2) Have you or your parents ever read articles, books, or essays published by these figures? (3) Have you or anyone in your family ever attended any public lectures by these figures? and (4) Have you or anyone in your family ever considered becoming a public theologian because of their public influence? Without such data, the lament over the perceived marginalization of academic theology based on critics' perceived loss of its public significance says a great deal about what canon of American theologians critics themselves value. However, it says little descriptively either about the historical and contemporary impact of academic theology on American public life or the state of the discipline within the American universities, colleges, divinity schools, and seminaries where most academic theologians labor.

Secularization and the Worldliness of Theology

I have referred to the marginalization of theology thesis with skepticism. However, I am not suggesting that many of the issues with which its advocates are concerned are unimportant. Rather, I think that the manner in which secular critics construe the secularization of the academy against theology is distorted by their negative dialectics. That is, the story of theology's crisis and struggle for legitimacy against secularism among the human studies from the late nineteenth century to the present has been couched all too often in terms of polemically exclusive theories of secularization. Under such theories, the crisis and struggle of theology are regarded as consequences of theology's secularization by a polemically exclusive other, whether "critical philosophy" or "science writ large." Critical philosophy is said either to usurp the meaning of theological ideas by transposing them into philosophical ones, or the distinctive meanings of theological ideas are shown to be "unreasonable" where the ascendancy of philosophy or science redefines the criteria of intelligibility among the human studies. Whichever the case, secularization signals a displacement or usurpation of theology's cognitive and normative legitimacy by its categorical other.

Recently, many of those who advance the marginalization of theology thesis, such as religious historian George Marsden, follow this negative account of secularization. Marsden describes secularization as "the removal of some activity of life from substantive influences of traditional or organized religion."[20] For him, methodological secularization means the bracketing of religious beliefs in the pursuit of knowledge or truth for the sake of gaining "greater scientific objectivity to perform a technical task."[21] However, when methodological secularization is extended to constitute an ideology, it amounts to the view that "all of life is best lived without reference to religious faith."[22] I take Marsden's theory of ideological secularization to be that theological beliefs or religious faith positions are categorically rejected in favor of nontheological descriptions of human life that commit the secularist to atheistic accounts of subjective meaning and value. Like Rorty, Stout, and others, I think that Marsden also substantively confuses the processes of secularization with a particular atheistic, secular philosophy and criticism when he tries to explain the historical differentiation of critical discourse from religious or theological influence. In Marsden's view, academic theology cannot be secular in either method or ideology because secularization is categorically understood in negative relation to organized religion and academic theology.

The problem with such a theory is that it often explicitly accepts the validity of positivists' convictions. It accepts into its secularization theory the inevitable progress of ideas via a history of negation, in which case science progressively ascends to negate metaphysics and theology. This theory of secularization also depends on Hegelian convictions about intellectual transcendence via a process of internal disruption and displacement. In this case, critical philosophy disrupts and displaces the explanatory functions of theology in understanding the advancement of human self-consciousness. No doubt some aspects of theology's crisis of marginalization may be owing to exclusionary accounts of secularization among competing discourses, for instance, in the physical sciences. However, critics also tend to beg the question of a secularization of theology internal to the discipline itself. Elsewhere, I have turned to Hans Blumenberg's conception of secularization in an effort to balance such negative dialectics.[23]

In Blumenberg's theory, twentieth-century academic theology and secular philosophy are historically connected within an intellectual world that both discourses inherited and now occupy different answer-positions in relation to historical and contemporary questions carried over and received into their continuous histories.[24] My task is to avoid interpreting the different answer-positions signaled by theology and secular philosophy in terms of the secularization of the one by the other, in which case secular criticism is regarded as the secular "other" of theology, and both discourses suffer hermeneutical violence.

Blumenberg asks us to conceive of the history of Western academic discourses as forming a system of interpretations about the world and human relationships. The system is not newly created every time new ideas ascend, no more than the intellectual world of late antiquity was radically made over by Christian theology. Rather, the legitimacy of theology has always been connected to its capacity to "[create] new 'positions' in the framework of the statements about the world and man that are possible and expected, 'positions' that cannot simply be 'set aside' again or left unoccupied in the interest of theoretical economy." Traditional theology is said to have occupied an answer-position to questions about the "totality of the world and history, about the origin of [humanity] and the purposes of existence" that were structurally antecedent in paganism. The ascendancy of theology, therefore, was functionally commensurate with its successful satisfaction of an intellectual vacancy created by the weaknesses and failure of other answers that also intended to satisfy the "budget of [human] needs in the area of knowledge."[25] The successful ascendancy of theology was based on its capacity to supply late antiquity with coherent answers to its classical questions.

For Blumenberg, secularization is a functionally heuristic category; it is not a substantive one. As I understand the argument, the position that theology occupied in the intellectual world of antiquity need not be construed as a displacement of paganism by its polemically exclusionary other, namely, Christian theology. Rather, patristic theologians saw in the answer-positions of paganism real possibilities for their own ascendancy in the economy of ideas. The secularization of paganism and the ascendancy of theology also need not be construed in terms of theology's usurpation of the content of paganism into its own self-understanding, expropriating the successful ideas of paganism as if by a transference of ownership. The ascendancy of various discourses is tied to their capacities to occupy "answer-positions that had become vacant and whose corresponding questions could not be eliminated."[26]

Blumenberg's theory of secularization by reoccupation does not mean that the various answer-positions that theology or secular criticism occupy are only a matter of intellectual inheritance so that no account of novelty of either questions or answers is possible. Blumenberg admits that historical interruptions (epochal thresholds) make such a conception of intellectual history problematic.[27] Rather, secularization by reoccupation helps critics to account for both the continuities and discontinuities between the often antithetical substantive positions taken by academic theologians and secular philosophers. The discontinuities are based on different receptions of historical questions and answers, and the differences of reception make it possible to account for the secularization of theology not only by its differentiation from philosophy and the sciences but also by an increasingly secular and, hence, worldly theological academy.

In such an academy, the world where theology reigned as queen of the sciences, controlling and determining the parameters of knowledge, meaning, and value in terms of a Trinitarian God who orders the world and who determines and fulfills its ultimate ends, is well lost to many academic theologians working in the twentieth-century North American context. Moreover, the philosophical world, where the controlling terms were system, order, law, and nature, has been displaced by the ascendancy of alternative notions such as time and change. Therefore, both academic philosophy and theology have become more secular and, hence, more worldly as standards of meaning and value have been shaped by the priority of change and time consciousness in critical thinking. Langdon Gilkey drives home the point when he says, "Change is basic in human experience and in the world that is experienced. To be in time, as we in our world are, is to be subject to changing moments as day replaces day, to new relations between the moving things in our world, to new and so to surprising combinations of what is around us."[28] Gilkey continues: "To experience change is to experience with inner immediacy our immersion in history. To understand and to deal with the change in which humans are engulfed, the passing of the old and the appearance of the new in time, to affect the shape and direction of historical process, are inescapable requirements for human thought and for human life alike."[29]

With Blumenberg and Gilkey, I also think that academic theology is enmeshed in the processes of secularization. In the historical processes of secularization, theology is worldly to the extent that its categories and critical thinking are constructed within the worldliness of experience, time, change, immediacy, history, process, movement, constancy, probability, and intersubjectivity. The historical processes of secularization render every theology that constructs its self-understanding within these categories a secular theology, or, following Dietrich Bonhoeffer, a worldly theology. For Bonhoeffer, Christian theological reflection is secular insofar as academic theologians are called to live out their lives "unreservedly in life's problems, successes and failures, experiences and perplexities."[30] The academic theologian interprets, analyzes, understands, and criticizes the world in which he or she lives with discipline and constant inquiry into the ways of the world.[31] The worldliness of theology is grounded in the theologian's concern with the things of this world: one's culture, its morals, its meaning, what it values, and its treatment of others. Referring to Bonhoeffer in this connection, Larry Rasmussen says, "It is axiomatic for Dietrich Bonhoeffer that Christian life—and reflection on it—happens most authentically in one's own backyard. If there are universals, they are best discovered by delving deep into one's own culture and living out its possibilities and responsibilities."[32]

A worldly theology and, hence, a secular theology, is one in which the categories of meaning and value are derived from a fundamental understanding of the purposes and motives of human life. Secular theology springs from human intentions, human negotiations of nature, experience, human relations, and religious life. The worldliness of theology recognizes that all human endeavors are bound between the natural limits of human finitude and the possibilities of transcendence from human fatedness. Again following Bonhoeffer, the worldliness of theology begins from "the temporal character of human life, its fullness and frailty."[33] In this context, academic theology provides theological interpretations, understanding, meaning, and value. And like secular philosophy, its public significance is tested by its explanatory adequacy.

To conclude, the marginalization of academic theology has been argued for by a number of critics as an inference from a theory of secularization that places secularism and theology in exclusionary answer-positions. I argue that such dialectical thinking produces more cognitive distortions about both ideas than it clarifies the real, substantive differences between critical philosophy and academic theology. Such dialectical thinking also fails to recognize the ways in which academic theology, like all the human and cultural studies, is involved in the secularization of the American academy. To be sure, as time, change, process, experience, finitude, history, tradition, and difference have ascended as ontological categories of the humanities, so in its critical thinking, academic theology also has become increasingly determined by such boundary conditions. Therefore, talk of secularization ought also to include the worldliness of academic theology.

I think that it is fair to say that the negative critique of academic theology's public significance follows upon an acute recognition of the increasing worldliness of theology. However, I do not regard such a state of affairs as lamentable. To my mind, the worldliness of academic theology is a challenge to and burden on American academic theologians. The recognition that theologians are *in the world and of the world* orients academic theologians' concerns for the things of this world. Such a worldliness places academic theologians socially within a wide matrix of mediating institutions of which institutional religion is one sphere among others, such as education, political affiliations, government, and labor.

The academy is but one mediating institution among the many that channel public discourse. However, the academic theologian's self-recognized worldliness suggests that he or she is free to participate in the great variety of communities of public discourse, including religion, political societies, communication organs, and government affairs. In such cultural spaces, the academic theologian is free to think, interpret public opinion, and spiritually and morally influence public actions, if not at a mass level then at least locally. There exists no spiritual, common, or statutory law in the North American context prohibiting such a worldliness. The commitment of the academic theologian to such social and cultural participation is a priceless inheritance of the secularization of the American academy. Fulfilling such a commitment through social and cultural analysis, criticism, and participation also constitutes the worldliness and secularization of theology.

Notes

1. Victor Anderson, *Pragmatic Theology: Negotiating the Intersections of an American Philosophy of Religion and Public Theology* (Albany, N.Y.: SUNY Press, 1998), and "The Pragmatic Secularization of Theology," in *Pragmatism, Neo-Pragmatism, and Religion: Conversation with Richard Rorty*, ed. Donald Crosby and Charley D. Hardwick (New York: Peter Lang, 1998).

2. Richard Rorty, *Contingency, Irony and Solidarity* (Cambridge: Cambridge University Press, 1989).

3. Ibid., xii.

4. Ibid., xiii.

5. Ibid., 16.

6. Ibid.

7. Jeffrey L. Stout, *Ethics after Babel: The Languages of Morals and their Discontents* (Boston: Beacon Press, 1988).

8. Ibid., 163.

9. Ibid., 163–64.

10. Van A. Harvey, "On the Intellectual Marginalization of American Theology," in *Religion and Twentieth-Century American Intellectual Life*, ed. Michael J. Lacey (Cambridge: Cambridge University Press, 1989), 172.

11. Ibid.

12. Ibid.

13. Ibid., 173.

14. Ibid., 172.

15. Ibid.

16. Cornel West, "The Crisis in Theological Education," in *Prophetic Fragments*, (Grand Rapids, Mich.: Eerdmans, 1988), 273.

17. Ibid., 274.

18. Ibid.

19. Anderson, *Pragmatic Theology*, 25–26.

20. George Marsden, "The Soul of the American University: A Historical Overview," in *The Secularization of the Academy*, ed. George Marsden and Bradley J. Longfield (New York: Oxford University Press, 1992), 16.

21. Ibid.

22. Ibid., 21.

23. Victor Anderson, *Beyond Ontological Blackness* (New York: Continuum, 1995), 31, 35–36.

24. Hans Blumenberg, *The Legitimacy of the Modern Age* (Boston: MIT Press, 1983).

25. Ibid., 64.

26. Ibid., 65.

27. Ibid., 66.

28. Langdon Gilkey, *Reaping the Whirlwind: A Christian Interpretation of History* (New York: Seabury Press, 1976), 3.

29. Ibid.

30. Dietrich Bonhoeffer, 21 July 1944, in *Letters and Papers from Prison* (New York: Macmillan), 370.

31. Ibid., 369.

32. Larry Rasmussen, with Renate Bethge, *Dietrich Bonhoeffer: His Significance for North America* (Minneapolis: Fortress, 1990), page v.

33. Ibid., 105.

Part Two

Theological Interventions
in Cultural Settings

6

Self (Co)Constitution

Slave Theology from Everyday Cultural Elements

Dwight N. Hopkins

This chapter examines how, out of their everyday cultural elements, enslaved African Americans attempted to coconstitute themselves aided by divine intent. That is to say, through their daily cultural practices, enslaved blacks perceived their ultimate concern, and this ultimate concern, or God, worked with them to refashion themselves within and, at times, beyond the confines of their chattel existence. Therefore, co-constitution is the God-human encounter working together for the forging of the new human being.

"Culture" here builds on Raymond Williams's notion of culture "as the study of relationships between elements in a whole way of life."[1] On the basis of the cultural lifestyles of enslaved African Americans, I modify Williams's definition in the following manner. Culture is always religious insofar as the way of life of all human beings entails some yearning for, belief in, and ritualization around that which is ultimate— that which is both part of and greater than the self. Culture is religious because the ultimate concern is both present in cultural material and transcends it. Therefore, for my purposes, culture refers to religious culture as a total way of life.

Furthermore, slave theology is defined here as a systematization of slave experiences of God in everyday religious cultural practices. If slave religion is the African American's yearning for, belief in, and ritualization around that which is ultimate, then slave theology is my attempt to seek some intentional normative practices located in slave religion. In this sense, slave theology for me as a systematic theologian entails an effort to order the manifestation of liberation in a more systematic way so that slave religion becomes a more ordered thought and practice, which could further enhance the faith and witness of those on the underside of any society.

As an initial attempt to detect the process of self coconstitution, I explore the possibility of teasing out elements of slave theology from two examples of everyday cultural elements—the experience of sacred word power and the experience of creating a syncretized religion.

Sacred Word Power

Regarding sacred word power, I would like to turn to the enslaved African Americans' encounter with the Bible (as written word), prayer (as words of hope), spirituals (as singing words), and naming (as words of self-definition). All four examples signify what sacred word power meant for enslaved black folk.

Enslaved African Americans seized the written word as sacred word power in order to gain literacy for reading and interpreting the Bible. Though legally restricted from learning how to read, black chattel subverted this mechanism of power (that is, the holy scriptures employed as a false instrument anchoring oppressive sermons, catechism, and ethics of the master and his paid clergy). They reappropriated and claimed the biblical word from their vantage as those at the bottom of the plantation political economy. Truly it was a seizure of power when slaves deployed the Bible; doing so helped them constitute themselves as self-initiating beings. Surreptitiously reading the biblical story enabled slaves to know the world for themselves, to be made whole by expressing their intellect, and to master a sacred text.

To maintain their divine power over black slaves, masters banned learning to read, particularly the Bible. When asked what would have happened if she had learned to read, former slave Ferebe Rogers replied, "I'd had my right arm cut off at de elbow if I'd a-done dat. If dey foun' a nigger what could read and write, dey'd cut yo' arm off at de elbo, or sometimes at de shoulder." Such mutilation of the black body resulted from the master's perceiving reading as contrary to the absolute mandates of God. Ex-slave Henry Nix had an uncle whose master removed a forefinger because the uncle stole a book. The theological rationale of this brutalized "sign for the rest" of the black servants was that, in the master's language, "Niggers wuz made by de good Lawd to work" and not to read and write.²

For the enslaved, reading the Bible resurrected the black intellect from the hell of darkness and ignorance. In his autobiography, runaway free man Henry Bibb termed the constrictions of slavery the "grave yard of the mind."³ The seizure of the sacred text symbolized a journey from imprisonment to a new religious being, one liberated, at least on the cognitive level, in a new space claimed within the physical bonds of captivity.

Frederick Douglass agreed that the Bible enabled the constitution of the new black person. Douglass received this revelation about the transformative power of the written text partly from overhearing his master's prohibitions against teaching slaves how to read. In denying Douglass instruction in reading, his master said, "If he learns to read the Bible, it will forever unfit him to be a slave. He should know nothing but the will of his master, and learn to obey."⁴ For Douglass, this statement was like a bolt of lightening from heaven, converting his old confused self into a resolute self bent on emancipation. In his own awestruck words, Douglass proclaimed,

> This was a new and special revelation, dispelling a painful mystery against which my youthful understanding had struggled, and struggled in vain, to wit, the white man's power to perpetuate the enslavement of the black man. . . . [F]rom that moment I understood the direct pathway from slavery to freedom.⁵

His discovery of the sacredness of reading removed Douglass forever from the power of his master and propelled him into a free space, both metaphorically in terms of his sense of identity and self knowledge and literally by impelling him to run away to the North. Reading the Bible made Douglass unfit to remain a slave. In this example, an enslaved black person recreated self and world by perceiving the master's language games and power dynamics and then deploying them for his own liberation. With his knowledge of the language, Douglass took care of himself on the road to freedom.

The power of the praying word, like that of the written word, enabled black chattel to be transported and to relocate themselves into novel horizons beyond the demonic clutches of those who would snuff them out. In a not uncommon scene, a group of slaves had assembled illegally in a slave shack to worship and enjoy some real preaching conducted by one of their own black religious leaders. But the religious exhorter "made more noise than we were aware of," thus attracting the violent arrival of nearby white patrollers. Armed to the teeth, the captain of the patrol entered, whereupon the assembled slaves fell to the ground "and prayed that God might deliver us." Indeed, the seemingly miraculous occurred. The captain's "knees began to tremble, for it was too hot, so he turned and went out." For the narrator of this tale, the divine presence had intervened in response to the victim's prayer: "As God had delivered us in such a powerful manner, we took courage and held our meeting until day-break."[6] Prayer could shake the foundations (e.g., exemplified by the knee trembling of the captain) and bring heat upon those who would sustain and nurture evil systemic restrictions on sacred words.

Consistently, ex-chattel recounted stories of heartfelt prayers receiving responses. The praying word reached God's ear and moved the divinity, who was power. Prayers, therefore, were not in vain. On the contrary, they yielded positive and effective results by humbling perpetrators of violence against those without wealth or political connections. Similarly, prayers reconfigured symbolic and metaphorical signs of potency, offering a language of reversal from the victims' vantage. Prayer, moreover, relativized hierarchical social relations and emboldened slaves born with the wrong color identity. Prayer aided the structurally marginalized to endure and to triumph in the end. The power of prayer was the certitude of faith.

The singing word (particularly the Negro Spirituals, the unique religious songs originating in the African American enslaved community) offered a spontaneity in creation leading toward black psychological wholeness, part of the dynamic of taking care of oneself. A former chattel recalled how his master ordered him to receive a hundred lashes. At the "praise meeting dat night dey [the other slaves] sing about it."[7] The communal absorption of the pain of the individual, though not necessarily lessening his mortal lacerations, allowed him a psychological reintegration derived from participation in community. The invention of a song provided a way to nurture and create the self in a communal procedure.

In the final analysis, the sacred power of the singing word, reflected not simply the solo effort of the enslaved. Indeed, the divine gift of potent song (in the words of one ex-chattel: all a black person "gotta do is open his mouth and a song jes nachally drops out"[8]) emanated from loftier heights. In the retrospective of former slave Rev. Reed: "Some of them old slaves composed the songs we sing now. God revealed it to them."[9] Thus, the revelation of divine lyrics and holy rhythm implanted in the aesthetic harmonizing of beautiful dark tongues signified the colaboring exertion of God and humanity in the reconfiguration of the black self. African American servants knew about themselves and how to take care of themselves.

The potency of the naming word exemplified some of the same attributes and theological import as reading, praying, and singing. Moreover, given the religious consequences of naming rituals in certain indigenous West African worldviews and practical witness, to give an enslaved African or African American a name had an ultimate significance for his or her self-identity, communal relations, and being in the world. As one Ghanaian theologian discussed traditional ways of life, the Akan of Ghana link divine naming to God's "love of justice and fairness." Quoting Akan sacred folk wisdom, he resumed: "Since God does not like wickedness, He gave every creature a name."[10] Indeed, black chattel (at least in South Carolina and Florida and probably in other areas) were aware of the West African practice of endowing names with the presence of the holy.[11]

Consequently, one fought to maintain one's accepted family name, not one's given slave name. Harry Robinson, after his sale to the Harper plantation, rebelled by holding on to his family surname. "My father was named Robinson, so I kept his name after I got free."[12] The master's name equalled slavery; a family name equalled freedom. Slaves lied to a dangerous extent to their masters about their true feeling regarding their names. To the white masters of the plantation, they presented the descriptions prescribed by the slavery system, while "among themselves they use[d] their titles."[13]

Creating a Syncretized Religion

"Stealin' the meetin'," what enslaved religious blacks called their secret (reinterpreted) Christian gatherings—commonly termed Invisible Institution—reflected the institutional location out of which a future black theology of liberation emerged. Such surreptitious congregations often reached huge numbers. The intricate dynamic of "stealin' the meetin' "—its types, content, and forms—located the syncretistic or hybrid reality of African American religious experience. It is in the Invisible Institution where a novel substance was molded from remnants of African indigenous religion, common folk wisdom, and a reinterpreted Christianity. Only in secret communion with God could black folk both speak freely about the God that had liberated the Hebrew people and act out the self that they created away from the presence of white power.

Types

Enslaved religious blacks configured several types of the Invisible Institution in the hopes of God making a way out of no way. One such example included secret societies. After the Civil War, one freedman named Robert Smalls responded with a common double talk and apparent contradiction (contradictory to the Christian slavemaster's logic) to the query, "Were there any societies among the colored people for discussing the questions of freedom?" Smalls replied, "I do not think there are any secret societies except the Church societies and they do not introduce that subject there. They pray constantly for the 'day of their deliverance.' "[14] Smalls probably saw no contradiction in his response. The white interrogator left the question open by not specifying particular societies. Thus, Smalls could answer that there were no general societies that spoke of freedom. However, there was a particular secret society that prayed for the deliverance of the African American. The master of both an unfettered thought pattern and linguistic acrobatics, Smalls could truthfully say that there were no general societies discussing freedom, but a secret religious one that prayed to God for deliverance.

African Americans knew that their God would not forsake them, so they sought all means and types of prayer opportunities. They actually believed a prayer was answered once lifted up to heaven. Sometimes they prayed in the fields ("We often waited until the overseer got behind a hill, and then we would lay down our hoe and call on God to free us"). When black chattel became too loud in their singing at night in slave shacks, plantation owner Dr. Little gave stricter orders for quiet. Consequently, in the report of ex-slave Mary Ferguson, "us tuck to slippin' off to a big gully in de pastur to sing and pray whar de white fokes couldn' hear us." Field praying was a sacred occasion positioning hearts in tune. While beseeching God's grace and glory at the top of their lungs, enslaved black voices were protected by the powerful silencing quality of the iron kettle:

> Meetings back there meant more than they do now. Then everybody's heart was in tune, and when they called on God they made heaven ring. . . . They would steal off to the fields and in the thickets and there, with heads together around a kettle to deaden the sound, they called on God out of heavy hearts.[15]

Another type of Invisible Institution was prayer in the woods. At an appointed hour, African Americans sneaked off in the blackness of night to the woods. Some simply had "a good time talking about their mistress and master." Others assembled around a big fire on the edge of the woods "whar deir racket wouldn't 'sturb de white folks," while others knelt and prayed with faces turned toward the ground to deaden the sound of their supplication and their heartfelt longings for themselves and future generations: "I know that day we'll be free and if we die before that time our children will live to see it."[16]

Illegal house prayer and worship embodied an additional expression of the African American attempt to recreate the self away from the white plantation owner's purview. Key to this dimension of self-constitution under divine presence was the overturned pot. At times the pot was positioned in the middle of the house to catch the sound before it travelled out to the master or overseer. An unnamed ex-chattel recalled: "I've known them to have to turn down a pot to keep the sound in. . . . I've never known them to get caught while the pot was turned down at my home." In one instance, the pot was stationed outside the door as if it contained a supernatural sentinel, one who had supernatural powers to silence the ecstatic expressions of the black worshipers and to warn the gathered of an approaching enemy. Mrs. Sutton, a former slave, recounted: "[T]hey would get a big ole wash kettle and put it right outside the door, and turn it bottom upwards to get the sound, then they would go in the house and sing and pray, and the kettle would catch the sound. I s'pose they would kinda have it propped up so the sound would get under it."[17]

Perhaps the most elaborate event of constructing a secret sacred place in which to develop their own Christian sensibilities and, thereby, recreate themselves away from the demonic Christianity of plantation ethos was the bush arbor gatherings. Bush arbors epitomized black hands and hearts creating space for the poor to encounter the holy in permanent structures of worship. Bush arbors, therefore, symbolized permanent seizure of space, invested with elaborate preparations and well-thought-out schemes. The architectural sacredness of the building complemented the holiness of the geographical location of the gathering. Pierce Cody, an ex-slave, offered the details upon which the following bush arbor picture was created:

> As a beginning, several trees were felled, and the brush and forked branches separated. Four heavy branches with forks formed the framework. Straight poles were lain across these to form a crude imitation of beams and the other framework of a building. The top sides were formed of brush which was thickly placed so that it formed a solid wall. A hole left in one side formed a doorway

from which beaten paths extended in all directions. Seats made from slabs obtained at local sawmills completed the furnishings.[18]

In the collective preparation to worship God, the poor fashion not only their secret and novel approach to the divinity, but resist and reinvent themselves over against oppressive strictures. Bush arbors denoted hidden holy conversations out of ear range, thereby allowing a domain of real preaching and testifying to unfold. While theologizing in liberation tongues, African Americans also formed a communal self unlike that ordained by their forced chattel existence. To boldly position a permanent "church" dwelling in the midst of slavery country, to organize the details of work to construct the edifice, and to take slabs from local sawmills without detection point to the ability of a people hemmed in to accept the empowering motivation of worship as grace. It appears as grace in the woods for free worship and grace engendering the constitution of new black selves: fearless, bold, and risk taking.

Content

Creating a syncretized religion—a Christian black faith of liberation—required definite content and explicit substantive claims on the part of enslaved African Americans. First, this new Christianity of spiritual and material freedom called forth a politics that seized space and place for those without wealth or resources. Politics here suggests the right of the poor to call on God to work with them in implementing their right of self-determination. The power of this space-place dynamic would make a way, a new location and a novel horizon where black folk could openly worship their God of freedom and be their freely created new selves. Bill Collins reminisced about this political right of self-determination regarding space and place when he recalled, "On Sunday we would go to the barn and pray to God to fix some way for us to be freed from our mean masters."[19] One could not be a new creation or embrace a God of power unless there were acts of deliverance. In fact the coconstitution of the self through politics can be seen in how their faith in God enabled the blacks to physically move to a new and safe place (i.e., the barn) in expectation, through prayer, that their God would then facilitate the ultimate deliverance from the realm of structural slavery.

The political content of black syncretized religion was never a selfish faith claim, individualistic witness, or provincial expectation. The movement out of the chains of "Egypt" and the realization of self-determination brought a universal note, if not for those gathered in immediate prayer, at least for their offspring and ultimately for all humankind. Alice Sewell remembered the arduous physical journey of moving from plantation pathos to penultimate free space and how hoping for the particularity of black freedom places encouraged free spaces for the unborn and more healthy social relations for people of all races: "We prayed for dis day of freedom. We come from four and five miles to pray together to God dat if we don't live to see it, to please let our chillen live to see a better day and be free, so dat dey can give honest and fair service to de Lord and all mankind everywhere."[20]

The content of black Christian syncretized religion included a cultural strand also. In this instance, culture signifies the ability of poor black people to realize the right of self-identity. Who has the right to name a person? Who has the right to contradict and subvert a person's belief that God grants the right to self-identify as part of the self-constitution process? Apparently, from his early years, former slave William Wells Brown grasped the identity and self-creation interplay around naming: "I received several very severe whippings for telling people that my name was William, after orders were given to change it. Though young, I was old enough to place a high appreciation upon my name. . . . So I was not only hunting for my liberty, but also hunting for a name."[21] Not simply the political right to determine space and place but also the cultural right to call himself whatever he wished empowered Brown to undergo repeated whippings for refusing to yield either right.

Furthermore, the right of self-identity in this instance meant a struggle for a name accepted by the oppressed and against one imposed by the oppressors. The name "William," accepted by Brown and denied by supporters of the plantation system, was part of a struggle over language power and metaphorical imaging. By holding on to his accepted name, Brown fought for all the polyvalent meanings such a title imaged, such as a language of free self-creation and self-initiative.

Moreover, the content of the hybrid Invisible Institution included the risk of theological marginalization, one danger in following a faith argument of "thus saith the Lord" against wicked spiritual and material powers. Being tainted as marginal by dominating theological norms is in reality the good news of apocalyptic deliverance and eschatological hope for dispossessed communities. Another former chattel suggests that what is marginal to mainstream public definers of theology is actually the Christian gospel of hope for the oppressed and subversive discourse for marginalized believers. His summaries of enslaved black preachers' sermons from the hidden margins of plantation life indicate such a critiquing and offer prophetic content for black theology of liberation:

> The preachers were inspired by this bright hope of freedom, and as it grew nearer its imagined fulfillment they preached it to their people with thrilling eloquence. "Taint no dream, nor no joke," cried one of these; "de time's a'most yer. Der won't be no mo' whippin', no mo' oversee's, no mo' patrollers, no mo' huntin' wid dogs; everybody's a gwine to be free, and de white mass'r's a gwine to pay 'em for der work. O, my brudders! de bressed time's a knockin' at de door! in dis yer world, bof white and black, is gwine to live togedder in peace."[22]

A true word preached from the margins transforms into the immediacy of a critical theological discourse harkening freedom and peace "in dis yer world."

Forms

Part of thinking about God differently (e.g., the construction of black theology) and recreating oneself in sacred space (e.g., the coconstitution of the black self) involved establishing novel forms of worship as celebration with God and resistance against evil's presence. In autobiographical reminiscences regarding secret slave meetings, Isaac Williams commented, "There would seldom be silence in our meetings, waiting for each other to speak, as I am told there is often in a white man's prayer meeting. We were always ready, that is the religious ones, to testify, and felt much better for doing so."[23] Jubilant continuous testimony delineates one form of black religious ingenuity. For blacks, silent moments in the presence of divine power and grace were supplanted by a total yielding of the self to spiritual possession. To keep silent (that is, to keep one's thoughts and joy to oneself) before God reflected a form of individualism in radical contrast to rejoicing in communal activity. Though each individual African American had to "come through religion" and be converted to the divinity by herself or himself, such an individual conversion embraced a communal context of an extended family of believers as well as an obligation to report back all sacred experiences to the public. In other words, the Invisible Institution, the secret, sacred "stealin' the meetin'" of black folk, marked the time for poor people to assert their voice openly and aggressively. It was the time to tell God all about their lives.

Jubilant continuous testimony was accompanied by a form of embodied ecstatic singing particular to black worshipers. Once free, James
L. Smith penned the following testimony in his autobiography:

> The way in which we worshipped is almost indescribable. The
> singing was accompanied by a certain ecstasy of motion, clapping
> of hands, tossing of heads, which would continue without ces-
> sation about half an hour; one would lead off in a kind of reci-
> tative style, others joining in the chorus. The old house partook
> of the ecstasy; it rang with their jubilant shouts, and shook in all
> its joints.[24]

In this novel form of communing with God, singing comes from the
body; in fact, the body sings praises to the divinity by the empowering
presence of the Holy Spirit. Embodied ecstatic singing is a theological
expression because the sacred immanence moves the poor community
to another worldly realm (e.g., to a horizon of a new self whose new
constitution begins in a spiritual plane) and then relocates this transcendent event in this world by reimpacting the physical bodily presence.

Singing is an extended family chorus, where one bonds with the
neighbor through words of songs. In this instance, former slave Alice
Sewell remembers that "when we all sung we would march around and
shake each other's hands." Indeed, another ex-chattel indicated that
this ritual of communal family feeling of comraderie was encoded in
song, as one verse said: "Our little meetin's about to break, chillen, and
we must part. We got to part in body, but hope not in mind. . . . We
walk about and shake hands, fare ye well my sisters, I am going
home."[25] Walking, physical movement united with the singing, buoyed
the gathered throng. The more they walked in the secret worship and
the more they sang, the more they unified as an extended family of
sisters and brothers in the presence of the Holy. The increased bonding
of the horizontal plane of human interaction coupled with the thickness
of the spiritual embrace from the vertical plane emboldened poor folk
and prepared them to enter the realm of evil plantation owners with a
renewed sense of faith and a newly constituted self blessed by the divinity. For bodies separated after secret meetings, the remembrance of
the song served as spiritual glue to recollect all who had gathered clan-
destinely.

The connection between the religious forms of the ring shout (of
enslaved African Americans in secret worship) and the drum (of their
West African ancestors) evinced the vital sacred relation between black

theology and the communal practices of the indigenous religions of West Africa. The ring shout-drum, an additional form of syncretized religion, shows that enslaved blacks knew who they were as African people. Such knowledge, derived from an African indigenous lineage, appeared consciously for those blacks closer to their West African heritage and unconsciously in the layered fiber of the newly created black religion in North America.

The drum became the object of virulent and rabid attacks from European colonizers in West Africa. In the analysis of one West African scholar,

> In the beginning of the colonial period, both administrators and missionaries waged a merciless war against the drum for various reasons. . . . Christian missionaries found in the drum an excuse to wage a war against African traditional possession cults. They took away and destroyed thousands of drums.[26]

White Christians feared the drum because it was an instrument in political resistance against the military attacks of Christian colonialists and was associated with the presence of divine powers. Another West African interpreter concurs: "Drumming accompanied most, if not all, religious occasions in traditional society."[27] Religion and the drum are wedded in West African indigenous religions because the high God saw fit to make it a priority in creation. According to one Akan saying,

> God in creating the world
> Has suffered to create.
> What did he create?
> He created the Drum.
> Divine Drum,
> Wherever you are
> In nature,
> We call upon you,
> Come.[28]

As God's creation, the drum is part of God, belongs to the sacred realm, and engenders human-divine relationship and recreative powers. The drum hinges the constitution of the self with the Holy. For the Akan of West Africa, the drum (a) summons the divinity and the ancestors to the worship event of the devotees, (b) conveys the message of God to those gathered, and (c) sends divine spirits and ancestors back to their place of dwelling.

Along with the drum, religious practices in Congo-Angola, Dahomey, Nigeria, the Gold Coast, Sierra Leone, and Togo (areas of origin for blacks in North America) involved movement in a ring as a form of religious ritual venerating ancestors. Specifically, the Ibos, Yorubas, Ibibios, and Efiks of southern Nigeria engaged in a slow, counterclockwise motion embodying a "wave-like ripple which runs down the muscles of the back and along the arms to the fingertips. Every part of the body dances, not only the limbs."[29]

Once Africans crossed the Atlantic and were denied by law the use of the drum and, therefore, were forced to worship God secretly, they incorporated the drum sound and function in their newly crafted ring dance. They performed the drum into a ring shout. One observer noted:

> The good-natured ingenuity of the Negroes in circumventing plantation rules speaks well for their ready wit, and it always rouses my admiration to see the way in which the McIntosh County "shouters" tap their heels on the resonant board floor to imitate the beat of the drum their forebears were not allowed to have. Those who hear the records of the musical chants which accompany the ring-shout . . . cannot believe that a drum is not used, though how the effect is achieved with the heels alone— when they barely leave the floor—remains a puzzle.[30]

The ring shout showed the theatrical alteration of poor Christians' state of consciousness and the syncretistic form of the Invisible Institution. It meant being possessed by the Holy Spirit's power of changing the old self into a new self. This partial remnant of West African indigenous spirituality grafted into a reinterpreted Christianity produced black theology.[31] This novel "New World" syncretism showed forth in the possessed feet-like drum's countercircling and the shouting of divine praises in a frenzy.

We return to the turned-over pot as a final form created by enslaved African Americans in their secret worship of God. Here, too, one could argue for a syncretistic synthesis between West African indigenous faith practices and a reconfigured Christian belief system. Based on extensive field work among African communities, in Suriname in particular, anthropologists Melville and Frances Herskovits link ecstatic dancing to the theological dimension of drums. They claim, first of all, that Africans perceived dancing as a sacred way of life. Next they observe the body positions of worshipers relative to the holy drums. Lastly they conclude that dancing around the drum signified an affirmation of God dwelling in these divine instruments. The religious dancers "face the drums and dance toward them, in recognition of the voice of the god within the instruments."[32]

There are similar associations between African American Christian worshipers and the sacredness of the turned-over pot, which suggests that one possible genealogical strand of the pot or kettle is the West African sacred drum. An unnamed former slave recalled, "Time has been that [slavemasters] wouldn't let them have a meeting, but God Almighty let them have it, for they would take an old kettle and turn it up before the door with the mouth of it facing the folks, and that would hold the voices inside."[33] Here this interviewee associates God's permission with an overturned kettle. Though slavemasters denied Christian worship, God held all might over all creation, including the earthly masters on the plantation. An old kettle protected the voices of those secretly praising the God of all might who enabled poor blacks to have safe time and ample space in which to forge their own theology. In another former slave's thought association, we find intellectual clarity as God's gift of grace: "In some places that they have prayer meetings they would turn pots down in the middle of the floor to keep the white folks from hearing them sing and pray and testify, you know. Well, I don't know where they learned to do that. I kinda think the Lord put them things in their minds to do for themselves, just like he helps us Christians in other ways."[34]

Knowledge to take care of themselves, in a situation where faith practices go on despite lethal threats from earthly slavemasters, is a pedagogical gift of God. Divine kindness (i.e., grace) instructs oppressed African American Christians to employ ingenuity to subvert evildoers who would prevent the spiritual self-care required in situations of subordination. In this sense, the pot or kettle becomes holy knowledge power to make a way out of no way for blacks. It therefore facilitates not only their taking care of themselves but gives them the time and space to coconstitute their theological worldview and forge a new humanity amidst deleterious circumstances.

This former slave's rhetoric juxtaposes evil's denial of worship, God's allowing a way for the oppressed, and the kettle's making real divine knowledge. At the same time, the ex-chattel's logic somehow links that mouth of the kettle to God's power. Pedagogy, rhetoric, and logic are embodied in the kettle's expediting the remaking of both a subversive Christian faith claim and a reconstituted slave status that affirms self-initiative.

More pointedly, Patsy Hyde remembered slavery days in which the turned-over pot indeed revealed directly the presence and power of God to those surreptitiously gathered in faith: "De slaves would tek dere old iron cookin' pots en turn dem upside down on de groun' neah dere cabins ter keep dere white folk fum hearin' w'at dey wuz sain'. Dey climed dat hit showed dat Gawd wuz wid dem."[35] The phrase "Gawd wuz wid dem" echoes the Christian notion of Emmanuel, an honorific title for Jesus the Christ denoting "God is with us." In their mindset, blacks were certain in their claim that divinity resided in their midst; this holy nearness of God's appearance was more powerful and more protective than any force on earth. And an old iron cooking pot had something to do with this sheltering, liberating power.

Conclusion

This chapter has provided a thick description of enslaved African Americans working with their perception of the divine in order to coconstitute themselves from everyday cultural practices. I have defined culture as the interaction of elements in a total way of life. Because blacks perceived an ultimate concern of freedom or liberation in these relationships between elements of a whole way of life, culture, in this instance, was religious culture. Out of this yearning for, belief in, and ritualization around that which was ultimate, I have begun a systematic ordering of normative slave beliefs and practices—what I call fragmented slave theology. Perhaps in the exploration of the interplay between theology and cultural analysis, the insights of black theology of liberation and Michel Foucault's accent on the everyday, microexigencies of life might offer some approaches to the academic study of one marginalized religious community struggling for liberation as the condition of possibility for the practice of freedom.

Notes

This chapter is part of a larger statement titled *Down, Up and Over: Slave Religion and Black Theology* (Minneapolis: Fortress, 1999).

1. Raymond Williams, *The Long Revolution* (Westport, Conn.: Greenwood Publishing Group, 1961), 63.

2. The Ferebe Rogers and Henry Nix references come from George P. Rawick, ed. *The American Slave: A Composite Autobiography*, Georgia, vol. 13, part 3 (Westport, Conn.: Greenwood Publishers, 1972, 1977, 1979), 215 and 144, respectively. Other accounts of slaves struggling to read can be found in "The Emancipated Slave Face to Face with His Old Master: Valley of the Lower Mississippi: Supplemental Report (B); American Freedmen's Commission by James McKaye," National Archives file 3280, 1863, roll 199, pp. 12–13; Rawick, *American Slave*, Georgia, vol. 12, part 2, 130–31; 274; vol. 2, part 2, 42; Henry Bibb, *Narrative of the Life and Adventures of Henry Bibb*,

an American Slave (Philadelphia: Rhistoric Publications, [1849] 1969), 31–32; Octavia V. Rogers Albert, *The House of Bondage or Charlotte Brooks and Other Slaves* (New York: Oxford University Press, [1890] 1988); and anonymous, Social Science Institute, Fisk University, *Unwritten History of Slavery: Autobiographical Accounts of Negro Ex-Slaves* (Nashville: Fisk University, 1968), 148.

3. Bibb, *Narrative of the Life*, xi.

4. Frederick Douglass, *Life and Times of Frederick Douglass* (New York: Crowell-Collier Publishing Company, [1892] 1962), 79–80.

5. Ibid., 79–80.

6. Quoted in *Five Black Lives*, intro. Arna Bontemps (Middletown, Conn.: Wesleyan University Press, 1971 [reprint]), 167.

7. Charles H. Nichols, *Many Thousand Gone: The Ex-Slaves' Account of Their Bondage and Freedom* (Leiden: E. J. Brill, 1963), 102.

8. Said by Callie Chatman, in Rawick, *American Slave*, Georgia, supplemental series 1, vol. 3, part 1, 195.

9. Quoted in *Unwritten History of Slavery*, 20–21.

10. Kofia Asare Opoku, "Aspects of Akan Worship," in *The Black Experience in Religion*, ed. C. Eric Lincoln (Garden City, N.Y.: Anchor Books, 1974), 299.

11. See Robert L. Hall, "African Religious Retentions in Florida," in *Africanism in American Culture*, ed. Joseph E. Holloway (Bloomington: Indiana University Press, 1990), 101, and Margaret Washington Creel, *"A Peculiar People": Slave Religion and Community-Culture among the Gullah* (New York: NYU Press, 1988).

12. Quoted in *Unwritten History of Slavery*, 122.

13. See the responses of former chattel Robert Smalls in microfilm roll 200, "Extracts from Debates on the Adoption of Freedmen's Inquiry Commission, 1863–64," National Archives, Washington, D.C., no page number.

14. National Archives, Washington, D.C., Microfilm Roll #200, "Extracts from Debates on the Adoption of the Federal Constitution, Relating to Slavery." American Freedmen's Inquiry Commission, 1863–64; no page number.

15. Quotes in this section on the praying in the field type can be found in Rawick, *American Slave*, 12, part 1, 174 and 328, and in Clifton H. Johnson, ed., *God Struck Me Dead: Religious Conversion Experiences and Autobiographies of Ex-Slaves* (Philadelphia: Pilgrim Press, 1969), 76.

16. Southern University (Boston Rouge, Louisiana), John B. Cade Library, no name, np, Texas; Redwick, *American Slavery*, Georgia, vol. 12, part 2, 333, and vol. 13, part 4, 192.

17. Quoted in *Unwritten History of Slavery*, 23 and 15.

18. Redwick, *American Slavery*, Georgia, vol. 12, part 1, 197–98.

19. Southern University, Cade Library, np.

20. Quoted in Norman R. Yetman, *Life under the "Peculiar Institution": Selections from the Slave Narrative Collection* (New York: Holt, Rinehart & Winston, 1970), 263.

21. Quoted in Gilbert Osofsky, ed., *Puttin' On Ole Massa* (New York: Harper Torchbooks, 1969), 217.

22. *The Kidnaped and the Ransomed: The Narrative of Peter and Vina Still after Forty Years of Slavery* (Philadelphia: Jewish Publication Society of America [1856] 1970, 160.

23. Isaac Williams, *Sunshine and Shadow of Slave Life: Reminiscences as told by Isaac D. Williams* (East Saginaw, Mich.: Evening News Printing & Binding Co., 1885), 67.

24. James L. Smith, *Autobiography of James L. Smith* (Norwich, Conn.: Press of the Bulletin Company, 1881), 27.

25. Albert, *House of Bondage*, 12. Alice Sewell's remarks are from Yetman, *Life under the "Peculiar Institution,"* 263.

26. Jacob K. Olupona, ed., *African Traditional Religions in Contemporary Society* (New York: Paragon House, 1991), 81.

27. John S. Pobee, *Toward An African Theology* (Nashville: Abingdon, 1979), 66.

28. Olupona, *African Traditional Religions*, 84–85.

29. Sterling Stuckey, *Slave Culture: Nationalist Theory and the Foundations of Black America* (New York: Oxford University Press, 1987), 11, 19–20.

30. Lydia Parrish, *Slave Songs of the Georgia Sea Islands* (Athens: University of Georgia Press, 1992), 16.

31. Creel, *"A Peculiar People,"* 299.

32. Quoted in Stuckey, *Slave Culture*, 20.

33. Quoted in *Unwritten History of Slavery*, 19–20.

34. Quoted in *Unwritten History of Slavery*, 10.

35. Quoted in Rawick, *American Slave*, Tennessee, vol. 16, 34.

In the Raw

African American Cultural Memory
and Theological Reflection

Anthony B. Pinn

In this chapter I explore how attention to cultural production can enhance theological reflection in the following ways: (1) I discuss current uses of cultural production—various sites of cultural memory—in African American theology; (2) I rethink collective memory and cultural resources by arguing that collective cultural memory is fragile if not fractured, and I assess the theological ramifications of fragile cultural memory; (3) I outline archaeological resources and the process of archaeological theology.[1] The relationship between theology and cultural analysis guiding this discussion is as follows. Theology, at its best, is dependent upon cultural production as a means to understand the expression and substance of religious experience. Theology benefits from cultural analysis because the latter helps theology explore cultural production in all its complexity. Furthermore, cultural analysis can benefit from the sensitivity to religious sensibilities that undoubtedly guide cultural productions.

African American Theology and Popular Culture

Liberation theologies are committed to cultural production as vital material for theological reflection. African American theological reflection is no exception. The first systematic treatment of black liberation theology by James Cone establishes this commitment to cultural resources.[2] Cone recognizes cultural realities as the materials through which divine revelations are manifest. To miss the importance and content of culture is to overlook the presence of God in the world.[3] In spite of the logic and rhetorical strength of Cone's argument, Cecil Cone has called into question the scope and depth of James Cone's attention to African American cultural production.[4]

According to Cecil Cone, black theological reflection is vulnerable because it relies on nonreligious orientations that are simply a reaction against European notions of freedom and community.[5] As a corrective, he suggests a conscious turn toward black religious experience and black cultural production, and the avoidance of white European approaches and cultural concerns. In this way, black theology becomes *black* by taking seriously claims to the revelatory value of black cultural experience and production. Blackness is dualistic in nature: It includes physical blackness as well as a unique set of cultural and historical realities.

In response to these critiques, many African American theologians have placed more emphasis on the cultural roots of the black church and the black community. However, this attention to cultural production as theological resource usually has not moved beyond those elements that are readily apparent and well documented—documented in ways that are often questionable and commonly christocentric. Even agendas that bring into question assumptions of theological normality do so using only the more visible resources—cultural production close to the surface of the cultural terrain. What develops is a static notion of cultural "blackness" based upon a limited collective cultural memory.[6] The work of Maurice Halbwachs supports this assertion. He writes that "the memory of the religious group, in order to defend itself, succeeded for some time in preventing other memories from forming and developing in its midst."[7] What ultimately occurs, then, is a sense of personal and cultural identity that allows for only a few cultural markers, and theology easily becomes apologia or advocacy for the religious implications of this reified cultural image.[8]

Dwight Hopkins and others bring this trend into question by rethinking black cultural production's content and shape of expression. Take for example Hopkins's article "Theological Method and Cultural Studies: Slave Religious Culture as a Heuristic."[9] Here Hopkins argues for an understanding of culture as a "total way of life" that entails an ever broadening terrain, beyond the forms of cultural productive experiences that reside on the surface of U.S. history and existential reality. He un-

derstands culture as complex conversation and exchange that take place
on a variety of levels. Hopkins's connecting of cultural production with
individual and communal identity is also useful: cultural production
develops with the development of personality, in light of various socially
constructed factors. This implicit appeal to social evolution and political
economy points to the difficulty of marking out the paths of black cultural production on the rough U.S. terrain.[10] Yet even this more complex
understanding of religious experience and the cultural foundations embedded in it seems troubling in its certainty about the location, content,
and meaning of African American cultural artifacts.[11]

Collective Memory and Cultural Resources

If my critique is correct, how is the complex range of cultural productions and activities uncovered and used in theological reflection? To
answer this question, one must begin by rethinking culture, cultural
production, and cultural memory.

Culture is a system of signs in motion, the meanings we develop to
explain how and where we live.[12] The Latin word from which "culture"
is derived means "to till the ground, to tend and care for." Yet, as Don
Cupitt notes,

> in antiquity it had already gathered the wide range of extended
> senses it still has today. Culture is the familiarized, tamed, gar-
> dened, version of the world. . . . It includes not only the *cultivation*
> of the soil, *agriculture*, but also the *culture* of new varieties of
> domesticated plant, the careful *cultivation* of acquaintanceships
> and skills, of one's own "person" and one's own soul, and
> therefore also *high culture*, the arts and sciences, and above all the
> *cult*, the care and tending of the gods. (Emphasis in original.)[13]

Culture understood in this way, in association with terrains, sociopolitical and economic knowledge, and artistic developments, points to cultural production's complexity. It also points to the importance of memory as cultural production's housing. Memory, in short, is the tissue
that explains and "connects" the various remnants and artifacts (i.e.,
cultural productions) we come across as individuals and as groups.[14]
Each time we interpret cultural memories, they move farther from the
moment of their conception and their concrete tie to cultural reality.
Direct contact with the context of cultural artifacts is lost because time
continues to move forward and representations replace realities.

Take the United States and the development of collective cultural memory here as a particular example of this memory distortion and loss. The early North American terrain held such untapped wonder and possibility, particularly with respect to the West. This created a sense of progress and possibility that overshadowed the importance of a historicized past. This also corresponded to the break between cultural artifacts and a consistently contextual story. Memory became disassociated from the (arti)facts.[15] Although this seemed beneficial at the time, selective memory and disregard for the past resulted in a shallow self-identity and consciousness that made the denial of African Americans and Native Americans easy. For example, prior to 1870, a few whites, then, at least considered the Indians' tragic part in the American past and present, even though they responded inconsistently to such issues— as friend or foe, victim or villain.

> By contrast, the African-American appears silently and unobtrusively in some historical art concerning the War for Independence. But any claims that might appear on behalf of black participation in national history would have to be made by blacks themselves and could expect to be largely ignored.[16]

With time, certain memories alleviated fears generated by an uncertain future and recent turmoil (e.g., Civil War, reconstruction, and strained ties between North and South).[17] Yet again, minority communities were forgotten. During the early twentieth century, this problematic use of memory made the philosophies of racial inferiority and separation that much easier to espouse. Keep in mind works by such figures as Thomas Dixon and the pseudosciences promoted during the late nineteenth and early twentieth centuries.

The ramifications of these revisionist efforts, such as the writings of Dixon, for oppressed communities are damaging and far ranging. This process does not completely obliterate cultural meaning and production within African American communities. Yet efforts to remove African Americans from the story of U.S. progress do result in fragile memory and decontextualized cultural artifacts.

African American communities have nurtured their own cultural production by making sense of their cultural memories (i.e., memory markers) damaged during years of bondage and continued discrimination. This massaging of collective cultural memory, or connective cultural tissue, is important. However, it does not entail a complete and linear transmission of cultural information. Pieces are lost along the way depending upon what groups and individuals consider important or unimportant moments and developments. Robert O'Meally and Geneviéve Fabre are correct: "Whether deliberately or not, individual or group memory selects certain landmarks of the past—places, art work, dates, persons, public or private, well known or obscure, real or imagined—and invests them with symbolic and political significance."[18] In short, the necessity of interpretation alters cultural memory. A clear and uncontaminated link between the past and present does not exist.[19]

Over time, what happens to the cultural artifacts that are not selected? Perceiving the world, as collective cultural memory does, always entails a loss of some pieces, the removal of what does not appear useful or helpful. As Toni Morrison writes,

> Over and over, the writers pull the narrative up short with a phrase such as, "But let us drop a veil over these proceedings too terrible to relate." In shaping the experience to make it palatable to those who were in a position to alleviate it, they were silent about many things, and they "forgot" many other things. There was a careful selection of the instances that they would record and a careful reading of those that they chose to describe.[20]

Cultural memory is again paradoxical because it is not only composed of cultural artifacts; we also use it to decode and interpret (i.e., place in meaningful context) those artifacts.

History is the cataloguing and filing away of cultural artifacts. It entails freeze-framing cultural production/artifacts that move throughout an undefined and unstable contextual framework. History is, at best, an inadequate way of presenting cultural artifacts called the past. It fains to remember and chronicle all, forgetting nothing of merit. In "organizing" cultural memories, history ultimately damages them through a faulty process of "clarification." Furthermore, as the earlier material on the United States shows, history is not a victimless crime. Even so, I would not want to settle too rigidly on oppressive social factors as the sole cause of ruptured cultural memory.

African American collective cultural memory is fractured for an additional reason connected to oppressive circumstances but not reducible to them. Sites of memory change due to generational shifts. Fabre and O'Meally explain that "certain sites of memory were sometimes constructed by one generation in one way and then reinterpreted by another. These sites may fall unexpectedly out of grace or be revisited suddenly, and brought back to life."[21]

Many African Americans overlook subtle cultural artifacts. That is to say, not every black person can play the dozens and appreciate the clever undertones of a Richard Pryor routine. The idea that some are unfamiliar with this information strengthens my argument. In addition, much of what has been collected concerning African American culture and cultural memory has gone through several translations before reaching print or some other final form. For example, many WPA workers received materials from generations who had forgotten (for many reasons) many nuances accompanying the cultural artifacts they shared. For example, descendants of slaves did not always know the significance of dietary restrictions they observed, or the religious connotations of colors in the quilts left behind by grandparents. In this way, standing both within and outside a cultural system has negative consequences. We must be mindful of Karen Fields's words:

> Nothing is more fully agreed than the certainty that memory fails. Memory fails, leaving blanks, and memory fails by filling blanks mistakenly. In filling blanks mistakenly, memory collaborates with forces separate from actual past events, forces such as an individual's wishes, a group's suggestions, a moment's connotations, an environment's clues, an emotion's demands, a self's evolution, a mind's manufacture of order, and yes, even a researcher's objectives.[22]

This in no way suggests that "fragile" memory is worthless. Yet I must agree with Fields, who goes on to say that "it is important to refine continually our methods of observing and thinking about memory as a matter of scholarly or scientific enterprise."[23] Progress can be made in theological reflection by recognizing the incomplete and fractured nature of collective cultural memory. We turn to Frantz Fanon and African American existentialism for help with this.

My intention is not to update the Hershovitz-Frasier debate over the survival of African culture in the Americas. That argument concerning cultural retention has been put to rest. Furthermore, my intention is not to take Fanon's analysis as a direct representation of conflict over African American cultural memory. Rather, I am suggesting Fanon's psychological and existential approach to cultural memory and identity in the face of cultural hostility is a useful tool. African American existentialism points to the necessity of understanding the condition of African Americans as an introduction to their collective cultural memory.

Early in *Black Skin, White Masks*, Fanon makes a statement that, in a symbolic manner, captures the existential dilemma: "The white man is sealed in his whiteness. The Black man in his blackness. . . . There is another fact: Black men want to prove to white men, at all costs, the richness of their thought, the equal value of their intellect."[24] According to Fanon, this dilemma results in a fracture of the human "soul": Memory is split between an urge toward blackness—conceived in cultural terms—and the continual presence of European cultural ideas.[25] Within this cultural quagmire, oppressed groups seek to resurrect cultural artifacts and place them in an identity-forming context. Though this is a seemingly Promethean task, Fanon does not give up on the ability of groups to reconnect or recover cultural realities that buttress a useful individual and collective identity. Referring to Africa, the words of Fanon are not lost on the U.S. context:

> Somewhere beyond the objective world of farms and banana trees and rubber trees I had subtly brought the real world into being. The essence of the world was my fortune. Between the world and me a relation of coexistence was established. I had discovered the primeval One. My "speaking hands" tore at the hysterical thought of the world. The white man had the anguished feeling that *I was escaping from him and that I was taking something with me.* (Emphasis added)[26]

"Cultural estrangement" is not complete.[27] There are cultural artifacts that the whitening of history does not erase. I cannot help but believe African American collective cultural memory is a matter of "escaping . . . and . . . taking something." Something, not everything, is taken. Intellectuals mistakenly think that they gather the substance of collective culture and construct firm cultural memory. But "[they] only [catch] hold of . . . outer garments. And these outer garments are merely the reflection of a hidden life, teeming and perpetually in motion."[28]

Fanon's observation sheds additional light on the ontology of fractured cultural memory.[29] The physical body itself is a cultural artifact, complete with scars, piercings, the memories housed in its essential form, and so forth. One could easily relate this understanding of body to Hortense Spiller's understanding of flesh as "that which holds, channels and conducts cultural meanings and inscriptions." According to Spiller, enslavement seeks to strip the body of its flesh. Instead, the flesh is transformed. It is hidden from view, covered by calloused and protective layers.[30] Ironically, flesh makes cultural memory visible but hidden. An additional problem emerges: The invisibility of African Americans has put their cultural artifacts up for grabs. They, the artifacts, are understood as belonging to no one, increasing acquisition and interpretation difficulties. This should spark new theological questions concerning collective cultural memory's locations and nature. In the words of Fanon, "O my body, make of me always a man who questions!"[31]

Theological Ramifications of Cultural Memory

Theological soundness is dependent upon the perpetual quest for cultural roots and epistemological soundness. The benefit of the cultural quest is uncertain, but it should drive theological reflection onward. Fanon's comments concerning the quest for an Aztec past by Mexican scholars fits here: "Because they realize they are in danger of losing their lives and thus becoming lost to their people, these [intellectuals], hotheaded and with anger in their hearts, relentlessly determined to renew contact once more with the oldest and most pre-colonial springs of life of their people."[32]

Such a task would be difficult enough if African Americans conducted this work in solitude, but it is complicated by the presence of a larger cultural norm (the dominant society) that often blocks this work by cooptation and the denial of the artifacts' importance. From Hegel to the present, African American culture and its manifestations have been questioned. Richard Wright covers this troubled terrain:

> Never being fully able to be myself, I had slowly learned that the South could recognize but a part of a man, could accept but a fragment of his personality, and all the rest—the best and deepest things of heart and mind—were tossed away in blind ignorance and hate. . . . Yet, deep down, I knew that I could never really leave the South, for my feelings had already been formed by the South, for there had been slowly instilled into my personality and consciousness, black though I was, the culture of the South.[33]

Wright rejected the dominant culture's rejection of him and went in search of cultural artifacts, cultural meaning—identity. But how do theologians engage in this same enterprise? How do we leave the metaphorical South (or North, East, or West for that matter) in search of cultural artifacts and collective cultural memory? The search should take us into new terrain and over old terrain with more critical insight.

African American writers have often taken the lead in pushing theological and otherwise religious questions and concerns. They have embodied in their writings hard investigation of cultural memory and artifacts. With this in mind, I look to Toni Morrison for assistance.

Morrison has come to realize that "memories and recollections won't give . . . total access to the unwritten interior life of these people [African American forebearers]."[34] At this point, Morrison employs imagination. She encourages theologians and others to recognize the fractured nature of collective memory. The procedure suggested by Morrison is of fundamental importance here: "[In] literary archaeology, on the basis of some information and a little bit of guesswork, you journey to a site to see what remains were left behind and to reconstruct the world that these remains imply."[35]

Archaeological Theology

Mindful of Morrison's words, I suggest an alternate way of viewing and deciphering African American religion and culture by theologically embracing the hidden and fragile, as well as the creative and life-affirming, manifestations of African American culture. I call this approach archaeological theology. This is a theological enterprise because theological concerns remain a high priority, and archaeological sensibilities and tools are used to enhance this theological agenda.[36] The first order of business is to outline the preliminary tasks in the development of archaeological theology. For the purposes of this essay, I concentrate on two: (1) attending to methodological shifts; and (2) rethinking the religious terrain, with hush arbor meetings as exemplar.

Initially, the term "archaeology" referred to the systematic and descriptive analysis of ancient societies.[37] During the nineteenth century, however, the term was expanded, and archaeologists became those who examined the material remains of perished civilizations.[38] In short, "the purpose of archaeology is to extract history from the monuments and artifacts of the past, to write history from the often inadequate relics that time has spared."[39] This took various forms and centered on various parts of the world, but a Eurocentric bias was usually obvious. Some archaeologists held an interest in non-Western cultural traditions and spent their careers exploring the "exotic," as it were. Others during the nineteenth century were concerned only with adventure and treasure, spending time only with pyramids and romanticized past civilizations.[40]

In the 1960s, "New Archaeology" developed and concerned itself with the manner in which people interacted with the environment and other groups, and the role of cultural production in facilitating this exchange.[41] Additional attention was now given to the politics of archaeology and the manner in which archaeological methodology could be fitted to the agendas of women, African Americans, and other marginalized groups.

I suggest an archaeological method of "cultural resource management" based upon political economy because it is mindful of the sociopolitical and economic factors influencing culture and archaeological analysis. Cultural management that accompanies the type of archaeological endeavor favored here—rescue archaeology—helps theologians move beyond present patterns of investigation by seeking not simply to absorb or add new materials, but to synthesize artifacts and "living" materials. Theologians can then work with materials that are usually excluded from the accepted record as well as familiar materials that must now be reevaluated.[42]

Because of the commodification of Africans through slavery, my sense of archaeological method also requires a cultural-commodity point of departure that is connected with political economy ideas. This approach suggests that every object can be commodified and its value made dependent upon a given location of exchange.[43] Borrowing from Charles E. Orser, I extend the meaning of value to include use, exchange, and aesthetics. Orser gives the example of iron pots found on sites once housing slave quarters. The use and exchange values of these pots are connected to kitchen or cooking services. But slave accounts indicate that these pots were also used to capture sound during worship services. This aesthetic value sheds additional light on cultural production during slavery.[44] In short, archaeological focus is on the manner in which religious rhetoric serviced economic agendas within the context of slavery. It demonstrates the ways in which cultural artifacts and memory point to untapped theological connotations. Attention to archaeological method can mean a richer understanding of African American life extending beyond a select and distorted representation, a movement away from current biases, for example, in the depiction of African American religiosity. This in turn can mean a broader and more complex theological analysis of cultural production and African American life in general.

I suggest beginning with a rethinking of hush arbor meetings. I have selected hush arbor meetings because of their central role in the discussion of cultural artifacts and memory within African American liberation theology and African American religion in general. William E. Montgomery depicts a typical hush arbor meeting:

> "If their masters refused to permit them to hold their own worship services, slaves would steal away into the woods and congregate in what they called hush arbors or brush arbors, which were

sanctuaries constructed of tree branches or in secluded cabins. . . . Black preachers related to them in their vernacular, and the singing and dancing provided them with excitement and pleasure."[45]

As Montgomery notes, not all hush arbor meetings were done without the knowledge of whites. In fact, at times whites gave slaves permission to hold such meetings in order to avoid having to share space. After emancipation many blacks built similar structures to use until more permanent locations were available. It is likely that these not-so-secret meetings were the early stages of black Christian churches in the South. Referring again to Montgomery, one sees this implicit movement from hush arbor to black Christian churches in the South. He writes, concerning the religious ramifications of emancipation:

> Control of their churches was as much a part of being self-reliant as owning their own land and exercising legal and political rights. . . . And it was dramatically stated in the action of the Reverend Morris Henderson, a former slave who was freed in February, 1865, and who led his Baptist congregation out of the church building in Memphis that whites had allowed them to worship in and moved into a rude shelter of tree limbs and branches known as a brush arbor. . . . They could listen to and react to their own preachers in their own way, singing, dancing, and shouting as the spirit moved them. And, of course, a church structure was already in place. It needed only to be formalized, in the case of the slaves' "invisible" church.[46]

Albert Raboteau provided one of the earliest and best treatments of slave religion, making explicit use of the Invisible Institution as a paradigmatic religious move on the part of enslaved Africans.[47] Raboteau argues that the Invisible Institution arose as slaves felt the need to develop their own religious thought outside oppressive structures of economically driven "false Christianity," to use Frederick Douglass's terminology. He does acknowledge some diversity of opinion within slave communities, yet it leads back to the Christian church. "During the closing decades of the antebellum period the so-called invisible institution of slave Christianity came to maturity."[48]

Too often we have thought in terms of Christianity to the neglect of other viable alternatives. Granted, Christian activity during this period is documented by slaves, but, keeping in mind prior statements concerning collective cultural memory, this does not mean that all occurrences were reported to curious persons. What was not reported may have been lost to cultural memory and housed in decontextualized and misunderstood cultural artifacts. My argument is not that secret slave meetings were non-Christian. I cannot be certain of this any more than others can be certain that Christianity dominated these meetings.

Assumptions commonly accepted concerning religious expression in slave communities are problematized by archaeological excavation. For example, in his work with a mid-nineteenth century village in Texas, archaeologist Kenneth Brown unearthed a room that "contained many artifacts similar to those used to fill *minkisi* [sacred medicines]."[49] Such findings point to the presence of Africa-Bakongo influence, particularly religious practices. During the 1960s there was increased interest in cultural artifacts of colonial African Americans, and this material is ripe for archaeological theology's probing. For example, Leland Ferguson, in *Uncommon Ground: Archaeology and Early African America, 1650–1800*, speaks of the excavation of slave quarters in a way that should spark interest in a theology based upon complex cultural artifacts:

> [W]hile objects like engraved spoons and African-style shrines seldom were mentioned in written documents, artifacts excavated on plantation sites, coupled with . . . discoveries of Bakongo-style marks on bowls from lowcountry sites suggest that the preserved remains of many shrines and rituals must be buried underground across the South. Archaeological evidence of African-style religious practices in America reinforces and makes tangible [a] sense that slaves brought to the Americas not only a variety of practical skills, but also elements of their African spiritual beliefs.[50]

Archaeological method applied to theology—archaeological theology—is useful because it facilitates hard questioning of assumed cultural history and theological reflection dependent upon it.

To get at this material and include it in theological analysis requires searching all angles: written historical records and autobiographical accounts, architectural information, folktales, folklore, fieldtrips to various sites, anthropological findings, archaeological findings, imagination, and so forth. That is, archaeological theology uses all available resources and recognizes that our findings always miss something. The framework is as follows: (1) decide upon issues and select work sites that are possible locations of cultural artifacts; (2) conduct surveys of the sites, suggesting initial theories and ideas; (3) record findings; (4) analyze the findings using an appropriate hermeneutic and appropriate theological sensibilities.[51]

Many argue that archaeology entails interpretative work. I, however, prefer to include an explicit hermeneutic in keeping with the basic principles of archaeological theology. I suggest "nitty-gritty hermeneutics."[52] Simply put, nitty-gritty hermeneutics is comfortable with disruption and breaks because it recognizes the flawed nature of memory and cultural artifacts. The artifacts, then, are less likely to be forced into contextual categories simply because the categories are widely known and embraced. "Its guiding criterion is the presentation of Black life with its full complexity, untainted by static tradition . . . [T]he term nitty-gritty denotes a hard and concrete orientation in which the 'raw natural facts' [in this case cultural artifacts] are of tremendous importance, irrespective of their ramifications."[53] It understands that the act of interpreting archaeological theology's "findings," like good lovemaking, is unpredictable, passionate, and messy.

Notes

A slightly altered version of this essay appears as chapter 5 in my book *Varieties of Religious Experience: African Americans Making Meaning* (Minneapolis: Fortress, 1998). I also plan to explore further the theological significance of cultural memory in another volume to be published by Fortress Press titled *Earth Bound: Toward a Theology of Fragile Cultural Memory and Religious Diversity.*

1. I should say a few words concerning my use of the term "artifact." I understand all cultural productions outside the creative moment as artifacts because they have become contextually uncertain. They are open to historical conditioning; they are no longer "owned" by their creators. Furthermore, historicization cannot be used to decide what is an artifact because history is conditioned. That is to say, history is subjective.

2. James H. Cone, *A Black Theology of Liberation*, 20th anniversary ed. (Maryknoll, N.Y.: Orbis, 1993), 27.

3. Cone does embrace, however, Barth's notion of the permanent and qualitative distinction between God and humanity. Cone, like Barth, wants to avoid the possibility of idolatry. Human words cannot be identified as God's words without the danger of theology becoming mere ideology, with limited liberating potential.

4. Cecil Wayne Cone, *The Identity Crisis in Black Theology* (Nashville: AMEC, 1975).

5. Ibid., 18, 142.

6. For example, critiques of homophobia and heterosexism in black churches and black theology revolve around rereadings of Scripture and the open nature of black religious community. Why not give attention to (whether ultimately fruitful or not) homoeroticism in black musical expression and other forms of black cultural expression that critique homophobia and heterosexism? Why not question the assumed heterosexual norm of black slave communities and relationships? How many theologians ex-

plore possible cultural artifacts that point to homosexuality in slave communities? Or are the images of mandingo, Jezebel, and the Mammie embraced in a bizarre and twisted reaction to white stereotypical depictions of blacks?

7. Maurice Halbwachs, *On Collective Memory*, trans. and ed. Lewis A. Coser (Chicago: University of Chicago Press, 1992), 93.

8. I make this argument as an extension of comments made by Don Cupitt concerning theology done in light of an understanding of tradition as whole and perfect. This theology he considers an exercise in advocacy. See Don Cupitt, *After Religion: The Future of Religion* (New York: Basic Books, 1997), 106–18.

9. Dwight Hopkins, "Theological Method and Cultural Studies: Slave Religious Culture as a Heuristic," in *Changing Conversations: Religious Reflection and Cultural Analysis*, ed. Dwight Hopkins and Sheila Davaney (New York: Routledge, 1996).

10. Ibid., 165.

11. Ibid., 168.

12. Don Cupitt, *After God: The Future of Religion* (New York: Basic Books, 1997), page xiii. For the purposes of this essay, I do not consider it essential to make sharp distinctions between folk, popular, and mass culture. My concern is with the function and format of collective cultural memory. However, those interested in such distinctions should see Susan Willis's "Memory and Mass Culture," in *History and Memory in African-American Culture*, ed. Geneviéve Fabre and Robert O'Meally (New York: Oxford University Press, 1994), 179.

13. Cupitt, *After God*, 22–23.

14. See Barry Schwartz's definition of collective memory in "Iconography and Collective Memory: Lincoln's Image in the American Mind," *Sociological Quarterly* 32, no. 3 (1991): 302, cited in Michael Eric Dyson, *Making Malcolm X: The Myth and Meaning of Malcolm X* (New York: Oxford University Press, 1995), 201, note 1.

15. Michael G. Kammen, *Mystic Chords of Memory: The Transformation of Tradition in American Culture* (New York: Knopf, 1991), 51–53, 59.

16. Ibid., 87.

17. Ibid., 281–82.

18. Geneviéve Fabre and Robert O'Meally, introduction to *History and Memory*, 7.

19. I draw from Dyson's discussion of collective memory. See Dyson, *Making Malcolm X*, 149–150.

20. Toni Morrison, "The Site of Memory," in Cornel West et al., *Out There: Marginalization and Contemporary Cultures* (Cambridge: MIT Press, 1990), 301.

21. Fabre and O'Meally, *History and Memory*, 8–9.

22. Karen Fields, "What One Cannot Remember Mistakenly," in Fabre and O'Meally, *History and Memory*, 150.

23. Ibid. Although Fields is, for the most part, talking in terms of individual memory, her comments are applicable to collective memory.

24. Frantz Fanon, *Black Skin, White Masks* (New York: Grove Press, 1967), 9–10.

25. Ibid., 18.

26. Ibid., 128.

27. I borrow this term from Frantz Fanon, *The Wretched of the Earth* (New York: Grove Weidenfeld, 1963), 210.

28. Ibid., 223–24.

29. I pull this sense of human beings as ambiguous from the work of Lewis Gordon, who, in turn, borrows from thinkers such as Simone de Beauvoir. See Lewis Gordon, "Existential Dynamics of Theorizing Black Invisibility," in *Existence in Black: An Anthology of Black Existential Philosophy* ed. Lewis R. Gordon (New York: Routledge, 1997), 72.

30. I draw from a discussion of Spiller's idea in G. M. James Gonzalez, "Of Property: On 'Captive' 'Bodies,' Hidden 'Flesh,' and Colonization," in Gordon, *Existence in Black*, 130.

31. Fanon, *Black Skin, White Masks*, 232.

32. Fanon, *Wretched of the Earth*, 209–10.

33. Richard Wright, *Black Boy* (New York: Harper & Row, [1937] 1996), 284.

34. Morrison, "Site of Memory," 302.

35. Ibid.

36. There is a natural link between archaeological inquiry and theological reflection. See Michael L. Blakey, "American Nationality and Ethnicity in the Depicted Past," in *The Politics of the Past*, ed. P. Gathercole and D. Lowethal (Boston: Unwin Hyman, 1990), 38.

37. Glyn Daniel, *The Origins and Growth of Archaeology* (New York: Thomas Y. Crowell, 1967), 1.

38. Ibid., 3.

39. Ibid., 20.

40. Brian Fagan, *Time Detectives: How Archaeologists Use Technology to Recapture the Past* (New York: Simon & Schuster, 1995), 25.

41. Stephen Sherman, "Cultural Transmission and Cultural Change," in *Contemporary Archaeology in Theory: A Reader*, ed. Robert W. Preueal and Ian Hoddler (Cambridge: Blackwell, 1996), 282.

42. Ibid., 312.

43. Robert W. Preucel and Ian Hoddler, "The Production of Value," in Preucel and Hoddler, *Contemporary Archaeology in Theory*, 106. Political economy, in short, can be defined as the study of the creation and use of goods, services and value (99).

44. See Charles E. Orser Jr., "Beneath the Material Surface of Things: Commodities, Artifacts, and Slave Plantations," in Preucel and Hodder, *Contemporary Archaeology in Theory*.

45. William E. Montgomery, *Under Their Own Vine and Fig Tree: The African-American Church in the South, 1865–1900* (Baton Rouge: Louisiana State University Press, 1993), 34.

46. Ibid., 52–53. Another example is found on page 94 of the same text.

47. Albert J. Raboteau, *Slave Religion: The "Invisible Institution" in the Antebellum South* (New York: Oxford University Press, 1978), section 11, chap. 5.

48. Ibid., 212.

49. Leland Ferguson, *Uncommon Ground: Archaeology and Early African*

America, 1650–1800 (Washington, D.C.: Smithsonian Institution Press, 1992), 116; also see 114–18.

50. Ibid., 117.

51. Examples of how to conduct this investigation are available in other areas such as history and philosophy. The work of Michel Foucault is a prime example of the archaeological method combined with other methodological approaches. His *The Archaeology of Knowledge and the Discourse on Language* (New York: Pantheon, 1972) offers both a model that archaeological theology can draw from and challenges to which it may want to respond. Those familiar with Foucault will notice my use of aspects of his understanding of archaeology, particularly his willingness to speak in terms of ruptures and fractures (169).

52. See Anthony B. Pinn, *Why, Lord? Suffering and Evil in Black Theology* (New York: Continuum, 1995), chapter 5. This chapter also appears, with some alterations, as "Message in the Music: On Interpreting the Contact between Religion and Popular Culture," in *Religion and Popular Culture in America*, ed. Bruce Forbes and Jeffrey Mahan (Berkeley: University of California Press, 2000).

53. Pinn, *Why, Lord?* 116.

8

Creating a Liberating Culture

Latinas' Subversive Narratives

Ada María Isasi-Díaz

The conviction underlying mujerista theology is that the religious understandings and practices of Latinas living in the United States have liberative value. Once again I have gathered the stories of these women and collected their insights, this time on issues of embodiment and sexuality.[1] These are women who struggle for survival and "un poquito de justicia," a little bit of justice.[2] Out of a sense of justice to Latinas whose voices, whose lives, are hardly ever taken into consideration by academics or by society at large, we have not wavered in our commitment to provide a platform for them in mujerista theology. Our faithfulness to their stories, to their understandings and insights, and our ongoing commitment to privilege their preferred future is also grounded in a firm conviction that it is precisely their vision of the future that will bring us closer to the kin-dom of God.[3] It is not that Latinas are morally superior. It is because they benefit so little from the present structures and arrangements, because they have so little to protect in the present, that they can really look for and see a radically different future, a liberating future.[4] We have included the voices of Latinas in our theological elaborations in mujerista theology because we believe in the ongoing revelation of the divine in the lives of the poor and the oppressed and because we believe that Latinas are capable of knowing and explaining what they believe and the role those beliefs play in their lives.

Almost always Latinas' stories of survival seem so ordinary that few value them. Few are willing to listen to them and understand that for Latinas, liberation/salvation is brought about and worked out in the ordinariness of *lo cotidiano*. Those of us who do mujerista theology have paid attention to Latinas' stories because, as Latinas ourselves, we perceive that those stories are a *tela*, a cloth, out of which our own beliefs and self-understandings are made. We have paid attention to those stories because we have heard and have been formed by similar stories told to us by our own mamas, abuelitas, tías, madrinas, comadres.[5] It is precisely in these stories that we have come to know the beliefs that are central to their lives and our lives.[6] As we have listened for no less than twenty years to the life stories of Latinas, the importance for us of these narratives has grown exponentially.

Very often besides the different themes explored in conversations with Latinas—the divine, sin and grace, conscience, morality—we have come to grasp and value several by-products of the sharing. One of them is a realization of the importance of the narratives that Latinas have woven out of their experiences for themselves and for all those willing to pay attention to them. Narratives are important for mujerista theology because, first of all, unless Latinas have a new narrative, a narrative in which we can see ourselves as moral agents, as subjects of our own history, we will not be able to conceive and work toward our preferred future, toward liberation. Our own narratives help us to imagine ourselves in a new way, and to imagine ourselves in a new way is to know ourselves in a different way from the way the dominant group knows us. A new narrative will help us to "read" ourselves in a different way because it talks to us about what we have not been able to see in ourselves or have ignored.

To us, it has become clear what the writers of the gospel stories knew long ago: People do not live or die for a creed, for this or that belief. Large-scale changes such as those that make liberation possible, which necessitate changes of the heart as well as changes of the mind, are not really possible on the grounds of reason alone. People need a story. A story puts sinews and flesh on the dry bones of reason and creed. People need a story, a narrative, that sets before us situations and understandings "by means of which we learn to join the ethical aspect of human behavior to happiness and unhappiness, to fortune and misfortune."[7] Discovering the stories of Latinas and elaborating a mujerista narrative is important not only because it helps us to conceive a just society, but also because it motivates us to remain faithful to the struggle for justice.

A third important learning has to do with how to make Latinas' narratives obvious to those who are willing to see and to understand precisely what it is that has challenged the hegemonic Western male center, what has called into question the different forms of oppression such as ethnic prejudice, racism, classism, sexism, heterosexism, and others. It is not the theories of the academy that call the status quo into question and challenge it. It is the struggles of marginalized and oppressed peoples. What has erupted and threatens to dislodge the subjugating aspects of the rationality of modernity is not theories of the academy or debates about postmodernity, but the insistence of subjugated people on being subjects of their own histories, on being central characters in their own narratives. Latinas' narratives weave into subversive stories their subjugated knowledge, which produce "epistemological earthquakes and psychic shocks"[8] that can become intrinsic elements of new canons—canons that are multiple and remain open.

Lived-experience

It has been our contention from the very beginning that mujerista theology has to do with the beliefs of Latinas in the United States, beliefs that ground and motivate their struggles and that are lived out in *lo cotidiano*. We base this on a very old dictum that conceives theology as "faith seeking understanding."[9] We are also motivated to focus on Latinas' beliefs by what is referred to in the Roman Catholic tradition as the *sensus fidelium*, that is, the ongoing revelation of God in the community of faith.[10] Based on these traditional understandings and the conviction that beliefs are integral to Latinas' experiences, mujerista theology claims the lived experience of Latinas as the source of our theological elaborations. This means, first, that claiming the lived-experiences of Latinas is more than the *locus theologicus*. Second, the lived-experiences of Latinas as the source of mujerista theology is what leads us to claim that our theological enterprise is not a critical reflection on praxis, but is a liberative praxis in and of itself.[11] Third, grassroots Latinas are "organic" theologians capable of understanding and explaining their beliefs.[12]

We use the hyphenated phrase "lived-experience" to insist on the inseparability of thought and action, of belief and action, which is why mujerista theology claims to be in and of itself a liberative praxis: reflective action that has as its goal the liberation of Latinas in the United States.[13] For us, thinking cannot happen apart from action.

There is no human activity from which every form of intellectual participation can be excluded: *homo faber* cannot be separated from *homo sapiens*. Each man [*sic*], finally, outside his professional activity, carries on some form of intellectual activity, that is, he is "philosopher," an artist, a man of taste, he participates in a particular conception of the world, has a conscious line of moral conduct, and therefore contributes to sustain a conception of the world or to modify it, that is, to bring into being new modes of thought.[14]

To counter the prejudiced view the dominant culture has of Latinas, a view that considers us less intellectually capable,[15] in mujerista theology we insist that

rational thinking cannot advance except through the dynamic interplay of thought and action within the process of inquiry itself. We cannot understand the nature of the world through some Cartesian meditation on the nature of reality. We can grasp the world only by interacting with it. Action, choice, decision, contribute something indispensable to the mind's conquest of truth. We must interact with the realities we think about in order to create the experimental situations that will validate or invalidate our hypotheses about them.[16]

Furthermore, "action enters into our very grasp of the constitutive nature of things."[17] In other words, we understand things when we grasp the "generalized tendencies" that ground their behavior. Only if we understand those generalized tendencies can we predict how things will happen and the circumstances under which they will do so. Moreover, the validation of any hypothesis about how something is going to happen cannot occur at a theoretical level but takes place only when it actually happens.[18] This means that "rational thinking advances only through the dynamic interplay of thought and action operating within the process of systematic inquiry,. . . . that the validation of a hypothesis cannot happen at the purely theoretical level,. . . . [that] the dynamic process of knowledge is never complete and always subject to revision," and that the meaning of a concept is its operational consequences.[19]

Lived-experience is, then, a process of interaction between thinking and action. Our actions concretize our experiences and make us present to the world since they are our evaluative response to it. Furthermore, our interacting with the world is the way we create ourselves, the way we become and express who we are. We cannot "act" ourselves into being apart from thinking, and we cannot "think" ourselves into being apart from action.[20] This intrinsic link between thinking and acting points to the fact that we emerge as subjects from our bodies, that we do not exist like some unchanging substantial essence.

The body provides the most immediate environment from which the subject emerges. It consists of physically assimilated parts of the larger environment with which the subject interacts. Physical assimilation successfully incorporates elements of one's world into one's total subjectivity in ways that sustain existence. Food recreates the body. Digestion sustains growth and perpetuates vital functions. "The body, then, anchors one in a world, in an enveloping environment of interacting physical forces of different degrees of consciousness and complexity. . . . Communities of persons, however, constitute the most significant and sustaining forces in the human environment."[21]

The centrality of the body in lived-experience acknowledges the materiality of our persons. Materiality makes it more difficult for the dominant group to ignore or silence marginalized groups. Whether the dominant culture likes it or not, the materiality of Latinas—our corporality, our bodies—affect this society in which we live. Our bodies, then, not only are essential to us, but they also are essential to society, if only because society needs the work produced by our bodies. It is precisely the exploitation of our physical labor that enriches the dominant group and provides for them the material base for their control and power. This is why during the last six years we have focused our conversations with grassroots Latinas and this study on Latinas' bodies—on corporality, embodiment, sexuality. These conversations indicate there is a subversion of the patriarchal understandings of corporality and embodiment operating in the lives of Latinas, in our lived-experiences.

The construction of the person through lived-experience is a key reason for making it the source of mujerista theology. But as a liberative praxis, mujerista theology does not understand lived-experience from a liberal individualistic perspective that ignores the role of our gender and our ethnicity. If we were to understand it this way, we would have to blame ourselves for the oppression we suffer. On the other hand, we do not claim that the lived-experience of all Latinas is the same. Instead of sameness we talk about "shared experience." Shared experience points to the fact that in talking about Latinas' lived-experiences we are not claiming a common identity, or common attributes for Latinas, or even common situations or experiences. The shared experience we have as Latinas does not define us but rather points to our common cultural matrix.[22] Since part of this cultural matrix is the marginality/oppression in which we live, "shared experience" also refers to the way we experience the world because of how others conceive us. It points to the way that our material environment of oppression and marginality conditions us. Each of us is our own person and acts in our own way. But we do so within certain limits and constraints set to a great degree by the racist/ethnic prejudice and sexism operative in the United States. Understanding Latinas' lived-experiences as shared experience, then, takes into consideration the social, political, and economic context of our daily lives, which does not determine or define us but certainly influences very directly our worldview. It is the background against which our lives unfold.[23]

It is important to point out that mujerista theology is about struggling against oppression, one of the key elements of the cultural matrix of most Latinas. There are Latinas who have the same countries of origin as we have, who speak Spanish, and who maintain in their homes Latino customs, but who do not identify with the Latino community. They insist that they do not suffer discrimination. They espouse a liberal individualistic stance and, by identifying with and accommodating to the dominant culture, they have managed to deal with the ethnic prejudice and sexism in the United States in a way that satisfies them. They certainly do not have a shared experience with the vast majority of Latinas in the United States. And they certainly are not the Latinas whose lived-experience is the source of mujerista theology.[24]

Focusing on the struggle against oppression helps Latinas to see ourselves as a group without having to claim that Latinas have some specific inherent attribute. To claim such would reduce Latinas to biological attributes and it would erroneously attempt to find essential social attributes in Latinas' actual lives.[25] On the other hand, if we fail to see ourselves as a group, it would not be possible "to conceptualize oppression as a systematic, structured institutional process"[26] and to organize ourselves effectively against it.

In understanding Latinas' lived-experiences and shared experience, we have struggled to stay away from any sense of inherent attributes while finding a way to be and to conceptualize ourselves as a group. We see Latinas' lived-experiences and shared experience as the key to this balance, since they indicate that daily practices, habits, *lo cotidiano*, which do not happen apart from reflection, are ways of articulating Latinas' subjectivity. Being Latinas, then, is not "a point to start from in the sense of being a given thing but is, instead, a posit or construct, formalizable in a non arbitrary way through a matrix of habits, practices, and discourses"[27] about us by others and by us about ourselves. Being Latinas signals "an interpretation of our history within a particular discursive constellation, a history in which we are both subjects of and subjected to social construction."[28] This means that our subjectivity as Latinas is a fluid understanding, since it is based on concrete lived-experiences and not on any kind of universal attribute. Our historical realities, our lived and shared experiences, central to our identity as Latinas, provide us with a powerful motivation for our struggles for justice and liberation.[29]

One last point needs to be mentioned about the lived-experiences of Latinas. Lived-experiences are not disconnected events. They are distinct events that form a continuum, a coherent picture, created by the person reflecting on how they are connected, and they often lead one to the other. Lived-experiences are woven into narratives, which make obvious the interaction between thought and action and the way persons emerge from *lo cotidiano*. It is to narrative and the role it has come to play in mujerista theology that we now turn.

Life Stories, Narratives

A narrative is a tool one uses to organize lived-experiences into meaningful episodes. "Narrative displays the goals and intentions of human actors; it makes individuals, cultures, societies, and historical epochs comprehensible as wholes; it humanizes time; and it allows us to contemplate the effects of our actions and to alter the directions of our lives."[30] Narratives allow us to link the distinct events of our lives by making us note that something is but a part of something else and that it is the cause or the effect of something else. Personal narratives, then, are stories of one's life that make it possible for the person to give meaning to her life and to interpret it within its historical and cultural context.

We always have been aware of how eager grassroots Latinas are to share and to interpret for us what they have experienced. We have noticed repeatedly how during the course of their time with us, usually a weekend, the women have given shape to their lives. While on Friday they have only related what has happened to them, by Saturday afternoon they are explaining the meaning for them of their experience. Furthermore, as the weekends progress, the women begin to make more and more explicit the conditions under which they have lived, the conditions that either helped them or kept them from doing what they wanted.

The women have not only revealed to us the facts of their lives; they have not only allowed us to come to know their world. As we have studied the tapes of the reflection weekends, we have come to see that these women have constructed a narrative; they have "invented" an image of their lives by creating characters out of those they have in-

teracted with throughout their lives, creating a character for themselves, and becoming protagonists of their own stories. What connects
their different lived-experiences seems to be not a theme or a linear
concept of their lives, but the character they have created for themselves, which allows one to see how they understand themselves.[31] The
characters they create for themselves are ones that lead to or emerge
from their present self-understanding. The characters of themselves
they create are very influential in determining what they communicate
during the sharing.[32]

In their narratives, Latinas share their understandings of how their
gender impinges on their lived-experiences, on who they are, on who
they have become. They explain cogently through their stories how
prejudices about women and the systems based on such prejudices have
come together to affect their lives. Their narratives show how they have
been conscious of having to adapt, to pretend, in order to survive and
how, in other circumstances, they have been unwilling to do so because
to act in such a way would have been a betrayal of who they were/are.
In their narratives, each of these Latinas makes obvious her heroic
attempt to respond to her situation in a positive way and create a person
that can confront the conditions of her life. This attempt is not a mis-
representation, nor is it trivial conceit. It is the self-expression of a
woman who is doing what we all do: struggling to make sense of events
that are beyond her control and to establish a place for herself in terms
of the things that are within her control, and doing so not only through
her actions but also through her representation of those actions via
language.[33]

The narratives woven by these Latinas seem to us to be subversive
in nature because they unveil what has been suppressed or ignored by
society and by the academy: how Latinas temporarily adapt and pretend, or do not think or feel or act the way they are "supposed to."
Latinas' narratives are subversive, then, because they are "countersto-
ries—narratives of resistance and insubordination that allow communities of choice to challenge and revise the paradigm stories of the
'found' [dominant] communities in which they are embedded."[34] The
narratives are "sources of counterhegemonic insight" because they expose how the understandings of the dominant ideology are not universal, because they reveal lives that defy or contradict the rules,[35] and
because they uncover quiet but effective forms of resistance. Their effectiveness may not be immediate; Latinas have not been very successful
in challenging the dominant community in any extensive way. But these
subversive narratives begin to break the hegemonic discourse by insisting that Latinas' lived-experiences and the narratives woven with them

are legitimate sources of knowledge and that as such they pass on from generation to generation understandings that make it possible for Latinas to live with a modicum of self-definition. The narratives that we have been privy to are full of instances of counterhegemonic insights that help Latinas to redefine themselves and the social institutions of society.

Here is an account of a conversation during one of the reflection weekends that exemplifies what we understand by subversive narrative. It is a topic with which we think many women will resonate. One of the women said that at times she pretends to experience orgasm for the sake of her husband, so he will not feel bad, "el pobre" (the poor man), she said to punctuate the reason why she does it. Other women joined the discussion, most of them tacitly or implicitly indicating that they had done likewise. There was only one who strongly indicated that she had not pretended and would not pretend in this regard.

At first this narrative might appear to indicate how women are oppressed by men. But it is a subversive narrative if one notices that none of the women thought they were obliged to pretend to have an orgasm. Their reasons for doing it or not doing it clearly show that they are aware of what they need to do to be able to live in situations they could not or did not want to leave. The ones who pretended did so to gain the goodwill of their husbands, or out of pity, or "para que me deje en paz" (so he will leave me alone). No one did it out of a conviction that she was obliged as a woman to make her husband believe his sexual performance was adequate. These woman did not blame themselves for not having an orgasm. They pretended for their own sake, and those who would not pretend acted for their own sake as well. From this perspective, one can reevaluate the perception that women who pretend to have orgasms are afraid of or controlled by their male partners. Instead, does it not show that Latinas claim the truth of their lives, that they act to protect themselves, for their own sake, and do not see themselves as failures because they do not have orgasms, even if they are aware of other versions of what the sexual performance of women should be? The narratives on this point that these Latinas shared with us show that Latinas are critical of "officially condoned untruths" because they consider them an injustice.[36]

The validity of Latinas' narratives is "not dependent on the approval of the established regimes of thought."[37] A mujerista narrative is made up of knowledge that the dominant group has "disqualified [it] as inadequate to their task or insufficiently elaborated," knowledge that it considers to be "beneath the required level of cognition or scientificity."[38] We believe, however, that a mujerista narrative shows the deficiency of any of "the centralizing powers which are linked to the institution and functioning of an organized scientific discourse within a society."[39] It also questions the methods used in setting such a discourse, and in questioning the methods used, it also questions the contents.[40]

The narratives of these Latinas are subversive because they show that the image they have of themselves is different from the one that the dominant culture has of them. Body size and weight is a good example of this sort of independent thinking of Latinas. At one of the reflection weekends, one of the facilitators shared feelings about her struggle to keep a positive self-image in spite of her big size. The women in the group immediately reacted in a very pastoral way and repeatedly affirmed her by saying she looked wonderful, "no estás tan gorda" (you are not so fat). But during the breaks, the women continued to come up to the facilitator, insisting that she should not have a negative view of herself because "en nuestra cultura" (in our culture) her body size would not be considered unsightly.[41]

The ability of Latinas to see the differences between how big women are seen in Latino and in Euro-American cultures reveals how conscious Latinas are of the meaning of their experiences and of the social conditions in which those experiences take place. It is precisely from the coming together of their lived experiences and the social conditions in which they live that Latinas draw their sense of reality.[42] Latinas' narratives reveal aspects of the human condition that are true not only for us. These revelations can aid other women who are not Latinas, if only they are willing to recognize that we are mirrors for them. If they can recognize that, they will be open to Latinas and our world, and they will be able to lay aside prejudices and to embrace differences.[43]

What role does social context play in Latinas' narratives? Social context is formed by the coming together of social understandings and values, including even what we would consider negative values, such as sexism, ethnic prejudice/racism, and classism. Within this context, societal structures and institutions figure prominently, and for Latinas here we would need to include the churches in a special way. But "context is not a script. Rather, it is a dynamic process through which the individual simultaneously shapes and is shaped by her environment."[44]

The narratives of Latinas point to the different elements that are interwoven in their social context. Perhaps the most obvious is the interpersonal one. Latinas' lives are shaped, and perhaps even made possible, by the way they mediate between themselves and others, by their relationships with others.[45]

This reliance may well be a function of women's relative powerlessness, their lack of access to more formal and institutional
routes to influence, and as such a survival strategy shared with
other relatively powerless groups. While it must be acknowledged
. . . that the relationships which contextualize the lives of the
women in question are forged, negotiated, and experienced within
the framework of larger social-structural forces and factors, the
significance of such relationships is *seldom revealed* in the analysis
of social structure per se, nor can they be explained through a
focus at that level. It is in looking directly at women's lives that
relationships come to assume contextual importance and interpretative power. (Emphasis added.)[46]

The interpersonal relationships of Latinas are a key element of our
social context, for we come from a culture that continues to function
in a very personalized fashion. By this we mean that Latinas' culture
has not been bureaucratized; we do not operate according to rules and
regulations but rather at the level of knowing someone who can help
you or who knows someone else who will find a way of assisting you.
This makes us see the interconnection that exists between the personal
and the political, a connection that has been so important in the development of feminist consciousness in the United States. For Latinas,
the individualism of the dominant culture in the United States is considered negative for any given person as well as for her or his family
and community. This individualism, it seems to us, is what undergirds
the false separation between the personal and the political that has so
effectively kept women and so-called women's issues out of the political
sphere. For Latinas, individualism is the antithesis of a true sense of
community without which we could not survive as a marginalized
group and without which we could not conceptualize liberation and
struggle for it. Understanding ourselves always within an interpersonal
context, then, helps us to grasp the power dynamics that exist in society.
It does matter who you know; it is not a matter solely of how good you
are at what you do or how hard you work. The importance we give to
the interpersonal helps us to see that central to societal structures are
networks of people who vouch for each other, who help each other, and
who do all they can to keep the benefits of society in the hands of those
who belong to "their kind." This helps to demythologize structures, the
level at which the political works, making clear that its elements and
processes are not so different from those that are present at the personal
level. This points to the need to insist that everything that happens at
the political level affects the personal, and that the personal is also
political. The differences between the two are more at the level of scale

and accumulation of causes and effects. Therefore, insisting on the importance of the personal and interpersonal in *lo cotidiano* is indeed an effective way of bringing about structural change.

A second element to consider when analyzing context is the intersection in Latinas' lives of their socioeconomic-political situation, the dominant culture in which we live, and the Latino culture and ideology that also frames and informs our daily living. In the narratives of Latinas, it is noticeable how they are able to juggle two cultural-ideological frameworks. What becomes obvious is that Latinas' lives and understandings of ourselves point to what is called "situational ethnicity," in which cultural change and ethnic persistence occur simultaneously."[47] To understand how Latinas deal with the cultural-ideological frameworks in our lives, it is best to consider a "multidimensional model of cultural change and persistence . . . [which takes into consideration] the study of the interrelationships of cultural, social and structural factors in historical perspective."[48] This means that for Latinas "the acceptance of new cultural traits and the loss of traditional cultural traits varies from trait to trait," with some traditional traits being retained, some new traits being adopted.[49] In other words, what Latinas do is pick and choose from each culture whatever can be beneficial to them, depending, among other things, on which of the two "worlds" they are operating in. It is precisely this picking and choosing that gives birth to "new cultural and social patterns created by migrants and ethnic minorities in the new society,"[50] which we Latinas call *mestizaje* and *mulatez*.

Mestizaje and *mulatez* is our most immediate context; it refers to Latinas' condition as racially and culturally mixed people, our condition of people from other cultures living in the United States, our condition of people living between different worlds.[51] *Mestizaje* and *mulatez* for Latinas is not a given but a conscious choice, made obvious as we indicate how we move in and out of Latino and Anglo-American cultures according to need and desire.

A third element of context to consider here is the expectations and understandings that Latinas bring of ourselves, of our lives, and of the telling of our life stories.[52] These expectations will lead us to use this or that point of reference for telling our stories, constructing meaning for ourselves and taking a stance, publicly or privately as we see fit. By expectations and understandings here we do not refer only to those a person had when she did or experienced something or when she has reflected on it in the past. We also mean, as indicated earlier, Latinas' intentions for participating in the reflection weekends, the way participants viewed themselves within the situation when they were sharing their stories, how they perceive their narratives will be used, what they believe their stories have to contribute, and how they think sharing their stories will benefit them.[53]

Two examples make this point clear. Cuquita participated in one of the first reflection groups we had. She is a 60-year-old woman born and raised in Mexico who has no home of her own. She works as a maid and, from what she said, we gathered that she lives in the homes where she works and has also one room in the house of one of her children, where she keeps "mis cosas" (my stuff). Her full name is María del Refugio Quevedo, Cuquita being her nickname. We are using her name because she wanted us to. Why? When she was young she fell in love with a man who had been to Texas and had returned to their village. He was in love with her, but he was financially better off than she was. Cuquita says that "no fue lo suficiente hombre" (he was not man enough) to go against his parents' wishes and marry her. She eventually left the village and married another man, but she never has forgotten the man from Texas with whom she has always been in love. She keeps hoping she will find him. At the end of our time together when we were explaining to the participants that if we were to quote them directly we would use a pseudonym, Cuquita told us in unequivocal terms that we were to use her true name: "Maybe my love will read this book and he will come for me."

Since this was at least one of the reasons why Cuquita shared her story with us, it has to be taken into consideration in analyzing her interpretation of herself and her life. Throughout she presented herself as someone who always has been and still is sexually passionate. In no way do we believe that she invented this. Nothing of what Cuquita said led us to believe this was not true. But we do think that her self-portrayal in this regard is linked to her desire to find the man she has always loved. How conscious she is of this desire is not possible to tell, but we believe that her expressed wish to use this opportunity to find him indicates that wanting him to find her is actively operative in the way she portrayed herself.

Another example concerns one of only two Latinas who said they were not comfortable with recording the sessions although they tolerated it. One woman, Rosario, came to see the importance of this project not only for herself but for Latinas in general, and, in spite of her initial reticence, she would lean into the microphone to be sure that what she was saying would be adequately recorded. Is it unreasonable to believe that what she shared was in part shaped by her desire to help other Latinas? We would venture to say that this most probably led her to a deeper reflection and analysis of her experiences. Wanting to help others by telling her story probably also gave her an added sense of con-

fidence in herself and her ability to relate her experiences in a meaningful way.

Conclusion

Our purpose as mujerista theologians is not only to provide opportunities for personal growth for each of the women who participated in
the reflection weekends—opportunities to review stories, evaluate them,
and be intentional about future actions—but also to help create a subversive community narrative, a mujerista narrative, that will make public the hidden traditions of Latinas. Our purpose is not to create a grand
narrative but rather a contextual narrative that is tied to and that grows
out of Latinas' lived-experience in the United States in the closing years
of the twentieth century. Our purpose is not just to help the participants
in the reflection weekends to evoke the past for the sake of the past;
our purpose is to provide an opportunity for them to interpret their
experiences so they can value them and thus make it possible to learn
from their past in order to look confidently into the future. Our hope is
that a mujerista narrative that gathers and weaves together Latinas'
stories can be instrumental in creating a "cosmos of meaning" where
we can develop new consciousness and creativity.[54] It is our belief that
by helping to form a collective identity, a mujerista narrative will contribute to form a vision of a just future for Latinas and our communities,
and motivate all of us to action.[55] It is our belief that a mujerista narrative can emotionally bind people together who have a shared experience, for "whether in touch with each other or not, the collective story
. . . provides a sociological community, the linking of separate individuals into a shared consciousness."[56]

Our goal is to make known Latinas' narratives so that our beliefs
and understandings can contribute to giving theological meaning to
and transforming social institutions, including the churches.[57] We are
convinced that Latinas' narratives gathered and recognized as a primary
source for mujerista theology make explicit the modes of thought and
subjectivity of Latinas and offer a specific historical analysis that "explains the working of power on behalf of specific interests"[58] that do
not include Latinas, as well as revealing opportunities for resistance
against such exclusion. The mujerista narratives point to the fact that
"subjectivity and consciousness, as socially produced in language . . .
[are] a site of struggle and potential change." Latinas' narratives indeed
suggest that meanings are social constructs and that language is not
an abstract system but is always socially and historically located in

discourses. Discourses represent political interests and in consequence are constantly vying for status and power. The site for this battle for power is the subjectivity of the individual, and it is a battle in which the individual is an active but not sovereign protagonist.[59]

At present, Latinas' narratives are not powerful discourses in society, for they do not have a firm institutional basis. We trust, though, that because of the important role of Latinas in our culture and because of the rapid growth of our communities in the United States, a mujerista narrative will begin to challenge understandings, practices, and forms of subjectivity that at present are staunchly supported by society even though they are oppressive. We continue to gather and circulate Latinas' narratives because we are convinced of their value and because we know that they will never have a social impact unless they are widely known and valued.

Notes

The women quoted have all given permission to use their quotations in this essay.

1. The religious understandings and practices of Latinas in their own words can be found in Ada María Isasi-Díaz and Yolanda Tarango, *Hispanic Women: Prophetic Voice in the Church* (Minneapolis: Fortress, 1992), and in Ada María Isasi-Díaz, *En La Lucha—In the Struggle: A Hispanic Women's Liberation Theology* (Minneapolis: Fortress, 1993).

2. See the essay by this name in Ada María Isasi-Díaz, *Mujerista Theology: A Theology for the Twenty-First Century* (Maryknoll, N.Y.: Orbis, 1996).

3. I do not use "kingdom," for it is a sexist and classist term. Furthermore, it is a term foreign to the reality we live at the close of the twentieth century. "Kin-dom" brings to mind the concept of family, which is important in Latina culture.

4. José Míguez Bonino, "Nuevas Tendencias en Teología," *Pasos* 9 (1987): 22.

5. Mothers, grandmothers, aunts, godmothers; *comadres* refers to the relationship between godmothers and mothers. I use Spanish here because English, our second language, cannot convey the meaning for us of these relationships.

6. Of course, we know that in the long run what we are dealing with is how we understand and value what they tell us.

7. Paul Ricoeur, *A Ricoeur Reader: Reflection and Imagination* (Hertfordshire, England: Harvester Wheatsheaf, 1991), 428.

8. I heard Elizabeth Minnick use this phrase at a conference.

9. This phrase captures a key methodological understanding of Anselm of Canterbury, who lived in the eleventh and twelfth centuries. "The purpose of Anselm's work is not therefore to attain unto faith through reason, but 'in order to rejoice in the understanding and contemplation of that which they believe, and also in order to be always prepared in as much possible,

to answer all who may ask for the reason of hope that is in all of us.' " This quote from Anselm's work, *Cur Deus Homo 1.1 (Why God Became Man)*, is cited in Justo González, *A History of Christian Thought—From Augustine to the Eve of the Reformation*, vol. 2, 2nd ed. (Nashville: Abingdon, 1987), 159.

10. In the hierarchical Roman Catholic tradition this understanding should be seen as a way of resisting attempts to make the pope and the bishops the exclusive conduit for the revelation of God. This traditional belief was reaffirmed in the Second Vatican Council. See "Dogmatic Constitution on the Church," in *The Documents of Vatican II*, ed. Walter M. Abbott, S J., (New York: American Press, 1966), 29–30.

11. Our understanding here is different from that of Gustavo Gutiérrez. See Gustavo Gutiérrez, *A Theology of Liberation*, rev. ed., trans. Sister Caridad Inda and John Eagleson (Maryknoll, N.Y.: Orbis, 1988), pages xxviii, 5–12.

12. For us to recognize the intellectual ability of Latinas to elaborate theology, to explain their beliefs, has to do with the fact one cannot speak of nonintellectuals, for, as Gramsci says, they do not exist. See Antonio Gramsci, *Selections from the Prison Notebooks of Antonio Gramsci*, ed. and trans. Quintin Hoare and Geoffrey Nowell Smith (New York: International Publishers, 1975), 6, 9, 330.

13. In reality, of course, both "lived-experience" and "reflective action" are tautological expressions, but we use them to insist on the reflective element of all action and on the action element of all reflection, particularly of all critical reflection.

14. Gramsci, *Prison Notebook*, 9. I used this quote from Gramsci to ground this understanding of mujerista theology in my first book (cowritten with Yolanda Jarango), *Hispanic Women*, 8–10.

15. I have used as my guide for the discussion that follows an article by Linda Alcoff, who is "half Latina and half white." See Linda Alcoff, "Cultural Feminism Versus Post-Structuralism: The Identity Crisis in Feminist Theory," in *Feminist Theory in Practice and Process*, ed. Micheline R. Malson, Jean F. O'Barr, Sarah Westphal-Wihl, and Mary Wyer (Chicago: University of Chicago Press, 1989).

16. Donald L. Gelpi, S J, *The Turn to Experience in Contemporary Theology* (New York: Paulist Press, 1994), 33. I am grateful to Dr. Robert Lassalle-Klien at the Jesuit School of Theology, Berkeley, whose unpublished article "Making Sense of the UCA Model for Christian Education: Thought on Practical Foundations for Theology in the Americas" has guided me in my study of Peirce's understanding of the intrinsic connection between thought and action, which was based on his understanding of how the rational mind works. See Charles Sanders Peirce, *Collected Papers*, vol. 5, ed. Charles Hartshorne and Paul Weiss (Cambridge: Harvard University Press, 1931 ff), 266–82.

17. Gelpi, *Turn to Experience*, 33.

18. Ibid.

19. Lassalle-Klein, "Making Sense of the UCA Model."

20. This is why we believe, together with Gramsci, that the lived experience of *lo cotidiano* is a key element in the political struggle over meaning. One of the greatest mistakes of the theologies of and struggles for liberation is that they have concentrated on societal structural elements to the point

of ignoring the lived-experience of *lo cotidiano*. We believe this is why the structural changes have not happened or, if they have taken place, have not been maintained.

21. Gelpi, *Turn to Experience*, 132. I have replaced Gelpi's word "self" with "subject" in this paragraph because "self" has tinges of Cartesian understandings that ignore the body and its social context as integral to the person. It also seems to me that "subject" places an emphasis on moral agency. I was motivated to present this clarification by Sidonie Smith, "Self, Subject, and Resistance: Marginalities and Twentieth-Century Autobiographical Practice," *Tulsa Studies in Women's Literature* 9, no. 1 (Spring 1990): 11–24. However, it seems to me that my position does not necessarily follow the one she presents in this article.

22. I have claimed that there are at least five key elements that form this common matrix or ethnicity for Latina *mestizaje-mulatez*: (1) the struggle for survival, (2) marginality as a socioeconomic reality within the United States, (3) the Spanish language, (4) popular religion, and (5) our *proyecto histórico* (what we hope for as Latinas living in the United States). See Isasi-Díaz, *En La Lucha*, chaps. 1 and 2.

23. See Iris Marion Young, "Gender as Seriality: Thinking about Women as a Social Collective," in *Social Postmodernism—Beyond Identity Politics*, ed. Linda Nicholson (Cambridge: Cambridge University Press, 1995), 187–215.

24. It is not my intention in any way to demean these women. I simply want to point out that individualistic solutions to oppression do not do away with oppression or prove that oppression does not exist.

25. Young, "Gender as Seriality," 208.

26. Ibid., 192.

27. Alcoff, "Cultural Feminism Versus Post-Structuralism," 321.

28. Ibid.

29. Ibid., 318–26.

30. Laurel Richardson, "Narrative and Sociology," *Journal of Contemporary Ethnography* (April 1990): 117.

31. This might be why the questions we pose in the reflection groups are not answered directly, though it might have to do also with the fact that the majority of the women who participated in the reflection weekends have limited schooling. We think this leads them to relate much more to the oral than to the written world. As Walter J. Ong explains, the world of orality is closer to life than the written world, which means that it is organized around relationships more than around discrete events that can be lined up in a sequential manner. See Walter J. Ong, *Orality and Literacy: The Technologizing of the Word* (New York: Methuen, 1981), particularly chap. 3.

32. Daphne Patai, *Brazilian Women Speak* (New Brunswick, N.J.: Rutgers University Press, 1988), 1–35.

33. Ibid., 33.

34. Hilde Lindemann Nelson, "Resistance and Insubordination," *Hypatia* 10, no. 2 (1995): 24.

35. The Personal Narratives Group, *Interpreting Women's Lives: Feminist Theory and Personal Narratives* (Bloomington: Indiana University Press, 1989), 7.

36. Ibid.

37. Michel Foucault, *Power/Knowledge*, ed. and trans. Colin Gordon (New York: Pantheon, 1980), 81.

38. Ibid., 82.

39. Ibid.

40. In this we disagree with Foucault, who sees subversive knowledges as not being primarily opposed to the prevalent methods and content but to how they are used. See Foucault, *Power/Knowledge*, 84.

41. See Christy Haubegger, "I'm Not Fat, I'm Latina," in *Reconstructing Gender: A Multicultural Anthology*, ed. Estelle Disch (Mountain View, Calif.: Mayfield Publishing Co., 1997), 175–76.

42. Ibid., 14.

43. Maria Lugones, "On the Logic of Pluralist Feminism," in *Feminist Ethics*, ed. Claudia Card (Lawrence: University of Kansas Press, 1991), 41–42.

44. Ibid., 14.

45. The elaboration of the first three elements is based on those (more than three) identified in Personal Narratives Groups, *Interpreting Women's Lives*, 20–23. We gained further insight into these first three elements from reading Ricoeur, *Ricoeur Reader*, 425–37.

46. Personal Narratives Groups, *Interpreting Women's Lives*, 20.

47. Susan E. Keefe and Amado Padilla, *Chicano Ethnicity* (Albuquerque: University of New Mexico Press, 1987), 191.

48. Ibid., 195.

49. Ibid., 15.

50. Ibid., 18.

51. Isasi-Díaz, *Mujerista Theology*, 64–66.

52. Ibid., 22–23.

53. See Marjorie Mbilinyi, " 'I'd Have Been a Man': Politics and the Labor Process in Producing Personal Narratives," in Personal Narrative Groups, *Interpreting Women's Lives*, 204–27.

54. See David T. Abalos, *Strategies of Transformation toward a Multicultural Society* (Westport, Conn.: Praeger, 1996), 7–19. Abalos's work gives great importance to stories, though he relies on literary fiction and uses as his lens, almost exclusively, the theory of transformation developed by Manfred Halpern.

55. Ibid., 30. Our educational/research project was not set up to organize the women for action. Several of the groups wanted to find ways to keep meeting, and at least three of the groups are ongoing groups that we hope will factor the experience of the meeting in which material was gathered for this chapter into their future projects.

56. Richardson, "Narrative and Sociology," 128. Richardson talks about "same experience" instead of "shared experience." See also Nelson, "Resistance and Insubordination," 23–40.

57. This is what Michel Foucault called a discursive field. I am indebted here to the presentation of his ideas in Chris Weedon, *Feminist Practice and Poststructuralist Theory* (Cambridge, Mass.: Blackwell, 1987), 35–42, 107–35.

58. Ibid., 41.

59. Ibid. I am not saying that it is only in language that subjectivity and consciousness are socially produced.

"We Don't See Color Here"

A Case Study in Ecclesial-Cultural Invention

Mary McClintock Fulkerson

A white member of an interracial church describes what is unique about his congregation, Good Samaritan United Methodist Church, with the claim, "We don't see color here." At its high point, Good Samaritan was remarkably diverse, with one-third of its membership African American, one-third African and Latino, and one-third Anglo-American. However, "we don't see color" is a rather ambiguous phrase, regardless of what Ray, the speaker, had in mind. While it *may* indicate that the kingdom has come at Good Samaritan, this expression has historically functioned to avert issues of racism and power.[1] The claim to color blindness appears accepting of the other, but may actually be a "strategy of condescension."[2] Such condescension is otherwise known as tolerance, a problematic form of inclusion for the reason that the one who is tolerant has the power to position the other in his or her sphere of influence within specific limits that he or she sets for the other. In Good Samaritan's case, Ray can fill the position of the tolerant and powerful because he has never had to see color for his own survival.

I put forward the story of a community characterized not only by diversity but also by the ambiguity of possible racial condescension in order to help think about a more abstract but fundamentally related issue, a theological account of identity. To characterize the distinctive

Christian identity of such a community, we need to be able to account for the complexities of such intentionally reconciliatory, but power-laden, practices as signaled by Ray's comment. To further complicate matters, the elements of a church's identity come from a variety of sources—regional, ethnic, national, secular, and religious. If we are to do justice to the complexities of the community, more is needed than the typical theological terms for distinguishing normative Christian identity. In too many conservative theologies, the term "culture" stands for something that is totally negative, that is outside the Christian community. In the case of postliberal theologies, culture refers to an impermeable system of meaning, a "Christian culture" set over against the negative culture of the "outside." Neither can accommodate the ambiguities of Ray's comment. We need an account of the relationship of theological assessments and culture that is capable of adequately portraying the ambiguous and liberatory aspects of this community.

In this essay, I will look at the language and practices of Good Samaritan United Methodist Church in order to begin to develop a theological account of Christian identity adequate to the task. "Christian identity" refers to at least three different concerns: (1) what holds a community together internally, (2) how it is distinctive from an "outside," and (3) what about it is in continuity with the Christian tradition.[3] This exploration will confine itself to an account of Christian identity in the second sense. Certain postmodern anthropological views appear more fully to evaluate the salient features of this identity than either the notion that an outside culture is a threat to Christian faith or that there might be a Christian cultural practice that is distinctive and self-originating. These postmodern views complicate identity by refusing strict discursive boundaries between theological and cultural signifiers. I conclude that identity is best described as emergent and transient rather than a result of a fixed consensus of belief or doctrine, and that the continuity of a community is best located in a (temporary) bodily *habitus*, clarified in critical events in a community's life. A look at one such event in Good Samaritan's life locates an identity of resistance, which may potentially counter the problematic aspects of the "we don't see color" remark. I offer it as an antidote to tolerance as condescension, which ignores the deep accumulated effects of racism so that white people get the advantages of proximity and of distance without actually changing anything.[4] This proposal is offered as part of a larger project of full normative assessment of Christian identity.[5]

A Brief Description of Good Samaritan

Dan, a white, middle-aged southern pastor, resurrected Good Samaritan United Methodist Church from a dying white Protestant church in an integrated working-class area of a midsize southern city.[6] Dan revitalized this community through a vision of its mission that first emerged in a Bible study of Acts 8, the story of the Ethiopian eunuch. Interpreting this story as a call to "go and find people who are different from us—the overlooked, the looked-over, and passed-over," the group reached out to African American and international people in the surrounding community. By 1996, there were 146 congregants on the roll, reflecting much diversity (i.e., a number of Liberian, Korean, and Latin American families, with a few mixed marriages). In February 1989, the community decided that "folks who are different from us" should include special needs people from nearby group homes. Good Samaritan began special services for a regular group of persons with moderate to severe handicapping conditions and also included them in its regular Sunday service.

This diverse group of Christians is always in debt. The church meets in a converted garage in one of the less fashionable places in town. (The per capita income in 1989 in the town was $13,376 for whites and $9,135 for African Americans.) Members of Good Samaritan include truck drivers, a letter carrier, pest control workers, elementary school teachers, clerical workers, and students. A few are on welfare, and a couple are university professors. The average income of church members about three years ago was $28,334.

Dan is assisted by his wife, Linda, a diaconal minister. Both are former Baptists with similar working-class backgrounds. Both have worked as social workers and counselors. Their style is intensely personal and folksy. Blacks and whites alike speak of their warmth and concern for members as individuals. Many say they joined precisely because of personal contacts from the ministers. The atmosphere of the worship services is highly informal, personal, and full of energy and movement. The services begin with conversations Dan initiates with the community, interspersed with self-deprecating remarks, jovial interchanges, and teasing. Linda takes this dialogical transition from ordinary time to sacred time to a more formal level with the singing of praise songs, accompanied by guitar. Africans and African Americans sway to the guitar and piano music; blacks and whites alike raise their arms during parts of the service. People following what some call "African time" come late consistently. Children wander around. Special needs folks cry out at all points in the service, sometimes laughing, sometimes yelling, as well as clapping and moving to their own rhythms.

Three topics reappear in Dan's services and give interpretive focus to the pleasurable physical experience that is worship. First is the celebration of the diversity of the community, which is never allowed to forget that its multihued nature reflects the kingdom of God. Paired with this affirmation is the second theme that "nothing is *our* doing; all the glory must go to God." A third, much repeated topic is God's care for the common person, the person without wealth or status or book learning. A kind of "redneck poetics" celebrating ordinary folks dominates the ministers' preaching and teaching.

Members' descriptions of the identity of the church center on its "difference." In a variety of ways, people identify what is special about Good Samaritan in terms of the way people of different races and nationalities are welcomed there. The language of inclusiveness is common, but also the appeal to a kind of self-evident logic: That is what the church should look like, they say. In addition, people tell a variety of stories about what attracted them to the church. A white professor who describes herself as a Marxist Christian with a southern Protestant background says the draw for her is the racial mix and the sense that the church is welcoming and nonjudgmental. A minimally employed African American woman credits Dan with creating a loving family. The convergence of freedom of movement, noise, and controlled chaos is key for several. A couple of African American women say it is the fact that their constantly moving autistic children are welcome in the space-time of worship that makes them stay.

There are strong webs of connection and accountability in the community; these seem to emerge from shared knowledge about hard times rather than shared doctrine. In response to a financial crisis for a woman on welfare, a collection is taken up. A member with cancer who cannot afford treatment also gets a collection. A young woman who makes foolish moves and loses her possessions gets a surprise house shower. A Ugandan woman stranded outside of the United States when her visa is stolen gets collections and prayer chains. The Africans and African Americans have extended families that draw them in and out of the community in noticeable ways. People keep up with one another's crises.

The situation is far from perfect, however, and the communal fabric is threaded through with lines of conflict and complaint. Some people with an intellectual bent (the idealistic students) leave because of Dan's Southern Baptist style. Dan says conflict is dealt with at a special worship time called "table-topping." Yet in my interviews, I hear conflict pass around as gossip that never reaches the public forum. Some white people worry among themselves that the church might get "too black." A social work student sees hierarchies and paternalism in the treatment of special needs people. Some like the altar call at the end of the service; some hate it. One African is known by other persons of color to be the kind of black who is an "Uncle Tom" in relation to the white members. There is mention of racism in my interviews with Africans and African Americans (moderated for my whiteness, to be sure), but rare mention of racism from the white members. A number of whites left at the earlier rejuvenation of the church. When in 1996 the bishop suddenly moved Dan to another church and replaced him with a man of color, a Bahamian, some feared the move would precipitate another white flight by many members.

The Hybrid Culture of Good Samaritan

How could an identity be adduced from the swirl of meaning and activity that is Good Samaritan? It would be difficult to pull out a stratum of controlling beliefs, a grammar, or even to attribute causality to ritual in order to catch up and unify what goes on there. Nor can the cultural elements in this mix be separated easily from the theological or faith elements. My first point about the nature of culture is that anything one might identify as traditionally Christian culture is best described as cobbled out of multiple worlds of discourse. It is a graft or hybrid—a mix of discourses, a new constellation of meaning.[7]

For example, some elements of the discourse of democratic liberalism, particularly that associated with the civic virtue of tolerance, repeatedly appear along with biblical references to God's love for all people as a way to talk about issues of race and difference. In part, the former is the discourse of official United Methodist programs, where inclusivity, discrimination, and representation figure. However, liberal discourses of "inclusive" community and its opposite, "exclusions," are like mantras that seem to have an unofficial status as the normative language of the church.

Therapeutic terms like "acceptance" also fill the brochures—"Whatever our color or background we feel immediately accepted here"—as they tell the stories of members joining the church. The search for real, true selves and Christian lives frequently frames sermon narratives, as does a regular admonition to honesty. While much of this discourse is biblical, it is grafted to more contemporary ideas of human potential or authenticity discourse. When such a classic virtue as the admonition to honesty is framed in terms of conflict resolution, particularly in the occasional ritual of table-topping, where the hidden conflicts and concerns lurking in the church are to be aired and resolved in public space, authenticity discourse takes on a contemporary resonance. These examples of combined regions of meaning—"hybrid" mixed discourse—exemplify the sense in which the theological and cultural are inseparable.

Considering the international makeup of the community further clarifies this judgment. With the arrival of Gerald Gray, the new minister, the popular culture of the Bahamas appears in the worship of Good Samaritan, as sermon illustrations draw on the wisdom of his home country. Such striking expressions of Bahamian corporateness as "all a we" have not become the language of the community, but they do add another set of associations to its cultural tool kit, a kit already lined with other international associations. Even between folks who look "the same color" from a white perspective, there are differences. For example, African Americans from Baptist backgrounds know that Liberian worship practices are different—the length of service, loudness of response, and kinds of prayers. Racial binaries (black and white) do not work here. In fact, the fragments of explicit identity discourse would disappoint a search for anything like a discrete or autonomous "black culture."

This hybridity, or graft of "Christian talk" with "worldly talk," would not be an issue in the theologian's search for a critical account of Christian identity, of course, if a controlling biblical or theological narrative or symbol system could be identified, thereby demoting the other realms of discourse to the status of secondary purgeable accretions. However, such is not the case. The church's self-definition as inclusive and multicultural is laced with terms from democratic liberal and therapeutic discourses. Moreover, its discursive trains of thought are not only *borrowed* from other communities; they trail or wander off into other realms of discourse, bringing other sometimes necessary associations with them. There is no clear direction of influence here; one cannot simply excise the borrowed associations because one thinks them corrosive of the Christian message. The full resonances of "inclusion as an equal" have particular importance for a recent escapee of Liberian political violence in this ecclesial space, for example, and do not inhibit her ability to say the confession of sin.

Hybridity does not translate into formlessness, however. The folks in the community know who they are and who belongs; they produce and practice a transformative identity. Let me suggest a way of identifying the ordering of hybrid discourses with a story about Kitty, a powerful woman who, with her family, had recently left the church over the United Methodist position on gay, lesbian, and bisexual people. The stated reason for leaving was her discovery that, although they may not be ordained, the United Methodist Church affirms these persons' sacred worth—a position Kitty and her family found unbiblical. In the attempt to make sense of this sudden departure, a group of United Methodist Women employed the language of "personal" and "private" to make an argument for the acceptance of gay and lesbian people in the face of what was perceived to be Kitty's open-and-shut case about the Bible. Insisting that Jesus wants us to love all people, one woman dealt with the biblical difficulty by noting, "What they do in bed is private. It is a personal thing." If culture were normatively identified with Christian signs, this conversation would be a perfect example of the encroachment of the secular distortions of liberalism. In such a view, the terms "private" and "personal" would reproduce the public-private domain of liberalism, thus excluding parts of life from God's redemptive presence.

I suggest, however, that such hybrids as the grafting of liberal and Christian love discourses function as what sociologists call "switchers."[8] Rather than merge two discourses, a switcher creates associations between different discursive terrains included in the experiential knowledge of a community's participants. Rather than bring together competing associations in a manner that vitiates the meaning of one, however, switchers operate so that certain symbols dominate and others are "switched" over to do new work. In this case, the speakers wanted to say there is room in the church for gay people, yet they had no biblical evidence to combat Kitty's complaint that the Bible is against gays and lesbians. Thus, the language of "personal" and "private" does work that is important to the honoring of the parties involved, and, one could argue, is dominated by a ready-to-hand narrative of God's love of all persons into which the speakers were habituated through their life in the community. The suspect terms thereby do the opposite of the expected negative work of liberalism.

I offer these examples to contest the idea that theological and normative Christian identity requires discursive practice that is "pure" from accommodation with the languages and practices of nonbiblical or nontheological realms of experience. While one must favor some discursive practices over others, one cannot distinguish something called Christian culture from the non-Christian by virtue of its content or, by implication, its source (biblical, doctrinal). That means that the conservative and related theological notions that define something called culture (or

Christian discourse) as a fixed impermeable entity do not make sense either.[9]

Cultural anthropology and cultural studies confirm my reluctance to identify any set of signifiers as either usefully identified as operating independently or as themselves constitutive of the normative identity of Good Samaritan. They do so with ethnographic disciplines' well-developed critique of holisms. Cultural holism refers to the notion that cultures are cohesive wholes held together by shared beliefs, symbol systems, or rituals that have a unidirectional causal force. Reviewing the effects of postmodernism on modern constructive culture, Kathryn Tanner critiques dominant theological positions on the matter of holism. Notions that cultures are identical with social groups, that they are cohesive self-enclosed cells, that the unifying causal force in a community is commonly held beliefs, or that the activities of a culture are caused by inner core beliefs of its members—all these are undermined by the impact of postmodern thinking on cultural anthropology.[10]

More persuasive are proposals that culture is emergent and contested (James Clifford), or that it is a "tool kit" or repertoire (Ann Swidler) from which participants appropriate pieces for different lines of action rather than a purified system that itself directs action. Or, as Betsy Taylor puts it, culture is an emergent performance, a temporary production of a shared way to go that is always shifting and emerging from a bodied, interactive negotiation.[11]

However, these corrections for false unity and completeness in an account of a communal identity still leave the question of regularity. *Something* continues in a community, however transient it may be; something must account for the switching of regions of discourse. Current postliberal cultural-linguistic models for Christian community account for regularity with a notion of the theological grammar (the rules) that should be ordering the community.[12] Regulative grammar purportedly holds the community together internally, distinguishes it from outside, and links it to the past. Tanner refutes this decisively, but I want to show in terms of this community why such a notion is problematic. Regularities that occur are best described as the results of a generative *habitus*, the feel for the game that gets generated in a community, rather than as rules about Christology, soteriology, or anthropology that are applied correctly (or not) by Good Samaritan congregants.

People learn as bodies, from interactions with other persons, objects, and practices from which patterns of association are built up, as Bourdieu says. This building up of interactive patterns creates cultural expertise as a habitus, that is, "systems of durable, transposable dispositions, . . . principles of the generation and structuring of practices and representations which can be objectively 'regulated' and 'regular' without in any way being the product of obedience to rules."[13] The notion of habitus highlights two crucial points: the fact that our convictions have to be rooted in bodily practices and the fact that agency is inventive and creative. As the "generative capacities of dispositions," habitus is an internalized sense of what to do that results from accumulation of bodied knowledge in a particular social world. It enables the practitioner to make her way in a new situation. Think, for example, of good piano playing. It requires cognitive, theoretical knowledge—the ability to read musical scores—but is actual only as physical kinesthetic knowledge. I come to know the feel of the spacing of an arpeggio, of what the physical force of the terms "forte" or "pianissimo" is, of the connection between shoulder placement and the power needed for a stunning crescendo. As this knowledge is gained, I acquire a habitus. Expertise accumulates in my body from practicing hours and hours every day for years. The result for the good practitioner is creativity. A good pianist can read new music at first sight. Having acquired a skilled knowledge for playing, a good pianist can improvise—can do the "same" thing in new ways.

In light of the habitus as a bodied form of regularity, the notion that doctrinal grammar functions like a system of rules to direct proper agency in a community is unsatisfactory. As a solution to the identity question, it fails by confusing a set of principles, a scheme, that is "constructed in order to explain the practice after the fact with a generative scheme functioning in a practical situation."[14] However it is that the resources of the Christian tradition are appropriate and necessary to the life and identity of a community, it is surely not by functioning in the unilateral way implied by the grammar image, either to hold the community together or to distinguish it from its "outside."

The strongest case for locating regularity in bodied habituation is the importance to racial reconciliation of the positioning of bodies in the formation of knowledge. The notion of habitus allows for the importance of the interaction of differently "raced" and abled bodies in the formation of Good Samaritan's congregants. For example, Good Samaritan's children are habituated in multiracial groups; white children experience African American children as the "experts" on certain topics (from common knowledges to specific ethnic knowledges, such as Kwanza) and all grow up experiencing bodies of many colors and degrees of able-bodiedness as "normal" in forming habits of mutual respect. The "we" of African American children in this community is complicated by a relation to African children. The "we" of the white children is more complex when they learn Bible stories about welcoming the stranger in a peer group that includes many faces that the larger society names "outsider."

In sum, it makes more sense to think of regularity as occurring in the form of a disposition, internalized as emotively oriented mental schemes that emerge as bodily learnings instead of shared beliefs/ideas or a system of "abstract principles" or rules that order Christian belief and behavior.[15] This is not to say that stories and language are not essential to interpret and reproduce certain dispositions. It is to say that to say and believe that we are a community that welcomes the stranger is not enough; it must be rooted in a feel for the other—the face-to-face bodied relation to the other in habitual situations of reciprocity.

For the final element in this proposal of an ecclesial identity, defined as the way in which a community is distinct from its outside, we require some source for the languages and stories that crystallize and interpret the knowledge of a habitus. I have preferred to think of culture as emergent, contested negotiating practices that are regularized as habituation, in tune with postmodern anthropologists. However, there is still the question of where to find the congealing of these processes of identity formation. Postmodern Indian anthropologist Veena Das argues that certain "critical events" in the making of a society or community provide the privileged locus for this. Critical events are ones that issue in "new modes of action . . . which redefine traditional categories" in a particular culture.[16] By surfacing the valued and "unsaid" in a community, Das's approach allows one to recognize the temporal and unstable nature of communities and societies, but also to glimpse something distinctive that congeals, even if only momentarily, into a set of commitments or character. Such an account of identity honors the changeable and ambiguous as well as the cumulative and constructive work of communities.

Critical Events in the Life of Good Samaritan

To account for Good Samaritan's distinctive identity, I will look at a couple of related critical events in its recent history. These events display what is most commendable in its Christian practice and thereby define what is critically or normatively Christian about it.

Most of the community's life has occurred under the pastorate of Dan and his wife Linda. However, in 1996, the bishop suddenly moved Dan to another church and brought in Gerald Gray, the man of color from the Bahamas, in his place. With the arrival of Gray a whole new

chapter began in the life of Good Samaritan. Coming from a more educated and statused family than the previous minister, Gerald not only
represented a new race in the leadership of the church, but be brought
a new style and new realms of discourse.

If one of the reasons to reject holism in a community is the presence
of dissent, the events following Gerald's arrival provide ample illustration, beginning with a wave of departures. Movement of folks because
of the pastor is nothing new at Good Samaritan. A group of white
members left in the first three years of the church over the changing
hue of the community and the pastor's obvious pleasure in it. Some
white university students who replaced them, drawn to Good Samaritan's racial mix, disappeared later because they were put off by Dan's
style. When word of Gerald's more "intellectual" discourse and formal
liturgical style got out, many of the students returned. However, I was
told that some people of color expect more white departures. Several of
the departures that occured in 1996 do not seem directly related to the
color of the new pastor. I return to the story of Kitty to explain.

Thinking that the community is well served by habituation into its
Wesleyan tradition, Gerald begins teaching a class on the Methodist
Social Principles. In a Sunday morning discussion, a white university
professor asks about the possibility of bringing her daughter's friend
to church along with her lesbian parents. The discussion turns to the
position of the United Methodist Church on homosexuality. Although
the church will not ordain gay, lesbian, or bisexual persons, Gerald
says, it is welcoming of all persons, regardless of sexual preference.
Kitty, a white woman formerly of the Church of the Nazarene, is
quite distressed over this. The following week she brings her Latino
husband and her children to the class. Armed with Bibles, they all express dismay at the United Methodist position. In a very short time
Kitty's family decides to leave the church, explaining to Gerald and
others that they cannot stay in a church with such a nonbiblical position, that is, a church that might welcome gay, lesbian, and bisexual
persons.

Soon afterward, an older white couple with a conservative background tells Gerald that, although they love the church, they are also
troubled by this position. After several conversations with Gerald they
leave the church, taking their adult daughter with them. Not long afterward, a white couple expecting twins tells Gerald that the 45-minute
drive to church is too long for them. Finally, a family of color leaves—a
conservative African American man and his Liberian wife.

While the reasons behind these departures are surely complex, the
apparent exodus contributes to a critical event of self-interpretation.

Several discussions of the departures occur, but one dialogue in particular stands out. At a Saturday planning retreat on the church's mission,
a most passionate discussion takes place on the nature of the church.
As such, it fits Das's notion of an event that makes new modes of action
possible. The community's self-understanding as inclusive and multicultural is at stake. Good Samaritan is a place where, as Brenda says,
"you are loved for who you are, not for your status or color." Having
been shaken by these departures, the community must rethink this self-
understanding.

Church Planning Retreat

There are seventeen folks at the planning retreat. It starts late, about
9:40, and is scheduled to go until noon. Present are Ray and his wife,
Wanda, two white graduate students (one at the center of the church's
life), two white divinity students, an African American graduate student, three Liberian members (Tarley, Aggie, and Lila), a Kenyan member (John), the first African American couple in the church (Sophie and
Ben), a single African American woman (Brenda), and Gerald and his
wife. After the typical joking and visiting that start up any Good Samaritan event, Gerald leads a meditation on Acts 1:1–8, a story of the
commissioning of disciples. Comparing the mission of the community
to throwing pebbles into a pond—the ripples imaging the purpose of
the church to go out to the world—he says that mission is to the Sa-
maritans, those considered "not like us," the different, the "least lovely."
Gerald then asks about a mission statement. A couple of folks venture
hesitantly, "We had one. . . ."

GERALD: But if you don't know it, then it isn't doing anything.
How about this: "We are diverse yet united disciples of Jesus Christ,
who are called to be faithful NOW (through Nurture, Outreach, and
Witness)." What do you think?

SOPHIE: In the mission statement before, a really important word
to me was "inclusive"—that we're different from other churches because of that. In other churches you get together because you're the
same economic level and for being comfortable, but I'm not to be comfortable in the church. I don't want this church to be like other
churches [nods of agreement].

BRENDA: Yes, the church has got to be where our comfort zone
is challenged. [A discussion follows where several—black and white—
craft the definition, being clear that just inclusivity is not the point. The
point is being faithful to God, and inclusivity comes with that.]

SOPHIE: I remember that we started out with Dan. First there were whites, and black people came and that was fine.

JOHN: [interrupts] FINE??!! [Laughter follows. "And a lot of white people left," someone continues.]

TARLEY: We have always said that we were inclusive, but I want to know what that *means*! Some things have been happening here. . . . [It is as if a dam has burst. Pent-up feelings come tumbling out from everyone, but mostly the people of color. The discussion turns to Kitty, her family and their leaving.]

SOPHIE: I am supposed to accept other people for who they are, sexual orientation or whatever. We are all the same and I'm not supposed to judge. If a homosexual person comes, I accept them; only later in the community I may show Scripture to them or they might come to know that something isn't God's will for their life, but we all have sins and it's not true that one is greater than the other.

BEN: [passionately] People—just as they are off the street—are supposed to be included. The bottom line is that Jesus never turned anyone away [nods all around]. Only God can judge.

SOMEONE: We have to reeducate people on what "inclusive" means.

GERALD: What is the common denominator to being included? Being human?

AGGIE: It's just being willing to work on your spiritual life. We all have sins and need to work on our relationship with God. That's all you have to have to be here.

TARLEY: I want to know about the Liberian minister who has two wives. What if he comes here? How will people react? Will he be included? In Liberia this is the custom. Is that what inclusiveness means?

SOPHIE: The question is whether it is of God.

ROB [white, gay divinity student, not "out" here]:   But it's important that people interpret what it means whether something is "of God," and Scripture is interpreted differently by different people. So the important thing is that we get together and struggle together over our different understandings of Scripture. [Several make statements of agreement: It's important to talk to each other, to tell each other our disagreements.]

GERALD: Yes, the Matthew 17 passage is very important here. When someone sins against his brother, the Christian is supposed to go to him.

JOHN: I have always worried that this was just a game, it wasn't real. Please, when I am doing something you think is wrong, you must tell me! How else will I know? [Goes on to repeat the feeling of anger at people for leaving without being honest with the rest of the community.]

SOPHIE: Regardless of who comes, I'm supposed to see that person with hope. There is hope that God will change them. The church is the place we all start—you come in just as you are, but you may not leave the same.

OTHERS: Yes!

TARLEY: Now we know what inclusiveness is, but we haven't even had any homosexuals.

SEVERAL OTHERS: Oh, yes, we did when Dan was here. There was a lesbian couple and people knew it. The problems for those people who left were always here. They just didn't bring it up before.

SOMEONE: Dan kept the peace. [Ray and Wanda agree.]

SOPHIE: Yes, Dan had a way of listening to people, and I could always tell when he disagreed. They would go on and on and say what they thought, and he would nod and say "uh-huh," but he kept the peace. They always thought he was agreeing with them when he wasn't.

SOMEONE: So homosexuality never got talked about?

OTHERS: No.

AGGIE: [angry] How can people feel this way and never discuss their differences?! I'm coming to distrust people who quote Scripture about things! [laughter]

SOMEONE: It is different with Gerald, because he is so direct.

The concluding words of the mission statement are "faithful and inclusive."[17]

Faithful Inclusiveness as Identity

There is no finish to this process of self-definition. However, if culture is emergent, negotiated, and partial, rather than unified, complete, and uncontested, then this "significant event" is a negotiation of a theological definition of inclusivity that qualifies as a temporary stabilization of identity. In this public act of self-definition, an ideal of reciprocity is being named and reiterated in smaller meetings and other discussions. It has been produced out of the many kinds of performances and ways of being embodied together that have given this group an intersecting set of dispositions. It is not reducible to a set of ideas or a pure realm of discourses. However, the forging of images, stories, and definitions in this gathering is crucial for its solidification.

Good Samaritan understands faithful inclusivity as follows: it is patterned after Jesus; anyone off the street should feel welcome; it involves loving acceptance of people for who they are; it attracts people; it is not the only purpose of the church; it is enabled by God; it requires reassessment again and again; it is not having no standards; it should unsettle the comfort zone of folks; it involves honesty; it is not continuing to be who you are; it involves transformation of sin, but no sin in particular. Some pieces are still not resolved: Will the Liberian polygamist be accepted? Will whites ever wonder why no one openly complained about the church being "too white" under Dan? Despite its open-endedness, a recognizable frame emerges from the group with which to flesh out what "faithful" adds to inclusive, a frame with which they can improvise in future situations.

In Betsy Taylor's terms, Good Samaritan's culture is an emergent performance, a temporary production of a shared way to go that is shifting and emerging from a bodied, interactive negotiation. In such a view, the way in which its members are others to one another in their various social identities in the United States is the necessary condition for the emergence of its "culture." The fact that they are of differently ascribed races (and able-bodiedness and sexualities) suggests that the heartbeat of this identity is the negotiation of social boundaries as a new way to be in relation and to define the human. This identity is invented out of languages that are borrowed from a number of the typical realms of discourse that circulate at Good Samaritan. Its "glue" is precisely the generative, creative power of a habitus; no doctrinal consensus could account for the knowledge displayed in the habitus of faithful inclusiveness.

The power of its logic can be seen in Sophie's discourse. Raised in a conservative black Baptist tradition (which taught her that homosexuality is a sin), Sophie has acquired dispositions related to being an outsider that enable her to extend the logic of welcome to a new situation (even though she intends to bring those she welcomes to another understanding). Shared belief in the principle of caring for all people or the "oppressed" does not create a "we" that honors difference in this significant and creative form. I am arguing that a feel for the other gained in the face-to-face relation to the other is crucial. Discourse of care for the stranger in habitual situations of reciprocity is essential to Sophie's habituation into this interpretive stance toward what is, for her, a new other. In her discussion of gay and lesbian persons, she displays what Bourdieu calls regulated improvisation, even if this new habit has not yet developed into a major challenge to tolerance.[18]

I have argued for the categories of postmodern anthropology on the basis of their capacity to display the character of Good Samaritan as both ambiguous and emancipatory. I find that the categories of emergent hybrid culture and the location of regularity in the bodied habitus are simply more adequate to display what is going on and what is important in a community. They open to view the conflicting, ambiguous, and messy character of human communities, and potentially honor the full-bodied way the gospel and sinful distortion are found in them. These categories disallow what we do not experience anyway—the positing of "pure" discourses or realms of experience that are free from other worlds of meaning and their mechanisms of power. Yet they also allow for recognition of continuities and emancipatory movement as that happens in communities. The category of regulated improvisation offers a way to think about the form Christian life takes when it resists sinful arrangements such as racism and the dishonoring of the *imago Dei* of the human family. Whether this habitus of faithful inclusivity deserves to be commended as *the* Christian identity of the community is a question requiring more discussion than can happen here—discussion about its relation to the larger social formations in which it is embedded and its continuity with Christian origins and with the larger tradition.

I close by indicating how "faithful inclusiveness" could be judged theologically in a preliminary way as a normative display of identity. I assess its normative possibilities in its potential as an alternative to toleration and its maintenance of asymmetrical relationships. Admittedly, addressing the power structures of racism and heterosexism in the community is unfinished; the "not seeing" of the privilege of whiteness and heterosexuality are signs of that. However, the features that distinguish the community's commitments from the strategies of condescension are several. First, the "we" of the community, in contrast to the power-based positioning that comes with strategies of condescension, is permeable, open to new strangers and new forms of accountability. Boundaries are being negotiated in this discussion and others in order to ascribe reciprocal regard and recognition that are not based on the socio-economic, racialized structures of the larger society. As Ben put it, "Jesus never turned anyone away." The only requirement for belonging is being willing to work on your spiritual life. Second, discomfort is normative for *everyone*; faithful inclusiveness requires self-transformation and confession of every member of the community and that it not be simply private. Third, the habitus of faithful inclusiveness is an implicit denunciation of the dynamics of tolerance insofar as it includes the requirement that each member be challenged by and accountable to the other.

I offer two conclusions. First, while not enough to dislodge the power to position the other that comes with tolerance, the distinctive way that faithful inclusiveness honors the *imago Dei* of all persons is an important element in the creation of an alternative. Insofar as this faithful inclusiveness is a tradition-formed, hybrid reciprocity that happens between persons with differently marked bodies and statuses, it has opened up a space for a "we" that refuses the sin of racism. It is not a completed project, but it is an honoring that matters. As the embodiment of the honoring of "those who are not like us," as Dan put it, this hybrid identity could foster new improvisational practices that mark the redeeming of more of God's creation. Second, I have also argued that this identity (the distinctive way they "don't see color" only appears when we open up the category of theological discourse to discern Christian identity as this complex set of meanings and bodied practices) is always coconstituted by the cultures of the context. Faithful inclusion is what distinguishes this community from its "outside," but it is a way of using that culture, not of avoiding it or denying its presence. That, to me, also honors God's creation and is the sense in which "we don't see color here" honors the *imago Dei* of all persons.

Notes

1. See Ruth Frankenberg, *The Social Construction of Whiteness: White Women, Race Matters* (Minneapolis: University of Minnesota Press, 1993).

2. Ghassan Hage, "Locating Multiculturalism's Other: A Critique of Practical Tolerance," *New Formations* 24 (1994): 30.

3. See Kathryn Tanner, *Theories of Culture: A New Agenda for Theology* (Minneapolis: Fortress Press, 1997): 61–96.

4. Pierre Bourdieu, *In Other Words* (Oxford: Polity Press, 1990), 127–28.

5. The larger project includes the other aspects of identity in the three that Tanner names. As only an element of the distinctiveness of Christian community from its "outside," this account requires additional consideration of the way this practice is embedded in and interactive with the larger social formation.

6. What follows draws from two years of interviewing and observing participants at the church.

7. I use the term "hybrid" in its most uncomplicated sense. For more complex accounts, see the work of Homi Bhabha, Trinh T. Minh-ha, and Robert Young.

8. The term is from Pierre Bourdieu, *Outline of a Theory of Practice*, trans. Richard Nice (Cambridge: Cambridge University Press, 1997), 114–30. Catherine Bell explains it in *Ritual Theory, Ritual Practice* (New York: Oxford University Press, 1992), 103–4. Some forms of opposition between realms

of discourse tend to act as "switchers" to establish relationships between various homologized activities. Inside/outside serves to link behind/in-front with female fertility/male virility connected with body and ritual. Thus, the argument would be that private/personal does not bring the entire baggage of liberalism when used this way; the combination of discourses simply function to let the major point or symbol—the full dignity of all persons in God's sight—be enacted. While switchers work to create certain kinds of fictive "wholes" and connections with the ritual-shifts that allow certain symbols to dominate, it seems to me a useful pursuit to see how for different social positions, different switchers and connections are operating. Thanks to Kelly Jarrett for calling this to my attention.

9. H. Richard Niebuhr's definition of culture as the worldview, beliefs, values, and practices of a society has been widely influential in supporting a distinction between Christ (or the idealized community) and culture. See H. Richard Niebuhr, *Christ and Culture* (New York: Harper & Row, 1951)), 32. See my essay criticizing three theological views, "Toward a Materialist Christian Social Criticism," in *Changing Conversations: Religious Reflection and Cultural Analysis*, ed. Dwight N. Hopkins and Sheila Greeve Davaney (New York: Routledge, 1996), 43–58.

10. Tanner, *Theories of Culture*, 38–58.

11. James Clifford, introduction to *Writing Culture: The Poetics of Politics and Ethnography* (Berkeley: University of California Press, 1986), 19; Ann Swidler, "Culture in Action, Symbols and Strategies," *American Sociological Review* 51, no.2 (April 1986): 277; Betsy Taylor, conversations with the author.

12. The best known is George A. Lindbeck, *The Nature of Doctrine: Religion and Theology in a Postliberal Age* (Philadelphia: Westminster, 1984).

13. Bourdieu, *Outline of a Theory*, 72, 82–83. This regularity is similar to Wittgenstein's notion of grammar as "knowing how to get on." Lindbeck, whose Saussurean examples make him sound like a structuralist, does not seem to use the concept of grammar that way.

14. Bourdieu, *In Other Words*, 67.

15. Bourdieu, *Outline of a Theory*, 10–15.

16. Veena Das, *Critical Events: An Anthropological Perspective on Contemporary India* (New York: Oxford University Press, 1995), 5–6.

17. I witnessed similar conversations on a smaller scale at United Methodist Women's meetings. These are gatherings of women who are core members of the community. The group discussed the events at several meetings, for Kitty had been their chair. A few expressed similar feelings of betrayal, but also concern for Kitty and her family. These were difficult conversations; some tried to figure out how they could still care for her and affirm the acceptance of gay people. They contributed to a process of clarification and solidification of the community.

18. Bourdieu, *Outline of a Theory*, 11.

Cultural Labor and Theological Critique

Serene Jones

In this chapter, I offer descriptions of two contexts within which I have used cultural theory as a companion to my work as a Christian theologian with Reformed and feminist sensibilities. The first finds its setting in the protracted struggle of three unions at Yale University to secure a contract to address the issue of the "casualization of labor." The second is a course I coteach with Harlon Dalton at Yale Law School on "Identity and Power in Theology and Law." In both of these contexts, I have found that cultural theory has helped me think through the relationship between the political and the theological in interesting new ways. Before turning to these examples, however, I want to first offer a brief history of my travels through the world of theology and cultural theory—the story of "how I got here." I hope this short genealogy will explain what I am referring to when I use terms such as "cultural theory" and "cultural studies" in the pages ahead.

A Cultural Travel Log

I first encountered the term "cultural theory" used in a theological context while studying with George Lindbeck well over a decade ago. At the time, I was still whirling from the cultural disorientation occasioned by my return to North America after living in South India for a period of time. In this context, I found Lindbeck's "Geertzian" approach to doctrine appealing because it challenged a reductively propositional and philosophically analytical approach to theology by bringing into focus the broader web of beliefs, actions, and attitudes within which doctrines find their meaning.[1] Lindbeck's critique of "expressivist" views of doctrine created a space within which I was able to think constructively about the radical cultural differences I had encountered while living in a small, Christian village in India. In addition to its methodological embrace of cultural specificity and radical difference, I also appreciated Lindbeck's warnings concerning the totalizing force that philosophical analysis of experience can exert on theological discourse.

I also found, however, that while Lindbeck's approach made sense of the enormous cultural differences I had experienced in Asia, I was frustrated with his cultural linguistic framework at another level. Although Lindbeck was able to take into account the constitutive workings of language and culture in the field of doctrine, he gave no account of the other complex negotiations that occur simultaneously. Lindbeck's object of analysis seemed an isolated person of faith, living in an isolated ecclesial community, whose isolated confessional and liturgical actions unfolded in a world untouched by power relations and complex cultural forces (such as the class relations embedded in a capitalist market). He had no analysis of the multiple power relations that course through the language of doctrine, and he provided no conceptual apparatus for seeing faith traditions as linguistic contexts within which political subjects, national subjects, gendered subjects, ethnic subjects, and religious subjects are constructed and deployed.

At the same time my critique of this cultural-linguistic assessment of doctrine was developing, I was doing parallel work in the fields of feminist theory and Marxist social-cultural theory, both of which were deepening my appreciation for the relationship between language, power, and identity formation. Lukács and Adorno exposed the intertwining mechanisms of cultural representations and the capitalist commodity form,[2] Gramsci pulled these mechanisms onto a terrain where political and economic battles took the form of cultural wars,[3] Foucault provided a rather unruly set of insights into the ways academic knowledges are inextricably implicated in such "wars,"[4] and Irigaray raised the specter of gender, that hidden subtext which, she argues, undergirds not only specific forms of discourse but discourse itself.[5] Although none of these critical theorists understood themselves to be cultural critics or even cultural theorists as we now use the term (they were more interested in constructing strategies of resistance appropriate to particular political struggles), they raised questions about representation that I felt Lindbeck's cultural-linguistic model could not ignore.

This material was not without its own limits, however, particularly with regard to its applicability in the field of constructive liberation and feminist theology. Not only did theological questions seldom arise in the works of these theorists (Irigaray is the exception here), but their conceptual apparatus also seemed ill equipped to handle normative questions—and doing theology, I believe, requires one not to be afraid of such questions. I felt this limitation at two levels. First, and most important, as a theologian who recognizes the normative function of doctrine, I was frustrated not by the relativism of these theorists (for it was clear that they were far too leftist to be cast as relativistic anarchists) but by their refusal to theorize the normative grounds upon which they stood when they resisted the pull of relativism. In other words, although I found that these theorists all engaged in the project of normative reflection, they seemed ill at ease in this world, and were thus of little use in helping me, as a theologian, think about the logic of foundational commitments.

Second, because of my involvement in ongoing local organizing work, I became increasingly convinced that while this kind of cultural theorizing provides useful descriptive accounts of given political situations, it could not provide political struggles with what they continue to need most desperately—an eschatological (normative) vision. To use a Gramscian metaphor, these theorists were good at analyzing the structure of the battlefield upon which liberation struggles were to occur. Similarly, they were able to provide the struggle with a strategic plan of attack. However, what they could not do was "rally the troops." To use another image that is popular in the union movement, these cultural theorists were good-hearted activists but not well-seasoned community organizers. Activists typically make strategic interventions based on the logic of critique, whereas local community organizers attempt to build enduring institutional networks that can mobilize groups of persons around a common vision of emancipatory change—and to do this, they must step into the arena of normative claims.

Given these limitations, I found myself in an awkward position with respect to cultural theory. On the one hand, in the Lindbeckian conversation, I found a model of theology that took culture seriously in its analysis of doctrine but refused to theorize power. On the other hand, in the cultural theory/poststructuralist conversation, I found theorists who were able to trace the complex workings of power relations but were unable to generate (much less even discuss) normative visions. Standing between these two moments, which I called "a rock" and a "hard place" in an earlier work, the challenge of negotiating the gap between them loomed large.[6]

At this point in my travels through the world of cultural theory and theology, John Calvin entered the conversation and, quite to my surprise, provided me with the model of doctrine that held these two moments together.[7] At the level of concrete social practice, Calvin was a lawyer-theologian whose acute ability to read culture and strategically analyze politics made him one of sixteenth-century Europe's most powerful political leaders. Correlatively, his deep belief in and facility for articulating a normative theological vision enabled him to engage in battles of cultural contestation that far surpassed those imagined by Gramsci. Thus, when it came to social practice, he seemed to negotiate well the gap between cultural criticism and normative theological intervention. Part of his ability to do so, I believe, was rooted in his lively understanding of the rhetorical character of theological language.[8] Drawing on Cicero's classical understanding of rhetoric as the art of political persuasion, Calvin gives us a model of doctrine that quite self-consciously holds together an analysis of power relations and language with a commitment to articulating normative truth claims.

Let me pause here and say a few words about Cicero's view of rhetoric, because in my own theological work, I continue to find rhetorical analysis a useful lens for thinking through the relationship between culture, power, language, and doctrine.[9] Put in the simplest terms possible, Calvin's "Ciceronian" understanding of theology as rhetoric was driven by the following insights: Language does things to people—it persuades them, and shapes them. In doing so, language creates and mediates relations of power; it can tear down cities just as it can build up nations. In order to use language wisely and effectively, a rhetorician must be attentive to two things: The audience's needs and desires, and the goal she or he wants to accomplish through persuasive use of rhetoric. With these two things in mind, a good rhetorician crafts language designed to move the audience's "heart and mind" toward the "good" she or he has determined. According to Cicero, the tasks of crafting persuasive prose and the ability to discern a "good" goal should never be torn asunder, for "wisdom without eloquence does too little for the good of states; but eloquence without wisdom is generally highly disadvantageous and never helpful."[10] My contention, to paraphrase Cicero, is that normative vision without cultural theory does too little for the good of faith; but cultural theory without normative vision is highly disadvantageous and perhaps even dangerous. For this reason, the conversation between theology and cultural theory remains an interesting one. If one follows the insights of Cicero, they are necessarily companionable wisdoms.

Given this brief account of the conceptual underpinnings of classical rhetoric, let me make two additional comments about why I continue to find it a useful framework within which to analyze and construct theological doctrines. First, when one does rhetorical analysis, one is not committed to any particular set of analytic tools for assessing the character of one's audience and the shape of one's language. Many different analytic tools can be used, each of which will be ultimately judged by its answer to the pragmatic question, Does it work? Rhetorical analysis thus avoids the totalizing proclivities of some forms of cultural theory whose analytic categories threaten to colonize the substance of theological discourse. As such, rhetorical analysis allows theological discourse to maintain its own cultural integrity. Second, I have found that rhetorical analysis works well within a community organizing model of theology because rhetoric offers a kind of "how to" manual for crafting persuasive doctrine. It makes you think about your audience, its cultures and the relations of power that structure them; it makes you identify the political-theological vision that drives the discourse (its end); finally, it makes you quite self-conscious about the shape of the language, metaphors, and images that you deploy and the effect they will have in the communities where your language is received. In this regard, rhetorical analysis takes you through a series of steps that are finally quite different from the steps embedded in cultural theory. Rhetorical theory demands that the rhetoricians be up front about their normative, political-theological agendas, whereas for cultural theory, the normative moment can be avoided in the name of either descriptive, critical distance or a preference for methodological reflection.

Having traced my rambling journey through Lindbeck's land of doctrine, the terrain of critical social theory, and the historical world of Calvin and rhetoric, let me wind up this travel log with a few comments on where I find myself presently with respect to cultural theory and theology. In my present work, I am interested in doing constructive feminist theology that remaps classical Reformed doctrines using a language that engages present-day Reformed sensibility in a practically emancipatory manner. Cultural theory helps me do this at a number of levels. At the broadest level, it gives depth and substance to my analysis of classical articulations of these doctrines by contextualizing them (it helps me understand the historical force of doctrine). Then it helps me conceptualize the cultural force of my constructive proposals by focusing my attention on questions of present-day audience (it helps me think pragmatically about the social force of contemporary theological images). I should say, as well, that cultural theory also humbly reminds me that as author, one does not finally control the cultural/ political use to which one's work is put.

More specifically, cultural theory has served to focus my constructive theological attention on the question, How do specific theological images shape and get shaped by individual and communal identities and practices? Critical race theory, particularly in its "Birmingham School" form and its legal theory form, has pushed me to conceptualize the "self" (who is formed by doctrine) as a "hybrid"—not as a stable, static self, but as a site through which multiple cultural identities are coursing. Theorists from these same schools have also impressed upon me the value of using not only linguistic but also spatial and visual tropes for analyzing the force of these cultural coursings. Similarly, recent work by feminist cultural anthropologists has provided tools for analyzing the diverse forms that gender articulations may take. And both critical race theory and feminist cultural anthropology have nuanced my understanding of what constitutes an act of resistance and the character of change.[11]

I should say in concluding this travel log that as a conversation partner, cultural theory has inspired me to take more seriously the form-ing character of theological doctrine, not just at a methodological level but at the level of my own theological practice. It has inspired me to proceed with the creative task of actually crafting cultural artifacts, like doctrines, in new and imaginative ways. This means, for me, taking seriously the pragmatic ecclesial function of doctrine and the theologian's and the church community's ongoing role in its articulation.

Two Case Studies

Against the backdrop of this brief travel log, let me now describe two contexts in which I have been using cultural theory as a companion to theological reflection.

David and Goliath: A Labor Conflict

At the center of my first case study stands a full-page letter that appeared in the *New Haven Register* on December 4, 1996. Entitled "David and Goliath," the letter is an urgent call for the New Haven community to intervene in what had become stalemated negotiations between Yale University and its unions. The letter was signed by over a hundred local clergypersons from Christian, Jewish, and Islamic religious communities and from pastors whose backgrounds ranged from Irish Catholic to Puerto Rican Pentecostal. In the weeks before the letter appeared, it looked to the public as if the stalemate would most likely be broken by union concessions. Morale was low and people were weary from the year-long struggle. A week after this letter appeared, however, things shifted dramatically. The unions held a rally that over three thousand people attended on the Yale campus and at which over five hundred people were arrested for civil disobedience, among them at least seventy-five clergy. Three days after the arrests and ten days after the letter first appeared, the university's administration suddenly ended the stalemated negotiations by offering a contract proposal that the unions were happy to approve. The unions felt their struggle had been victorious. According to many accounts of these events, ranging from those in the *New York Times* to the *Christian Century*, it was the clergy letter that turned the tide in this protracted struggle. As a participant in these events, I found it helpful to use cultural theory (along with theological reflection) to understand the reasons why this letter seemed to accomplish this rather unexpected turn of events.

In order to describe how it helped, let me first offer some background. Yale has a long history of labor/management strife. In years past, it has been a litmus test for new unionizing strategies in the service sectors of North America, just as it has also been the symbolic beachhead that corporate America has been determined not to lose in their ongoing disputes with labor over new forms of work. The 1996 contract struggle was no different on both scores. The central issues for the unions were subcontracting and the casualization of the work force, both of which are issues that labor is wrestling with on a national scale. On the other side, management wanted to secure their ability to subcontract and to have the option of creating part-time positions with no benefits as a way of cutting labor costs. Management was quite aware that the unions would reject these proposals, and they had wisely put in place an administrative structure that could supposedly sustain the university in the event of a strike by the unions. The economy of New Haven was at a low, and replacement labor was easy to secure.

Given this situation, the unions had to think creatively about their tactics of resistance—they had to think beyond the model of traditional "strikes." What they came up with was a series of work stoppages: Local 34 would go out for three weeks and then return to work just in time for Local 35 to enact their own work stoppage for three weeks, and so forth. It took a great deal of coordinated effort to pull off this rather unusual strategy. This effort gave all of us involved a chance to experience—up close and personal—the challenges of a coalitional politics of difference because the three groups involved represented three very different cultures and, hence, three distinct community identities.

The oldest of the three is Local 35, composed of maintenance and dining hall workers. Its makeup is predominately African American and Latino men. It has been in existence since the early 1960s and has very traditional, old-style views about labor. At the core of its union identity are the issues of race and class. In negotiations, its representatives typically focus on economic issues (the bottom line), and in its strategies of resistance, 1960s-style civil rights actions predominate. Local 34, the union of clerical and technical workers (the largest of the three unions), was formed in the early 1980s and consists primarily of Euro-American and African American women, although the number of Latina workers is growing rapidly. This group was organized by the Hotel and Restaurant International as a vanguard model of service sector unions. Although the members of 34 are quite aware of class issues (the women in 34 originally made significantly less than the members of 35), their unionizing slogans have traditionally focused on the issue of respect. They identify strongly as a women's union, and thus gender plays a central role in their communal self-understanding. The third group is GESO (the Graduate Employees and Students Organization).[12] One of the first groups of graduate students to organize and press for recognition at a private university, GESO's membership is split about evenly between male and female students from middle- and upper-class backgrounds. The students are predominately white, although, historically, students of color have played a significant leadership role. Although class, race, and gender issues usually appear on their platform, their principal agenda has been self-representation in decision-making processes related to their work as teachers. Their desire is to set up structures of accountability that challenge the system of favoritism and cronyism that they believe presently rules graduate student life.

As one might expect, coordinating actions that drew all three of these very different cultures together was quite a challenge. Each group had originally organized around different "narratives of identity" and had developed a history of actions that were appropriate to their communal self-understanding. When the maintenance workers were in charge of a rally, the tone was usually loud and militant, with the language aggressive and often caustic, and the music consisted of gospel-style protest songs, many of them from the 1960s. When the clerical workers organized a rally, they wanted to hear other women tell individual stories about disrespectful treatment at work. The tone of their gathering was less angry, and the music was quieter and always involved holding hands. When the graduate students organized a rally, they focused on getting committed faculty to speak, who offered sound and authoritative arguments about why the students were being treated unjustly. They seldom had music, never held hands, and strenuously tried to avoid anything that sounded religious. When rallies were held where all three participated, one would inevitably hear the maintenance workers complaining that the secretaries were not aggressive enough, while the clerical workers would express their offense at the "inappropriate, loud language" used by the maintenance workers. And both 34 and 35 would complain about the snobbery of GESO and their boring talks and elitist views toward political action. Members of GESO, in return, could always find something that was terribly "politically incorrect" in the speakers and songs from both of the other unions.

Given the well-planned nature of management's response to the unions, the pressures of organizing were enormous, and the differences between the unions presented a significant challenge. The differences were the source of their strength (they represented a wide range of interests at the university and by working together wielded a great deal of power), but the differences were also the occasion of their weakness. It was hard to create a common rhetoric that could mobilize such a diversity of cultural sentiments.[13] After seven months of stalled negotiations and rapidly declining union attendance, it looked as if the coalition might break and the unions would concede to the university's contract proposals. The fracturing politics of identity had, in one sense, immobilized these three communities in the face of a unified foe as strong and well organized as the management they confronted.

And then the letter came along. What did it do? How did the letter work as an organizing tool, and what does it tell us about the power of a theological narrative as cultural critique? The first point to make about the rhetorical power of the letter is that it served to unify the base of political resistance by constructing a cultural space within which a "coalitional politic" could unfold. In earlier, failed attempts to build a rhetoric that could sustain a coalitional base among these groups, organizers took as their starting point the three varied, internal "politics of identity" and tried to cull a unifying narrative of identity out of these three pools of images. These attempts kept failing because each group understandably worried that such points of commonality would efface the particularity of their hard-earned and still fragile communal identities.

In this context, the letter offered the unions a different option—a narrative that required that they give up nothing in terms of their particular identities because the principal focus was on acting against a designated opposition in the name of a greater good. In other words, everyone found that in this story, they could be "David"—the marginal underdog who fights for the good of his community over against Goliath. His identity unfolds according to the logic of his act of resistance against a gargantuan foe. Hence, three of the most salient features of the narrative are (1) there is an unjust power relation, (2), the less powerful side of the power relation decisively acts against the more powerful; and (3) this act of resistance is positioned on morally high ground. In these moments, the unions found points around which the diverse narratives of race, class, and gender could coalesce (in terms of power relations), as could the diverse histories of varied acts of resistance (in terms of David's oppositional position). What the letter provided, in short, was one of those old-fashioned "grand narratives" into which our varied stories could be read without reducing our particularities, while simultaneously providing a common base from which to act. From this, the unions learned that when working with coalitions in which there is no internal centralized power and little in the way of coercive power or common identity, it is critical that some form of narrative reinforce the bonds of solidarity.[14] On this particular point, it is also important to note that it took a grand narrative to describe a foe that is as grand as the multinational corporate interests represented by management.

Let me make two additional observations about the function of the letter. First, it worked because it drew sharp, hard lines. In the language of poststructuralism, it thrived by virtue of its ability to inscribe a totalizing binarism in which one term was clearly privileged. When looked at from the perspective of sheer strength and status, the university's management appeared to be the championed term, but an inversion occurred because, according to the gaze of the letter, the unions stood on the higher ground, as the resisting margin. To make this inversion, the letter quite intentionally demonized the administration, and in doing so, made it impossible for people to be neutral in the conflict (which is what many of the New Haven clergy wanted to be). At the level of cultural theory, what this suggests to me is that the poststructuralist's theoretical assumptions that binarisms are always oppressive and that demonizing the other is inevitably counterproductive are assumptions that do not necessarily hold up well under the pressure of concrete political struggles where "dismantling the power of demons" appears to be a necessary strategy.

A second and related observation is this. It is important that according to the logic of this grand narrative, David won. He won decisively. He did not sit down at a table and come to a communicative consensus about conditions for just relations with Goliath. We know from the story that Goliath had no intention of negotiating with this subjugated second term, and given David's relatively weak position, David did not have the power to bring Goliath to the table. This is a scenario with which the unions could easily identify. And by inserting the moment of David's victory into the rhetorical culture of the union battle, the letter created an imaginative horizon upon which the possibility of victory seemed quite plausible. In the telling of this story, the unimaginable becomes a real political goal. What this suggests to me at the level of cultural theory is that in our present political climate we cannot underestimate the political function of an eschatology of victory, an eschatology where there are clear winners and not an eschatology that is content to articulate only visions of communicative conversations where dialogical consensus is the best one can imagine. This is not to say that dialogical consensus is never useful; it is only to say that it alone is not sufficient to cover all forms of political negotiation and contestation.

One last word about the letter. What about its theological function? Did it matter that it used a story from the Jewish and Christian Scriptures? Or was it just a good, cultural grand narrative that happened to be religious? To this question I often found myself wanting simply to shrug my shoulders and say, "I don't know." It is clear that for different people it provoked different readings, but the common thread that seemed to run through those readings was an act of contestation on behalf of the marginal against the powerful. If we want to find its theological significance, then perhaps it is here that we should look— to the actions it effected, the liberatory actions it called forth. Herein may lie its "truth"—the particularized action it incarnates.

But there is more to be said about its theological significance than this. When one approaches the story of David and Goliath from a faith perspective, one immediately sees that the story is more complicated than the version I laid out above. In addition to the two sides I have traced, there is a third actor in the conflict—God. According to the story, David's ability to stand up to and win against Goliath was undergirded by his faith in God, his belief that God was with him (and the people of Israel) in that struggle, that God was on his side. For some participants in this labor conflict, I am certain this divine presence was an acknowledged part of the process by which they read their lives into the story. But for many others—particularly members of GESO and the activist but secular faculty who participated—there was a clear discomfort with this aspect of the story, a discomfort manifest mainly in their silence with respect to the place of God in the story. However, it is also clear that the power afforded the narrative by this divine actor gives the story its ability to place David on the moral high ground, a high ground that these students and faculty were quite willing to occupy.

What does this mean about the cultural function of theology in these events? The answer to this question is far from simple (and deserves more attention that this essay can offer). Does it mean that these supposedly nonreligious people were acting as closeted believers when they imagined themselves into the space of David? I suspect they would rightly reject this reading of their actions. I imagine that at a general level they had no problem reading themselves into a story that did not completely agree with their professed commitments. We do it all the time. It is a necessary art form practiced by all of us who live in pluralistic, postmodern North America. I imagine further that they had little problem being normatively shaped by the story in a manner that elicited from them a certain form of social practice—in this case, attending the rally and, for many, getting arrested. What interests me in this context is this: What if these practices—and not doctrine—became the starting point for conversation with such people about theology? In the history of Christian theology, much has been written about the forming power of the liturgy in Christian communities. Perhaps the letter constituted the outline of such a "liturgy"—the script of a performance that its participants enacted. When cultural theory is used to help us better understand the complexity of such practices and performances (in their broadest sense), it may well be that new interesting ground will emerge for cultural conversations about the nature of belief and its place in the lives of North American communities standing on the edge of a new millennium.[15]

Theology and the Law

Let me now briefly explore another context in which cultural analysis and theory have provided a useful lens for conceptualizing the relationship between theology and politics. As noted earlier, I coteach a course at Yale Law School entitled "Identity and Power in Theology and the Law." Harlon Dalton, my fellow teacher, is a founder, with Lani Guinier, of the Critical Race Theory Group, which focuses on questions of race in the law and public policy.[16] We decided to coteach after being billed together as speakers at a clergy conference. In the course of our public conversation, it became clear that not only did we share a set of very strong political commitments, but also that these commitments had prompted us to approach our respective disciplines in a manner that took cultural theory quite seriously.

In his recent book, *Racial Healing: Confronting the Fear between Blacks and Whites*, Dalton uses neighborhoods in New Haven as a context for thinking through the ways in which our culture creates interactive expectations and instigates institutional forms that mediate our "raced" relations in often hidden but nonetheless normative, fear-filled ways.[17] He also offers a different vision of community interactions—one in which that which is culturally hidden is put on the table so that real conversation and healing action can begin. This work has resonated with my interest in doing constructive, feminist theology informed by cultural analysis. Out of our conversations about these issues grew our course.

The most distinctive mark of this course is its departure from the usual "Religion and the Law" class that takes as its central task the exploration of the varied calculuses one might employ to negotiate questions of church/state relations—calculuses that usually take First Amendment rights as their starting point. In contrast to this model, the conversation we are pursuing takes as its starting point the observation that both theological discourse and legal discourse in North America serve as normative contexts within which notions of personhood and community are constructed and, at times, contested. In other words, we explore the internal, cultural-linguistic structures of these two worldviews and ask the question, How do their narrative frameworks both situate their subjects and negotiate relations of power? While we both recognize that neither theology nor the law can be reduced to a single cultural narrative, we nonetheless believe it is critically important to get a handle on central normative moments in both, for some of the reasons I explained in the previous section on grand narratives. For me, the context of theological reflection is the Reformed tradition; for Dalton, the legal context consists of a combination of constitutional law and critical race theory. I should say here, as well, that our conversation remains a lively work in progress.

For the purpose of this chapter, I want briefly to highlight two parts of our conversation thus far. The first concerns the view of the human person that sits at the heart of both conceptual worlds. At the core of legal discourse is the founding conception of a subject who is "self-owned," an agent who is internally self-constituted, self-defining, and capable of acting out of that self-definition. The substance the subject "owns" (when one owns oneself) in legal discourse is defined as a collection of abstract, universal rights. In order to universalize these rights, this self-owning subject is not allowed to claim any distinct specificity. Devoid of particularity, the subject is figured as disembodied. As such, at the center of legal discourse, at least in its constitutional form, stands a person who belongs to no one other than himself.[18] At the center of theological discourse, on the other hand, one finds a conception of the self that is principally "other defined." The core of Reformed anthropology is often summed up in Calvin's famous phrase: We do not belong to ourselves; we belong to God.[19] And in belonging to God, we are freed to belong truly to our neighbor. Further in this narrative framework, this "self who belongs to God" is defined both as the creaturely self whom God claims as concretely particular and embodied, and the redeemed self whom God claims, despite the power of sin, through the power of a grace that forgives. Hence, in this discursive world, one meets a self who is defined from a space beyond the self as an embodied, particular, fallen but forgiven self. In this context, it must be noted further, to be self-possessed and self-defined is to be a sinner. What are we to make of this difference? As Dalton and I have pursued this question, the connections between this theological vision and racial and feminist legal theories' interest in group rights and communal understanding of identity have become increasingly apparent.[20]

Let me pursue this point by turning to a related issue that has arisen in our conversations. It concerns the relationship between Christian understandings of the atonement and juridical theories of punishment.[21] At the heart of North American jurisprudence sits a model of retributive punishment that considers "atoning for crime" in the following way. This self who owns himself, and hence is invested with certain rights, may at times act in ways that violate the rights of other self-owned persons.[22] Because the acts of this self are entirely self-generated, the self alone must bear responsibility for the harm done. They must be punished by the state, which represents all subjects' rights, in a manner that matches the seriousness of the crime. Because this self remains a disembodied, nonparticular self, however, there is little discussion in U.S. legal theory of the ways in which this punishment is wrought upon real, particular people for the purpose of causing them suffering. In other words, by crafting a legal discourse of retributive punishment that universalizes and disembodies the self, the discourse is able to hide the fact that it is real people, in specific bodies, that are intended to suffer as a result of violence inflicted by the state.

Now let us compare this discourse on punishment with classical Christian views of the atonement, the doctrine that inscribes notions of punishment and retribution. At the center of this story sits a subject who is punished for the crimes of others—an innocent subject who suffers what humanity on the whole should suffer given the force of their crime, namely, the fall. The subject is punished by a God who, in order to maintain the integrity of divine justice, must exact a payment for the crimes committed. When punishment is depicted in this story, the figure is not disembodied but is portrayed as physically suffering; his flesh is "torn." Furthermore, this narrative of punishment depends upon an acknowledgment of this person's historical specificity. He is Jesus of Nazareth, a person who has been perfectly obedient to the law of God. And it matters that he is this person and not another. He is not infinitely replaceable. Hence, the central narrative structure of classical atonement theory demands that the viewer not only see that punishment involves suffering but that it involves the suffering of a specific person that we know. In fact, when confessing this doctrine in its classical form, we are required to say that the person on the cross should be me—this is the punishment I deserve.

Given this difference between legal and theological discourse, what are we to say about the relationship between them? It seems to me that a useful place to start is to explore the ways in which both narratives often simultaneously structure the way in which Christians (and others) visualize the character of retributive punishment in our culture. Both images—the pristine, disembodied self who feels no pain and the suffering sinner who has her or his own unique history—are frequently sitting side by side. As such, they can often be played off of one another in rather interesting ways. For example, it could be that the silences and repressions of the juridical understanding of retributive punishment are exposed when one's eye moves from that pristine scene to the scene of the cross. In this way, the atonement could serve to culturally contest the hidden violence of state punishment.[23] This is a particularly important exposure to make given the present-day reality that African American men and women receive harsher penalties than Euro-American men and women for the same crimes. What this reveals is that, in fact, the specificity of one's body does play a role in sentencing—a role the state hides.

Reading the relationship between these two narratives could also move in the other direction, allowing the legal discourse to throw light on often shadowed parts of the Christian narrative of atonement. When the figure on the cross is placed beside the morning newspaper's account of the harsh sentencing of a drug addict who robbed a local sandwich shop, the newspaper's account could be used to make us painfully aware that the doctrine of atonement seems to describe an act of violence perpetrated by a God who seems to care little for the suffering he has wrought—an image at which we should be profoundly alarmed. In this way, reading juridical culture into theological culture may help us get some much-needed critical leverage against traditional understandings of atonement.

Conclusion

As I hope this example (and the example of the union struggle) suggests, the relationship between theology and cultural theory is complex. On the one hand, cultural theory has much to teach theologians about the unpredictable and diverse character of theological meaning and the multifaceted relations of power it constantly negotiates. Learning to better appreciate the many ways theological language creates and is created by distinct cultural forces, I believe, cannot but help theologians in both the diagnostic and constructive aspects of their endeavors. For theologians such as feminists and liberationists who have long been interested in the political dimensions of theological reflection, cultural theory promises to complicate their understanding of what constitutes the political by highlighting the ways the seemingly most innocent or commonplace play of images remains loaded with meanings that mediate multiple relations of power—and that do so in often unstable and quickly shifting ways. For theologians who purportedly eschew the realm of political reflection, cultural theory serves to remind them that such eschewals are not only naive but dangerous, for the political lives in the very texture of the cultural forms they inevitably inhabit.

On the other hand, theology has much to teach cultural theory about the character of normative claims and the nature of eschatological visions. In particular, theologians can help cultural theorists who have chosen to engage in critical cultural analysis for the purpose of furthering concrete emancipatory struggles to appreciate better the place of normative visions in those struggles—and consequently in their own work. I have long thought that in the world of cultural theory, more theologians should claim their place as the oldest and perhaps most adept of our present-day normative constructivists, for many are, like Calvin, well trained in the art of handling truth claims that seek to move the hearts and minds of those who embrace them. To occupy this position effectively, however, theologians must be bold enough to converse with cultural theory in a manner that is not embarrassed by but applauds the particularized logic of theological discourse. If in the course of conversation theology concedes its distinctiveness to the potentially consumptive logic of cultural criticism, it will have little left to offer. If it resists this temptation, then the conversation promises to be exciting. In addition to helping progressive cultural theorists figure out how to engage in normative reflection, theologians may be challenged to articulate the uniqueness of their enterprise.

Notes

1. George Lindbeck, *The Nature of Doctrine: Religion and Theology in a Postliberal Age* (Philadelphia: Westminster, 1984). See also Clifford Geertz, *Interpretation of Cultures: Selected Essays* (New York: Basic Books, 1973). For a feminist critique of Lindbeck, see Amy Plantinga Pauw, "The Word Is Near You: A Feminist Conversation with Lindbeck," *Theology Today* 50 (April 1993): 45–55.

2. See Theodor Adorno, *Minima Moralia: Reflections from Damaged Life*, trans. E. F. N. Jephcott (London: New Left Books, 1974); idem, *Negative Dialectics*, trans. by E. B. Ashton (New York : Seabury, 1973); György Lukács, *History and Class Consciousness*, trans. R. Livingstone (Cambridge: MIT Press, 1971); idem, *The Theory of the Novel: A Historico-philosophical Essay on the Forms of Great Epic Literature*, trans. Anna Bostock (Cambridge: MIT Press, 1971).

3. See Antonio Gramsci, *An Antonio Gramsci Reader: Selected Writings, 1916–1935*, ed. David Forgacs (New York: Schocken Books, 1988); idem, *Letters from Prison*, ed. Frank Rosengarten; trans. Raymond Rosenthal (New York: Columbia University Press, 1994).

4. See Michel Foucault, *Power/Knowledge: Selected Interviews and Other Writings*, trans. Colin Gordon (Brighton, England: Harvester Press, 1980).

5. See Luce Irigaray, *Speculum of the Other Woman*, trans. Gillian C. Gill (Ithaca, N.Y.: Cornell University Press, 1985); idem, "Divine Women," in *Sexes and Genealogies*, trans. Gillian Gill (New York: Columbia University Press, 1993).

6. Serene Jones, "Women's Experience Between a Rock and a Hard Place," in *Horizons in Feminist Theology: Identity, Tradition, and Norms*, ed. Rebecca Chopp and Sheila Greeve Davaney (Minneapolis: Fortress, 1997).

7. John Calvin, *Institutes of the Christian Religion*, ed. John McNeill (Philadelphia: Westminster, 1960).

8. For discussions on Calvin's relation to the rhetorical tradition, see William Bouwsma, *John Calvin: A Sixteenth Century Portrait* (New York: Oxford University Press, 1988); Don Compier, *Denouncing Death: John Calvin's Critique of Sin and Contemporary Rhetorical Theology*, unpublished dissertation, Emory University; Serene Jones, *Calvin and the Rhetoric of Piety*, (Louisville, Ky.: Westminster John Knox, 1995); Olivier Millet, *Calvin et la Dynamique de la Parole : Étude de Rhétorique Réformée* (Geneva: Slatkine, 1992).

9. For Cicero's perspective on rhetoric, see his three major works on the subject: *De inventione, De Oratore*, and *Orator*.

10. Cicero, *De inventione*, I.I.I., p. 2 (Loeb Classical Library), trans. H. M. Hubbell (Cambridge: Harvard University Press, 1949).

11. For an example of critical race theory, see Paul Gilroy, *The Black Atlantic: Modernity and Double Consciousness* (Cambridge: Harvard University Press, 1993). For examples of feminist anthropology, see Lila Abu-Lughod, *Veiled Sentiments: Honor and Poetry in Bedouin Society* (Berkeley: University of California Press, 1986); idem, *Writing Women's Worlds: Bedouin Stories* (Berkeley: University of California Press, 1993); Anna Lowenhaupt Tsing, *In the Realm of the Diamond Queen: Marginality in an Out of the Way Place* (Princeton: Princeton University Press, 1993); Anna Lowenhaupt Tsing and

Gayle Ginsburg, eds., *Uncertain Terms: Negotiating Gender in American Culture* (Boston: Beacon, 1990).

12. I call it a "group" because although they have been successfully voted in as a union by their constituency, the university has not yet officially recognized them as a bargaining unit.

13. See the following literature on new social movements: Nancy Fraser, "Social Movements vs. Disciplinary Bureaucracies: The Discourse of Social Needs," CHS Occasional Paper No. 8, Center for Humanistic Studies, University of Minnesota, 1987; Alberto Melucci, *Nomads of the Present: Social Movements and Individual Needs in Contemporary Society* (Philadelphia: Temple University Press, 1989); Alain Touraine, *Critique of Modernity*, trans. David Macey (Oxford: Blackwell, 1995); Alain Touraine, Michel Wieviorke, and Francois Dubet, eds. *Workers Movement* (Cambridge: Cambridge University Press, 1987).

14. See Frederic Jameson, *The Political Unconscious: Narrative as Socially Symbolic Act* (Ithaca, N.Y.: Cornell University Press, 1981).

15. On the relation between performance and normative claims, see Lynne Huffer, "Luce et Veritas: Toward an Ethics of Performance," *Another Look, Another Woman: Retranslations of French Feminism; special issue of Yale French Studies* 87 (1995): 20.

16. See Lani Guinier, *Lift Every Voice: Turning a Civil Rights Setback into a Strong New Vision of Social Justice* (New York: Simon & Schuster, 1998); idem, *The Tyranny of the Majority: Fundamental Fairness in Representative Democracy* (New York: Free Press, 1994).

17. Harlon Dalton, *Racial Healing: Confronting the Fear between Blacks and Whites* (New York: Doubleday, 1995)

18. See Carol Pateman's critique of this image of self-ownership in *The Sexual Contract* (Cambridge: Polity Press, 1998).

19. Calvin, *Institutes of the Christian Religion*, 690.

20. For examples of the kinds of feminist legal theory I refer to here, see Martha Fineman and Nancy Sweet Thomadsen, eds., *At the Boundaries of Law: Feminism and Legal Theory* (New York: Routledge, 1991); Catharine MacKinnon, *Feminism Unmodified: Discourses on Life and Law* (Cambridge: Harvard University Press, 1987); and Martha Minow, *Making All the Difference: Inclusion, Exclusion, and American Law* (Ithaca, N.Y.: Cornell University Press, 1990).

21. See Robert Cover, "Violence and the Word," *Yale Law Journal* 95 (1986): 1601–29.

22. When this happens, the juridical subject is capable of seeing that he or she would not want to be treated as such, and, as a result, this morally culpable self feels guilt.

23. This question of punishment is particularly important when thinking about race and the law given that African American men are statistically likely to get a much harsher penalty than white men who are punished for the same crime.

Votán-Zapata

Theological Discourse in Zapatista Political Struggle

Mark Taylor

> *Discourse is not simply that which translates struggles or systems of domination, but that for which, and by means of which, struggle occurs.*
>
> Zapatista Subcomandante Marcos
> (citing M. Foucault, *The Order of Things*)

With these words, Marcos, the major spokesman for the Zapatista guerilla movement, showed his profound respect for discourse and language. His quote from Foucault came at the beginning of his 1980 *licenciatura* thesis in the School of Philosophy and Letters (UNAM—National Autonomous University of Mexico), when he was known as Rafael Sebastién Guillén Vicente.

Fifteen years later, after some years in the classroom and ten more in the jungle learning the ways of social transformation from poor indigenous communities, he emerged as an active guerilla leader. His awareness of the power of discourse, though, remained very much in evidence. In fact, it may be his power of the pen—writing stories for children, creating narratives of self-parody, retelling Maya mythology, issuing communiqués over the Internet—which has presented a new vision of leftist struggle that has captured the imagination of much of

Mexico and the world. Marcos has been described as "the other ladino," the person of Spanish descent in Mexico who, unlike the Spanish conquerors who stole and burned early Maya's written words, now restores the word, the discourse, to the Maya, and in a way that enables Maya political struggle.[1]

Marcos and the Zapatistas burst upon the scene in their uprising of January 1994, when they took control of seven major towns in Chiapas, Mexico's southernmost state. In the five years since, they have issued a discourse that at times troubles traditionalists of the right and the left, and baffles both political activists and scholars of ancient Maya belief. Amid the political tumult of contemporary Mexico, these armed (but now largely nonviolent) communities in rebellion often invoke the ancient Maya gods of Chaacob, Kuilob Kaaaxob, Kisin, and others, but with new meanings.[2]

The Zapatistas, therefore, offer an example of political struggle with a notable theological dimension. I do not mean that they feature an elaborate use of Christian doctrinal concepts and systems. There is, however, theology in the sense of discourse (*logos*) relating to what a people holds to be sacred (*theos*). This discourse is made up of a host of symbols and stories that are both ancient in their legacy and retold with new meanings. In the case of Maya political struggle, this discourse of the sacred is not just "about" their struggle, translating (to use Foucault's term) a people's political reality into some linguistic, theological discourse. No, more importantly, the discourse is itself an agent of the struggle, a means by which that struggle occurs. The meaningful cultural practices that cluster around this theological discourse constitute the spirituality that often sustains and constitutes features of Maya resistance and struggle.

Christian liberation theology has long argued that peoples' sense of divine presence and will is articulated not only through sacred scriptures and doctrine, but "also in the diverse stories of believing peoples,"[3] in their popular religiosity. Here we will see that such diverse stories abound at the very heart of Maya understandings of their intense political struggle. This essay, after a brief introduction to the Zapatista movement today, examines one of the most powerful symbols in the theological discourse of Zapatista political communiqués—Votán-Zapata.

This symbol, as I will show, thrives in relation to the great myths of the plumed serpent, Quetzalcoatl or Kukulcan, of the Nahua, Aztec, and Maya traditions of Mexico and Central America. Many of the liberating meanings of this symbol, however, have been developed in the context of decades of work by priests, catechists, and others who imbibed and taught liberation theology in Chiapas. More than thirty years of work by the Catholic diocese in Chiapas, inaugurated in the 1960s by Bishop Samuel Ruiz García, yielded hundreds of catechists who interpreted the gospel as one of liberation and a diocesan plan to "facilitate knowledge and support of popular movements struggling for justice."[4]

When diocesan workers were charged with instigating the 1994 Maya uprising, they denied the charge. Even though liberationist Bishop Ruiz has been described as more responsible than anyone else for the way indigenous communities have recently evaluated and organized themselves to struggle for their rights,[5] he toured the mountainous jungles and canyons to counsel against armed uprising.[6] The guerillas have also distanced themselves from the church's liberation theology. "We are the liberation without the theology," said one. Nevertheless, one of the fully Maya leaders of the Zapatistas, Comandante Davíd, has said that "the moment came when those very same indigenous *pueblos* started to make themselves aware of their reality by means of reflection and analysis, *and also by studying the word of God,* and thus they began to wake up"[7] (emphasis added). A full account of the theological dimension of indigenous struggle in Chiapas, then, would include an analysis of the role of Christian liberationist belief and practice in the emergence of the revolt. We cannot ignore, however, the distinctively Maya symbols and stories, especially those pertaining to Votán-Zapata. This is the theological discourse that has been more to the fore of the Zapatista movement, and understanding this discourse of struggle is the crucial prerequisite for understanding how Christian liberationist belief may also have played a role.

Who Are the Zapatistas?

Here we are, the forever dead, dying once again, but now in order to live. (January 1, 1994)

This was the announcement by which Maya communities in 1994 revealed their indigenous army, the Zapatista Army of National Liberation (EZLN). The revelation came on the very day of the implementation of the North American Free Trade Agreement (NAFTA), which had just been approved by Mexico, Canada, and the United States in the fall of 1993. When Mexico's President Carlos Salinas de Gotari attached his signature to NAFTA, the Zapatistas felt he had signed away the force of a constitutional provision, Article 27, which until then had kept indigenous peoples' land under their own control. NAFTA also made little provision for protecting the three nations' environmental habitats or the rights of workers to land, fair wages, or free movement across the borders of the three countries. Beginning January 1, 1994, big capital could move freely southward to find the lowest wages, but masses of workers could not move northward to chase even a fair working wage.[8]

On New Year's Eve, therefore, while the presidents of Mexico and the United States were at parties, five hundred Zapatista troops took over city hall in San Cristóbal de Las Casas. Then on the morning of January 1, they "declared war" (somewhat more theatrically than in fact) against the Mexican government on behalf of "the miserable and dispossessed."

> Mexican brothers and sisters, we are the product of 500 years of struggle: first against slavery; then in the insurgent-led war of Independence against Spain; later in the fight to avoid being absorbed by North American expansion. . . . We are denied the most elementary education so that they can use us as cannon fodder and plunder our country's riches, uncaring that we are dying of hunger and curable diseases.[9]

In San Cristóbal, the major result of the Zapatista incursion was the symbolic burning of the records of corrupt officials in the city hall. Simultaneous actions of a similar nature were undertaken by the EZLN in at least six other Chiapas towns, involving nearly three thousand indigenous people.

The EZLN had carefully built up its mass support in southeast Mexico's Lacandón jungle. Nearly fifteen years earlier, Marcos and a small group of *mestizo* revolutionaries entered the area, but were retrained by the Maya over time in the ways of revolutionary cultural movements. EZLN spokesman, Marcos, has frequently stressed that he and his group came teaching revolution but were transformed into a social movement for and by the Maya communities. Through the EZLN, the Maya expressed their rage and pain as sufferers of five hundred years of exploitation. They routinely issued information about their current situation:

> Three fourths of the indigenous people remain illiterate.
>
> 20 percent of its adults are unemployed. 60 percent draw less than the minimum wage of four dollars a day.
>
> 55 percent of Mexico's electric power is produced in Chiapas, while only 30 percent of its homes have electricity.[10]

Crucial to the galvanizing of this revolutionary consciousness was Zapatista development of a "Women's Revolutionary Law" in 1993, the year before the uprising. It proclaimed and enacted key reforms for women in its communities: to exercise leadership in its armies, communities, and homes; to be free from rape, forced labor, and forced childbirth; and to be free to choose for or against marriage and to select their own spouses.[11] By 1999, the success of these reforms for women was much debated, but the intensity of the debate signals just how important the dimension of women's freedom is to Zapatista struggle.

With the January 1994 action, these often invisible poor of Mexico splashed onto the front pages of first-world newspapers like the *New York Times*, thus dramatizing the fact that Mexico's poverty still ran deep and wide. The *Times* even ran an op-ed essay accompanied by a sketched map of Mexico that was drawn like a grand carpet unrolling from North America and smothering the skulls of Mexico's impoverished dead.[12]

NAFTA was supposed to have been Mexico's badge of belonging to the bright world of corporate culture. Mexico had been the darling of free market visions of third-world development, having deployed IMF structural adjustment plans in the 1980s. President Salinas was even being groomed to head the World Trade Organization. Mexico's fine economic image, however, started to crumble in the wake of the 1994 uprising. In coming months, the Zapatistas and "the Chiapas effect" would be one factor in producing a near wholesale collapse of the Mexican economy in late 1995. "Just when we were telling the world and ourselves that we were looking like the U.S., we turn out to be Guatemala," said one Mexican writer,[13] referring to the militarized country to the south where a ruthless elite routinely repress indigenous poor communities.

After occupying the Chiapas towns, the Zapatistas quickly retired from them, losing over 145 of their soldiers. Dead guerills and prisoners were transported in U.S.-made helicopters. Supposedly provided to Mexico to fight the drug war, they were apparently used for "logistical support" in Mexican actions against the EZLN.[14] Those helicopters were just one sign of U.S. military assistance to the Mexican government as it sought to quell the uprising and as its troops encircled Maya communities. Some 60,000 Mexican troops remain in Chiapas at the time of this writing in 1999.

Since withdrawing into the jungles, the Zapatistas have remained an almost constant feature in Mexican news and politics. The EZLN maintains itself as a voice from indigenous Chiapas with an agenda for *all* of Mexico. After the government's announced cease-fire in 1994, the

Zapatistas and the Mexican government have been in various states of negotiation and breakdown of dialogue. The Mexican government still often initiates military incursions into indigenous communities, such as in February 1995 when over 20,000 indigenous families were forced to flee their destroyed villages to hide in the mountains. The more recent tactic is the use of "low intensity warfare," which combines military occupation with the sponsorship of paramilitary operations. At present, between eight and fourteen different paramilitaries now divide and harass Zapatista communities.[15]

The Clinton administration, like U.S. administrations before it that permitted Indian genocide and forced removal within its own borders, has lifted no voice on behalf of the Zapatistas. After all, the EZLN, by helping to destabilize Mexico, also countered the positive spin the United States continually had given to NAFTA. Instead, the United States provided military aid to the Mexican government (under the guise of fighting drugs) and also helped in providing intelligence about alleged Zapatista conspirators.

In addition, major banking industries in the United States expressed their nervousness about the Zapatistas. One Chase Manhattan representative even suggested that because of possible investment instability in Mexico, it was desirable to "eliminate the Zapatistas," in order to demonstrate the Mexican government's "effective control of the national territory and of security policy."[16]

In spite of these modes of retaliation by political and economic forces, the Zapatistas have been incredibly resilient. They have mobilized public referenda on the future of Mexican citizens, which have drawn participation in almost all of Mexico, and with voter turnouts greater than referenda sponsored by the government.

The Zapatistas have couched their revolutionary discourse in a simple plea for land, justice, freedom, and dignity, moving from a predictable Marxist rhetoric to a more popularist one, and thereby catalyzing mass rallies of tens of thousands of people in Mexico City. In September 1997, 1,111 Zapatista representatives marched out from within their military encirclement in Chiapas to Mexico City, drawing crowds of upwards of 100,000 participants. In 1995 and 1996, the Zapatistas carved arenas out of the jungle to host conventions on the global market's damaging effects and rights of indigenous peoples that drew hundreds and, in one case, thousands of activists from Mexico and from nearly every continent. They have organized Zapatista solidarity groups throughout the world, including in nearly every large city in the United States.

In March 1999, the Zapatistas traveled throughout Mexico, organizing a public referendum in which almost three million voted their opinions on the future of indigenous peoples.[17] In May of the same year, they coordinated their resistance with the impressive student movements at UNAM in Mexico City. While the Zapatistas technically refuse to lay down their arms because they see themselves as still under mortal threat from the Mexican government, their most effective strategies have been in nonmilitary types of action: supporting new coalitions of civil society in Mexico; organizing civil disobedience by women, children, and peasant men against Mexican military power; capturing media interest through ruse, story, humor, and political analysis.

In all this, the Zapatista aim has been neither to destroy the national government in Mexico nor to opt completely out of the international market. Rather, it has been to create a life-giving autonomy for indigenous peoples over their lands, which would then generate alternative understandings of the national government's sovereignty and equally alternative understandings of how to participate in global trade. Mexican historian Adolfo Gilly has described the revolt as seeking an "other modernity," a true "Mexican modernity" that includes those that Enlightenment modernity has routinely excluded.[18]

A new modernity seemed to dawn, indeed, when on July 2, 2000, Mexico's voters sent the dominant party candidate, Francisco Labastida, down to defeat, thus ending some eighty years of authoritarian control by the party known as the PRI (the Institutional Revolutionary Party). His rival, Vicente Fox, assumed the presidency in December 2000 and promptly ordered some troop withdrawals from Chiapas, the release of approximately eighty Zapatista prisoners, and new dialogues with Zapatista leaders. While attending the global economic forum in Davos, Switzerland, in February 2001, Fox announced that his government wants "Peace, peace, peace."[19]

For his part, Marcos says that peace does seem closer than ever before since 1994. He and twenty-four Zapatista rebel commanders even planned a march to Mexico City, in February or March 2001, to test the new promises of dialogue. The march has much public support in Mexico, but some political leaders still declare the Zapatista leaders to be traitors, worthy only of the death penalty. Foreign observers were to be allowed into Mexico to observe the march, but were to stay only for ten days. Moreover, if they actively participated in the march, they would be expelled and forbidden to return for at least ten years. At this writing in March 2001, therefore, *Zapatismo* abounds with new hope, but still faces an uncertain future.[20]

Who Is Votán-Zapata?

He took his name from those who have no name, his face from those with no face; he is sky on the mountain. Votán, guardian and heart of the people. And our road, unnameable and faceless, took its name in us: Zapatista Army of National Liberation.

Communiqué of the EZLN, April 10, 1995

The distinctive spirituality of contemporary *Zapatismo* is energized by its complex symbol, Votán-Zapata, and the movement's staying power is intricately bound up with it. I will present four dimensions of meaningful cultural practice that coalesce around this symbol, drawing primarily from two communiqués of astounding literary beauty, written in 1994 and 1995 by Marcos but issued under the name of the entire Maya leadership of the EZLN.

The Cosmological Dimension

The name "Votán" signals a first dimension of meaning that calls forth a deep connection to the cosmological traditions of Mesoamerica. Votán is a cultural hero of Maya groups whose legendary actions in history and culture were bound up with some of the most ancient traditions of Aztec and Maya myth.

Votán was often referred to as the "heart of the sky, the heart [and guardian] of the people" who was propitiated by Maya peoples on the third day of their agricultural calendar.[21] The hero played a key role in inciting indigenous revolts, so much so that in 1690 a nervous bishop, Francisco Nuñez de la Vega, burned every trace of Votán's deeds and the memory of his miracles, which were guarded throughout indigenous communities of Chiapas. This did not work in 1690, nor could it work today, because this cultural hero and his accompanying cosmology do not abide in that which can be burned. They dwell in the daily world of Maya life, practiced in the house, the cornfield, and the community.[22] So it is that the culture hero, and memories of him, could ignite ever new cycles of revolt against oppressors.[23]

Votán's historical actions as culture hero are consonant with a larger paradigm of the mythic hero Quetzalcoatl of Nahua and Aztec tradition. Votán is a culture hero linked to narratives of Quetzalcoatl, the feathered serpent-god who comes and appears in many forms, and to Kukulcan, the Maya analogue to Quetzalcoatl.[24]

Whether connected to the mythologies of Quetzalcoatl or to those of Kukulcan, Votán seems to be a figure who came from some unknown place (sometimes thought to be Phoenicia, sometimes Africa[25]). Legends have him traveling up the Usumacinta River to found Palenque. Irene Nicholson stresses that

> it is evident that he was a great enough leader to have extended his religious beliefs through a vast Maya-Nahua territory. . . . It is a universal tragedy that we know so little of this great religious leader, Quetzalcoatl-Kukulcan-Votán: plumed serpent, quetzal bird, Venus the sun god, who sacrificed himself that true manhood might be created.[26]

This summary by a Mesoamerican mythologist is echoed in a 1994 communiqué of the EZLN:

> Brothers and sisters, we want you to know who is behind us, who directs us, who walks on our feet, who dominates our heart, who rides in our words, who lives in our deaths. . . . From the first hour of this long night on which we die, say our most distant grandparents, there was someone who gathered together our pain and our forgetting. There was a man who, his work traveling from far away, came to our mountain and spoke with the tongue of true men and women. His step was not of these lands; in the mouths of our dead, in the voices of the old wise ones, his word traveled from him to our heart.[27]

This one who comes from afar, however, also comes from the Maya realm of the dead. He lives "in the mouths of our dead." In the same communiqué, there are these words: "He is and is not in these lands: Votán Zapata, guardian and heart of the people. Votán Zapata, timid fire that lived 501 years *in our death*. Votán Zapata, name that changes, man without face, soft light that shelters us"[28] (emphasis added).

Maya scholars in Mexico, therefore, stress that Votán is often linked to the particular forms of Quetzalcoatl that can also be transformed into Xolotl, the lord of the dead. Xolotl had a particular mission: to go to the place of the dead and to gather up remains of the dead to be made into humanity. Quetzalcoatl, in this way, gives birth to humanity. At the same time that humanity is thus birthed, so also are corn and fire brought by Quetzalcoatl to humankind.[29] Sometimes the association of Votán with this fire-bringing Quetzalcoatl yields the formulation, "Balun Votán," which signifies Votán as "of the inferno."[30] Votán is a figure, then, who gives life to humanity, bringing corn and fire from the obscure and infernal realm of the dead.

This realm of the dead is called "Mictlan" in Mesoamerican cosmology, and Chiapas has traditionally been understood as the geographical location of Mictlan. That tradition is reinforced by the fact that one of the major Maya groups of Chiapas, the Tzotziles, adore Xolotl, lord of the dead. Seeing themselves as "bat-people," these Chiapas dwellers are the "sons of obscurity" or "those who walk in the night."[31] EZLN communiqués often refer to their actions in defense of the poor as the emergence of a healing shadow, a renewing that comes from the realm of the dead, and from dark places. They spread "shadows of tender fury," bringing pain to their enemies but comfort and tenderness to the centuries-long sufferers of colonialism.[32] They come, like many rebellions in Chiapas over the centuries, with a spirit of what García de León termed a "nocturnal tenacity." The Zapatistas' predawn raids on Chiapas towns on New Year's Day of 1994 only dramatized that legacy.

Votán is a figure, then, who reaches deep into Maya traditions of spirit to highlight heroic cultural actions born from the realm of the dead. From a communiqué of March 15, 1994, the entire EZLN comandante leadership writes, "We are shadows of tender fury; our dark wings will cover the sky again, and their protective cloak will shelter the dispossessed and the good men and women who understand that justice and peace go hand in hand. If they deny us our rights, then our tender fury will enter those fine mansions."[33] If you can hold at once the coincidence of opposites in this Maya discourse of struggle, we might say that these heroic renewals of Votán are, as with Quetzalcoatl, shadowy and obscure eruptions of a dawn. Fire is brought. There is both stealth *and* stunning action in the revolutionary process. There is tenderness *and* fury.

The Political Dimension

A second dimension of meaning concerns the political rebellions long featured in the history of Chiapas. The two important EZLN communiqués on Votán-Zapata were released on the seventy-fifth and seventy-sixth anniversaries of the assassination of Emiliano Zapata. When Votán and Zapata are linked, Zapata, the revolutionary general of Mexican history, is suffused with the cosmological meanings of Votán:

> Today we again remember the struggle which gave us our name and face. . . . Emiliano died, but not his struggle nor his thinking.

Many Emiliano Zapatas were born afterwards, and now his name is not that of one person. His name is the name of a struggle for justice, a cause for democracy, a thinking for liberty. In us, in our weapons, in our covered faces, in our true words, Zapata became one with the wisdom and the struggle of our oldest ancestors. United with Votán, Guardian and Heart of the People, Zapata rose up again to struggle for democracy, liberty and justice for all Mexicans.[34]

Zapata, then, becomes one who, like Quetzalcoatl, comes from afar. Thus, there can be many Zapatas. Zapata cannot be killed. He will always rise again.

Joined with Votán, the General Zapata who died in 1919 can now travel in mythic time—forward to be embodied in many subsequent struggles, such as the 1994 uprising, and backward to 1521, when he is said to have sustained resistance in the heart of indigenous peoples during the first days of conquest.[35] Zapata, like Votán, even attains the ability to travel from the underworld, yielding up all the creativity and renewing force of the indigenous dead.

This fusion with Votán not only bestows mythic character upon Zapata, but also politicizes Votán in particular ways. This occurs in two senses. First, Votán is said to dwell now in the contemporary Zapatista army. As cited at the outset, "Votán, guardian and heart of the people . . . took its name in us, the Zapatista Army of National Liberation."

Tender fury that arms itself. Unnameable name. Unjust peace that becomes war. Death that is born. Anguish made hope. Pain that laughs. Silenced scream. One's own present for another's future. Everything for everyone; for ourselves nothing. The unnameable, we, the forever dead. We, stubborn dignity, forgotten corner of our country. We, Zapatista Army of National Liberation.[36]

Here, the ancient spirit Votán is politicized, now alive and embodied in the Maya revolutionary collective, the EZLN. Alejandro Moreno Corzo stresses that the Zapatista combatants are able to see themselves as an integral part of Votán, and thereby to possess a psychic liberation from their humiliating conditions in order to acquire the ability to change their lifestyles and communities.[37]

In a second sense, Votán is also politicized by being set in opposition to the arrogance of wealth and power. Coupled with Zapata, Votán is set against the treasonous ones who lured Emiliano into ambush and assassination in 1919.[38] Votán becomes a force among indigenous peoples against those who traffic in money, lies and treason in any epoch.

The powerful and arrogant ones include dominant forces such as the Spanish conquistadors, ranchers, ladino and mestizo oppressors of every era, and especially today's "neoliberalism," the word that the EZLN and many in Latin America and the Caribbean use for the exploitative dynamics of global capitalism.[39]

Votán had been politicized many times in the past. García de León makes this clear in his commentary on Votán's role in indigenous revolts during the centuries of repressive colonization in Mesoamerica. Today's EZLN has seized this politicized Votán and followed its mythic force into full-scale encounter with some of the most powerful corporate and military forces that European and North American cultures can muster.

The politicized Votán or, conversely, the mythologized Zapata, have not only enchanted much of Mexico, but allowed that country and much of the rest of the industrialized world to face its own repressed consciousness of indigenous roots. The Zapatistas have forced to the surface the collective shame, we might say, that usually remains buried by the collective amnesia of nation-states. The culturally therapeutic effect of this mythos of political revolution has been well summarized by García de León:

> [I]n reality what was being carried [in this revolt by the EZLN] were our own sufferings, the crimes of an entire society lacking in democracy and justice. It is for this reason that the call of the jungle penetrated so deeply into the heart of all Mexicans of every region. It is for this reason that their hidden faces appeared before us as a mirror, in which we could contemplate our own imprisoned face.[40]

In a similar vein, Guillermo Michel, philosopher at the Iberoamerican University, sees the symbol as a vision for "a new relation of person to person, of a people to people, most especially the relation of all of us to our indigenous peoples."[41] Adolfo Gilly sees Mexico building a new, more inclusive modernity through an act of self-recognition, one galvanized by today's indigenous struggle in Chiapas. Even amid today's complex political order, Mexico can know the return of its "enchanted world."[42]

The Natural Dimension

A third dimension of meaning involves the domain of nature. *Zapatismo* is neither a revolutionary mythos alone nor a revolutionary politics

alone. In the *Zapatismo* view, all of nature conspires to guide and infuse
human efforts of resistance and hope. *Zapatismo* thus includes, but
moves decisively beyond, the rhetoric and analyses of class struggle and
warfare, and, indeed, beyond any primarily anthropocentric concepts of
cultural and political change.

This, too, is clearly signaled by the communiqués regarding Votán-
Zapata. The 1994 communiqué speaks of Votán-Zapata having made
his home in the Mayas' mountainous terrain and in the night as nature's roof for the people. Votán-Zapata is also "timid fire" and "soft
light that shelters us."[43] Votán-Zapata not only rides in great generals
like Emiliano, but also flies in "the little bird," like the Tapacamino
species native to the Lacandon forest.[44] Almost all the communiqués
are signed by the EZLN as "from the mountains of the southeast."

Votán-Zapata names, however, not just a natural habitat of Votán,
but a veritable *conspiracy by nature itself* to work revolution. This is clear
from some of the earliest writings of the EZLN, especially the one entitled, "Chiapas: The Southeast in Two Winds, a Storm and a Prophecy,"
where the political struggle of the Zapatistas is seen as "a clash between
these two winds."[45]

The first wind is "imposed from above," largely coming from the
North (Mexico City, the industrialized region of northern Mexico, the
United States), where the tyrannies of dominance and power are most
acutely sensed. The second wind is "from below, the wind of rebellion
and dignity." In a communiqué written in 1992, two years before the
well-known uprising, Marcos puts it like this:

> [W]ind is the fruit of the earth, and it has its own season, and
> matures in the breasts of those who have nothing more than their
> dignity and their will to rebel. . . . This hidden wind is content for
> now to blow through the mountains and the glades, without yet
> going down into the valleys where money commands and lies
> govern. This wind, born below the trees, will come down from
> the mountains; it whispers of a new world, so new that it is but
> an intuition in the collective heart.[46]

"Now the wind from above rules, but the one from below is coming,
the storm rises. . . . [S]o it will be." Marcos's letter adds yet another
ending in the form of a prophecy: "When the storm subsides, when the
rain and the fire leave the earth in peace again, the world will no longer
be the world, but something better."[47] The Maya sometimes see this
clash of the winds as an effect of the very rotation of the earth itself.[48]
This rotation makes special use of the "wind from below," which, in

turn, works with the other forces of nature, such as mountains and birds. *All* of earth, therefore, is included in this renewing wind from below. "The wind," after all, "is the fruit of the earth," says Marcos.

Marcos portrays the rising up of a poor Maya campesino, Antonio, who becomes motivated to fight for land, justice, truth, and dignity. Antonio does so by looking to natural forces like the sun rising over the earth from the east. Then it is that "a wind comes up and everything stirs. . . . [T]he land [is] agitated by a terrible wind. . . . Now, it is time to wake up."[49]

The sun in relation to the earth, especially when the sun is seen "greeting the East" at dawn, is a special coconspirator with wind in nature's uprising for Antonio's people. The wind that clashes with the cruel, "neoliberal" North is generally southerly, but it has its origin in the East, where the sun rises at dawn to chase away the shadows of oppression. For the Maya, "the representation of the East wind is the planet Venus, which is also Kukulcan, the Maya analogue of Quetzal-coatl and thus, also, Votán."[50] So it is that revolutionary nature is extended into all the cosmos.

Votán-Zapata's connection to the sun, the dawning of which occurs in the East and comes with both light and wind, may be its most important reference to natural phenomena. In 1993, before their uprising, Maya shamans journeyed on March 21 to observe a ritual to commemorate the beginning of a whole new epoch, "the sixth Sun." This new epoch marks the beginning of the liberation of indigenous peoples and the end of domination by foreign powers.[51]

Votán-Zapata, then, is not only a mythic person, nor is Votán-Zapata just the resurrected political hero, Zapata. The symbol encompasses both mythic person and political leader in relation to a dynamic synergy of nature's conspiring forces, drawing from sun, earth, and wind. If we keep in mind all of Votán's mythic themes, Votán as rising sun can also be seen as the force coming from the dark underworld of the dead, bringing forth fire and corn for a new humanity. Sun, earth, wind, and fire—all four are present and are born from the worlds of the dead to bring a healing storm for those who endure a living death.

The Unitive and Coalitional Dimension

A spiritual vision arises, then, in which mythic heroes are taken as historical actors, where the dead cycle in and out of the realms of the living, where both military generals and little birds make revolution. The elements of nature (sun and wind, for example) not only shine and blow in mythic narrative, but also on the world stage of global markets and politics. Moreno puts the matter clearly: "Votán is the historical incarnation of mythic time. He represents the end of a time of death by being the herald of a new dawn."[52] In Michel's terms, Votán-Zapata is "incarnating the conjunction of a mythic person in a movement of recovery that gives shelter to *all of those who have been excluded*."[53]

With these words, Michel brings forth the final dimension of meaning in Votán-Zapata, the unitive and coalitional. By these terms I suggest that certain features of the myth create, on the level of cultural practice, new unities and coalitions among contemporary groups. The creation of these coalitions has given *Zapatismo* a distinctive and forceful impact throughout Mexico and the world. Mesoamerican scholars have noted that "symbolisms associated with the somewhat mercurial figure of Quetzalcoatl have often given rise to coalescing movements, interregional and pan-ethnic in character."[54] I provide three examples of this coalition-building propensity in the complex symbol, Votán-Zapata.

First, there are the discourses about the color and race of Votán-Zapata. Some of the stimulus for this discourse is rooted in the fact that the origins of the EZLN are partly due to mutual interaction between lighter skinned *mestizo* revolutionaries and darker skinned indigenous of the Lacandón jungle. The 1995 communiqué mentions this directly: "The Powerful say that the people of light skin bring bad ideas to the indigenous because they talked to them of struggle against injustice."[55] The communiqué then addresses these powerful ones, insisting that this revolution is not simply the work of lighter skinned folk:

> The struggle for democracy, liberty and justice does not come from one color of skin or one language; it comes from the land, for our dead who seek a dignified life for their death. . . . Votán-Zapata has *all the colors and all the languages*; his step is along all of the roads and his word grows in all hearts. . . . Brothers and sisters, we are all Votán-Zapata; we are all the Guardian and Heart of the people. They can kill us, drive us to the mountains to shut up our voices, to make big lies like jails to hide our truth. But we are all the dead of always, those who died to live.[56]

This unitive embrace of all colors and languages was even more directly addressed in a 1995 letter from Marcos, reporting another of his conversations with Antonio. The letter discusses long-standing traditions that depict Votán-Zapata as having united with "Ik-al Zapata," thus fusing within Zapata both light and darkness, both day and night, both white and black, such that a "black Zapata" and a "white

Zapata" are both "the same road" for "the true men and women," as
the highland Maya often call themselves.[57] Here is a crucial passage:

That Zapata (Emiliano) appeared here in the mountains. He
wasn't born, they say. He just appeared just like that. They say
he is *Ik'al* and *Votán* who came all the way over here in their long
journey, and so as not to frighten good people, they became one.
Because after being together for so long *Ik'al* and *Votán* learned
they were the same and could become Zapata. And Zapata said
he had finally learned where the long road went and that it was
the same, Votán Zapata and Ik'al Zapata, the black Zapata and
the white Zapata. They were both the same road for the true men
and women.[58]

Not all the meanings and logic of this passage are clear, but the
interplay of light and dark, of white and black around Votán-Zapata is
consonant with the ways the symbol can effect coalition building. In
1999, Marcos drew from the diversity of colors at work in the symbolism, to dramatize the solidarity of "brown" and "red" peoples with
"black" liberation struggles in the United States, as when he wrote of
Zapatista support for the African American journalist on death row,
Mumia Abu-Jamal.[59]

A second feature of the Votán-Zapata symbol that yields a coalition-
building discourse is found in the way the EZLN has proposed the symbol pertaining to nonindigenous communities. The 1995 communiqué
on Votán-Zapata is again the important starting point for seeing this:

Even though he is of indigenous blood, Votán-Zapata does not
struggle just for the indigenous. He struggles also for those who
are not indigenous but who live in the same misery, without
rights, without justice in their jobs, without democracy, for their
decisions, and without freedom for their thoughts and words. . . .
All of us are one in Votán-Zapata and he is one with all of us.[60]

This attempt to make Votán-Zapata available to a wider community
has in fact been accepted. Votan-Zapata was invoked at the August 1996
Intercontinental Encounter that brought two thousand of the world's
activists into the Lacandón jungle to plan alternative strategies to neoliberalism. Activists from diverse continents reported that the symbol of
Votán-Zapata had meaning for them.[61]

Third, and finally, there is the famous communiqué that was released
by Marcos amidst the 1994 rumors that he was gay. Marcos, the masked
spokesperson for the equally masked EZLN, embodied the diffuse spirit

of the Zapatistas in the answer that he sent to the Mexican press. It was a response that not only reflected the kind of presence that is signified by the Votán-Zapata symbol, but it was a response that also invited the practice of a coalitional politics:

> About this whole thing of whether Marcos is homosexual: Marcos is gay in San Francisco, black in South Africa, Asian in Europe, Chicano in San Isidor, . . . Palestinian in Israel, Indigenous in the streets of San Cristobal, . . . rocker in CU [the enormous City University in Mexico City], Jew in Germany, . . . feminist in political parties, Communist in the post–Cold War era, prisoner in Cintalapa [town in Chiapas], pacifist in Bosnia, Mapuche [resisting indigenous of Chile] in the Andes, teacher in the CNTE [National Coordinating Committee of Educational Workers], artist without gallery or portfolio, housewife on any given Saturday night in any neighborhood or any city of any Mexico, Guerillero in Mexico at the end of the twentieth century, striker in the CTM [Mexican Workers Confederation], . . . woman alone in the metro at 10 p.m., retired person in planton [sit-ins in public places], in the Zocalo [public square], campesino without land, . . . unemployed worker, doctor without a practice, rebellious student, dissident in neoliberalism, writer without books or reader, and to be sure, Zapatista in the Mexican southeast. In sum, Marcos is all the minorities who are untolerated, oppressed, resisting, exploding, saying "Enough!" . . . *that* is Marcos.[62]

Both the rhetoric of Marcos in this passage and the lists of actual groups participating in solidarity with the EZLN over the past years (which include middle-class Mexicans infuriated by rising interest rates) display the penchant of *Zapatismo* to build diverse coalitions from the unitive discourse that flourishes in its communiqués and especially in its theological discourse about Votán-Zapata. It is a strikingly broad coalition of people's movements, and, happily, it has yet to generate a corrupting self-worship. In fact, new members who come into solidarity with *Zapatismo* are often attracted precisely by the inspiring character of a movement that does not enforce conformity. Precisely that kind of commonality is the spirit of Votán-Zapata. Frank Bardacke, a California farmworker in the UFW, ended his faithfully compiled volume of Zapatista communiqués in these words. I could not end this essay with better words.

It is a mistake to ask too much of Marcos and the Zapatistas. Marcos tells the convention, "We neither want, nor are we able, to occupy the place that some hope we will occupy, the place from which all opinions will come, all the answers, all the routes, all the truths." The Mexican left must accept that, and the U.S. left even more so. It is inspiring to witness the persistence of revolutionary will and action. It is encouraging to see a promise of what a democratic revolutionary movement might look like and sound like. That is what Marcos and the Zapatistas can do for us: inspire and encourage.[63]

Notes

1. Armand Bartra, "Prologo: Mitos en La Aldea Global," in *Relatos de El Viejo Antonio* by Subcomandante Insurgente Marcos (San Cristóbal de Las Casas: CIACH, 1998), 7.

2. Ibid., 11.

3. Ibid. (translation mine).

4. John Womack Jr., *Rebellion in Chiapas: An Historical Reader* (New York: New Press, 1999), 206, cf. 23–37.

5. Ibid., 23.

6. Ibid., 41.

7. *La Jornada*, November 21, 1996. Cited in Adolfo Gilly, *Chiapas: La razón ardiente* (Mexico City: ERA, 1997), 83 (translation mine).

8. Gilly, *Chiapas*, 63.

9. "Declaration of the Lacandon Jungle: Today We Say 'Enough!'" in *Shadows of Tender Fury: The Letters and Communiqués of Subcomandante Marcos and the Zapatista Army of National Liberation*, ed. Frank Bardacke (New York: Monthly Review Press, 1995), 51.

10. Marc Cooper, *Starting from Chiapas: The Zapatistas Fire the Shot Heard Around the World* (Westfield, N.J.: Open Magazine Pamphlet Series, 1994), 7.

11. See "Women's Revolutionary Law," in *Viva Zapata! The EZLN in Their Own Words*. Produced by the Zapatista Solidarity Committee, February 11, 1994, New York City.

12. Jeffrey Rubin, "Mexico—A Tale of Two States: One Represses, the Other Doesn't," *New York Times*, January 7, 1994.

13. Cooper, *Starting from Chiapas*, 2.

14. John Ross, *Rebellion from the Roots: Indian Uprising in Chiapas* (Monroe, Mass.: Common Courage Press, 1995), 102–4.

15. Carlos Fazio, *El Tercer Vínculo: de la teoría del caos a la teoría de la militarización* (Mexico City: Joaqín Mortiz, 1997).

16. Riordan Roette, "Mexico—Political Update," Chase Manhattan's Emerging Markets Group Memo, January 13, 1995, 2. See A. Cockburn and K. Silverstein, "Mexico and the Banks," *Nation* (March 6, 1995): 306–11.

17. "Votaron cerca de tres millones en la consulta," *La Jornada* (March 22, 1999).

18. Gilly, *Chiapas*, 111, 118.

19. Mexico Solidarity Network, Weekly News Survey, January 22–31, 2001 (online publication, February 2, 2001).

20. Ibid.

21. Antonio García de León, *Resistencia y utopía* (Mexico City: Ediciones Era, [1985] 1997), 39.

22. O. Moreno, "La Utopía India," *La Guillotina* (Summer, 1994): 6–7.

23. García de León, *Resistencia y utopía*, 40.

24. Neil Baldwin, *Legends of the Plumed Serpent: Biography of a Mexican God* (New York: Public Affairs, 1998), 120–21.

25. Ivan Van Sertima, *They Came Before Columbus: African Presence in Ancient America.* (New York: Random House, 1976), 50–51, 58–59.

26. Irene Nicholson, *Mexican and Central American Mythology* (New York: Peter Bedrick Books, 1987), 140–41.

27. Berdacke, *Shadows of Tender Fury*, 196.

28. Ibid. (emphasis added).

29. Moreno, "La Utopía India," 7.

30. A. M. Corzo, "La Llamada de la Selva," *La Guillotina* (Summer 1994): 17.

31. Ibid., 14.

32. Berdacke, *Shadows of Tender Fury*, 175.

33. Ibid.

34. "Votán-Zapata se levanto de nuevo, 16 de Abril de 1995," in *EZLN 2: Documentos y comunicados* (Mexico City: Ediciones Era, 1995), 307 (translation mine).

35. Ibid.

36. Berdacke, *Shadows of Tender Fury*, 197.

37. Corzo, "La Llamada de la Selva," 17.

38. *EZLN 2*, 307.

39. See Martin Hopenhayn, "Postmodernism and Neoliberalism in Latin America," in *The Postmodernism Debate in Latin America*, ed. John Beverly et al. (Durham, N.C.: Duke University Press, 1995), 93–109.

40. Antonio García de León, "Prólogo," in *EZLN 1: Documentados y comunicados* (Mexico City: Ediciones Era, 1994), 14–15 (translation mine).

41. Guillermo Michel, *La Guerra que vivimos: Aproximaciones a la rebelión de la dignidad* (Xochimilco: Universidad Autónoma Metropolitana, 1998), 40. Cf. 61–63, 66–67, 91–92, 117–18 (translation mine).

42. Gilly, *Chiapas*, 50.

43. Berdacke, *Shadows of Tender Fury*, 196.

44. Ibid., 197.

45. Ibid., 50.

46. Ibid., 47.

47. Ibid., 51.

48. Moreno, "La Utopía India," 8.

49. Berdacke, *Shadows of Tender Fury*, 50.

50. Moreno, "La Utopía India," 8.

51. Ibid., 9. Cf. E. Z. Vogt, "Possible Sacred Aspects of the Chiapas Rebellion," *Cultural Survival Quarterly* (Spring 1994): 34.

52. Moreno, "La Utopía India," 8.

53. Michel, *La Guerra que vivimos*, 67 (translation and emphasis mine).

54. H. Campbell, *Zapotec Renaissance* (Albuquerque: University of New Mexico Press, 1994), 16. Cf. Baldwin, *Legends of the Plumed Serpent*, 47.

55. *EZLN 2*, 308 (translation mine).

56. Ibid., 307 (translation mine and emphasis mine).

57. García de León, "Prólogo," 31–32.

58. *EZLN 2*, 162 (translation mine).

59. "To Mumia Abu-Jamal," from Subcomandante Marcos, April 24, 1999, in *Prison Radio* (www.prisonradio.org).

60. *EZLN 2*, 307 (translation mine).

61. From my personal interviews with activists.

62. Berdacke, *Shadows of Tender Fury*, 214.

63. Ibid., 216.

Index